Story Hour

Contemporary Narratives
by American Poets

Story Hour

Contemporary Narratives
by American Poets

Sonny Williams, Editor

Story Line Press
2004

Published by Story Line Press, Three Oaks Farm
PO Box 1240, Ashland, OR 97520-0055
www.storylinepress.com.

This publication was made possible thanks in part to the generous support of our individual contributors.

Cover art by George Hitchcock
Book design by Claudia Carlson
Cover design by Sharon McCann

Library of Congress Cataloging-in-Publication Data
Story hour : contemporary narratives by American poets /
Sonny Williams, editor.
p. cm.
Includes index.
ISBN 1-58654-035-1 (pbk.)
1. Narrative poetry, American. 2. American poetry--20th century.
I. Williams, Sonny, 1967-
PS593.N2S76 2004
811'.030805--dc22
2 0 0 4 0 0 2 0 4 3

Table of Contents

Introduction

BY SONNY WILLIAMS

More than twenty years have passed since the latest revival of narrative poetry in America began to be noticed by readers and critics. After spending much of the twentieth century in neglect, narrative poetry is once again an important and vital art form. This form has rejuvenated poetry by providing poets with greater flexibility and more options to connect poetry to a larger community. Narrative poetry's success can be measured by the critical attention it has received, the numerous literary journals that now welcome it, and the number of poems and books devoted to telling stories in poetry. However, no defining anthology has been produced by which readers may see the cumulative result of this success. This book attempts to rectify that absence.

Everybody loves a story and *Story Hour: Contemporary Narratives by American Poets* represents fifty years of poets writing stories in verse. It chronicles the early influences of Robert Penn Warren and Elizabeth Bishop and the accomplishments of present-day writers like Mark Jarman and Kim Addonizio. Though earlier anthologies have included narrative poems, no other anthology exists that is devoted to contemporary American narratives.

I have arranged the poets chronologically by birth, and I have chosen poems that were published from the late fifties on. This is not an arbitrary time frame, for it was during the late fifties through the sixties and seventies that the short confessional poem and the deep image lyric dominated American poetry. This prevalence of the lyric mode originated in the nineteenth century and in the principles of Modernism. Though verse narrative never completely disappeared, the aesthetic principles of Modernism significantly challenged the form's viability. By definition, Modernism was predicated on challenging the reader's expectations of coherence, experimenting with conventions, and dwelling on fragmentation, ambiguity and uncertainty. The "feeling" of poetry was best expressed through the lyric, and stories were best left to prose fiction writers. Coupled with the tenets of Symbolism and Imagism, the High Modernists were unable or unwilling to write complete, coherent stories. This may be understood in the context of World War I, discoveries in science, the Great Depression, and other events which made the world seem a bloodier and more confusing place. The once viable organization of a unified perceiving consciousness seemed to prevail no longer. Many artists believed that a different kind of art was required to express chaotic and fragmented existence.

Modernism had repudiated the American examples of Henry Wadsworth Longfellow, John Greenleaf Whittier, and Joaquin Miller, viewing them as quaint representatives of a more innocent age. Even as poets such as Stephen Vincent Benét, Edward Arlington Robinson, Robert Frost, and Robinson Jeffers were writing verse narratives, telling stories in poetry steadily gave way to personal meditations—the essay in verse—and brief confessions. By the middle decades of the century, movements such as Beat, Black Mountain, Confessional, and Deep Image had become so influential that the dominant mode of expression for the next several decades was through the short, free verse lyric. These poems concentrated on subjective, private, and autobiographical materials. This rejection of traditional forms and narrative was expressed in a number of essays and manifestos. In 1950 Charles Olson, in "Projective Verse," reveals this attitude when he states, "Yes, yes, we must, must, *must* get rid of the drama, at all costs—I mean, even get rid of narrative—the temptation, you hear?"

If one wished for stories in verse, one had to turn to popular music. Influenced by the Blues, songwriters such as Woody Guthrie, Bob Dylan, Tom Waits, Lucinda Williams, Willie Nelson, and many others continued to write and perform ballads or stories in verse.

A few poets, though, also found storytelling a viable and necessary alternative for communicating their experiences. Instead of focusing on their interior landscapes, these poets included other characters and situations in an attempt to witness the world as it is and appeal to a larger audience. So it is appropriate that this anthology begins with Robert Penn Warren and Elizabeth Bishop, who wrote against the grain and influenced many poets to come.

The foundation for this narrative revival was also created by publishing venues throughout the country. At *The Hudson Review*, editors Frederick Morgan and Paul Deitz began to publish new narrative poems in the early eighties. After *The Kenyon Review* was reestablished in 1979, editor Frederick Turner did the same in its pages. Between 1980 and 1989, editors Mark Jarman and Robert McDowell published their controversial magazine *The Reaper*, which excoriated poetry and criticism that ignored any of poetry's options, especially storytelling. Adopting The Reaper as a pseudonym, the editors in a series of compelling essays emphasized honest criticism, humor, and storytelling-in-verse. In 1984, Jarman, McDowell, and the painter Lysa McDowell created Story Line Press, an independent literary publisher that provided one of the first venues for poets practicing narrative.

The resurrection of verse narrative would later become known as the New Narrative. At times it is coupled with the New Formalism under the umbrella term, Expansive poetry (a term referring to poetry written with more than a specialized audience in mind). This vital recovery appealed to a broad popular audience, not solely an academic one. Beginning in the mid-eighties, people began to gather annually in Elko, Nevada to attend cowboy poetry readings. They celebrated ballads and verses of the Western cattle drive, life on the range, and the contemporary reality of ranch life, especially as perceived by ranch women. This and other festivals throughout the U.S. led to a dynamic revival of cowboy poetry.

In the West Bronx of New York City, rap music in the seventies began to emerge as a new urban art form. Artists such as Run D.M.C. and the Sugarhill Gang were alternative and underground, yet they employed traditional meters and rhymes to tell stories from an urban black perspective. Among Hispanic communities in the American Southwest, corridos, or border ballads, have long provided people with an "alternative discourse."

All of these activities satisfy the general culture's need for stories told in the memorable, compressed language of verse.

*   *   *

The most important criterion for selecting the poems was that they must tell a story. There are many theories as to what constitutes a narrative poem, and important questions must be asked in order to develop a narrative aesthetic. For example, how does one write narrative verse without becoming prosaic? What forms and styles must be enlisted or invented to tell our stories? What kind of narrative poems does our moment in history call for after Modernism, the rise of the motion picture, and the cultural upheaval that has most defined our world over the last sixty years? The selection of the poems found here was based on some general principles with these questions in mind.

To be considered a narrative poem, the work must be more than just a journalistic report, a character portrait, or merely anecdotal; it must imply a belief or an idea that the poet deems necessary for the reader to understand. There must be a beginning, middle, and an end, though not necessarily in that order. There must be dramatic action, and there must be dramatic resolution. The action must be compressed, and time must be controlled. Whether poets tell their stories in traditional forms, free verse, or non-metrical prosodies, they must maintain the integrity of the poetic line; otherwise, the author risks losing the rhythm and becoming prosaic. Form is the language system or prosody chosen by the poet, as well as the pattern, structure, and design of the story. Richard Wilbur says that the poet "should choose the form whose logic will provide it with precision, economy, and power." The poet must choose the form in which meaning and sound coalesces. By ignoring form, poets reject rhythm and reject time and any possibility of a story dies. All of the aforementioned aspects must be considered in terms of their relationship to the overall design.

All human experience can be expressed through narrative poetry, for it is an art of inclusion. It includes both public and private experience. The poems collected here include some of the most intense lyrical and meditative passages in American poetry, lyrical and meditative passages that are in service to the story rather than being the focus of the poem. The narrative poems included in this book are as entertaining and as accessible as the best contemporary prose fiction. They offer the pace and appeal of cinema and maintain the intensity of language and imagery of lyric poetry.

The verse forms offered here are as various as the subjects. They intensify the drama, making the poems more compelling, more memorable. For those who work in academia or those who are cultured hobbyists, for those who are web designers or farmers, anyone who loves a good story will find the narrative poems in this book illuminating, surprising, and most of all, enjoyable. Should any poets thumb through this book and discover inspiration for writing their own stories, I will be thankful.

For more detailed discussions of narrative poetry's revival, I recommend the following: *The Reaper Essays* by Mark Jarman and Robert McDowell, *New England Review and Bread Loaf Quarterly Volume VIII, Number 1, Autumn 1985* (which includes a symposium on narrative poetry edited by Mark Jarman), *New Expansive Poetry: Essays on the New Narrative & the New Formalism*, edited by R. S. Gwynn, *Sound and Form in Modern Poetry* by Harvey Gross and Robert McDowell, *The Ghost of Tradition: Expansive Poetry and Postmodernism* by Kevin Walzer, *Missing Measures: Modern Poetry and the Revolt Against Meter* by Timothy Steele, *After New Formalism: Poets on Form, Narrative, and Tradition,* edited by Annie Finch, *The Secret of Poetry* by Mark Jarman, *The Poetry of Life and the Life of Poetry* by David Mason, *The Oxford Companion to Twentieth Century Poetry* edited by Ian Hamilton, *Poetry After Modernism* edited by Robert McDowell, and *Dictionary of Literary Biography, Volume 282* edited by Jonathan N. Barron and Bruce Meyer.

The compilation ends with an appendix, which contains a number of novels-in-verse, long narrative poems, and epics that could not be reprinted here but are important enough that they needed mentioning. I have written short critical summaries that I hope will give the reader some sense of the story as well as lending insight to the poet's technique. Of course, reading the stories is the best way to experience them.

After a reading, a woman from the audience approached the speaker, the poet Edwin Arlington Robinson.

"Mr. Robinson," she asked, "what is the best way to read one of your long story poems?"

"The only way I know," Robinson replied, "is to read them one word at a time."

This anthology would have been impossible without the vision and efforts of Robert McDowell. I thank him for his critical eye and his faith. I am also grateful to Dana Gioia, Frederick Turner, and Mark Jarman for their advice, suggestions, and encouragement.

1

Robert Penn Warren (1905–1989)

Audubon: A Vision

To Allen and Helen Tate

Thou tellest my wanderings: put thou my tears into thy bottle: are they not in thy book? —Psalms: 56, 8

I caught at his strict shadow and the shadow released itself with neither haste nor anger. But he remained silent. —Carlos Drummond de Andrade: "Traveling in the Family" Translated by Elizabeth Bishop

Jean Jacques Audubon, whose name was anglicised when, in his youth, he was sent to America, was early instructed in the official version of his identity: that he was the son of the sea captain Jean Audubon and a first wife, who died shortly after his birth in Santo Domingo, and that the woman who brought him up in France was a second wife. Actually, he was the son of Jean Audubon and his mistress during the period when Jean Audubon was a merchant and slave-dealer in Santo Domingo, and the woman who raised him was the wife his father had left behind him in France while he was off making his fortune. By the age of ten Audubon knew the true story, but prompted, it would seem, by a variety of impulses, including some sound practical ones, he encouraged the other version, along with a number of flattering embellishments. He was, indeed, a fantasist of talent, but even without his help legends accreted about him. The most famous one—that he was the lost Dauphin of France, the son of the feckless Louis XVI and Marie Antoinette—did not, in fact, enter the picture until after his death, in 1851.

I
WAS NOT THE LOST DAUPHIN

[A]
Was not the lost dauphin, though handsome was only
Base-born and not even able
To make a decent living, was only
Himself, Jean Jacques, and his passion—what
Is man but his passion?

Saw,
Eastward and over the cypress swamp, the dawn,
Redder than meat, break;
And the large bird,
Long neck outthrust, wings crooked to scull air, moved
In a slow calligraphy, crank, flat, and black against
The color of God's blood spilt, as though
Pulled by a string.

Saw
It proceed across the inflamed distance.

Moccasins set in hoar frost, eyes fixed on the bird,
Thought: "On that sky it is black."
Thought: "In my mind it is white."
Thinking: *"Ardea occidentalis,* heron, the great one."

Dawn: his heart shook in the tension of the world.

Dawn: and what is your passion?

[B]
October: and the bear,
Daft in the honey-light, yawns.

The bear's tongue, pink as a baby's, out-crisps to the curled tip,
It bleeds the black blood of the blueberry.

The teeth are more importantly white
Than has ever been imagined.

The bear feels his own fat
Sweeten, like a drowse, deep to the bone.

Bemused, above the fume of ruined blueberries,
The last bee hums.

The wings, like mica, glint
In the sunlight.

He leans on his gun. Thinks
How thin is the membrane between himself and the world.

II

THE DREAM HE NEVER KNEW THE END OF

[A]

Shank-end of day, spit of snow, the call,
A crow, sweet in distance, then sudden
The clearing: among stumps, ruined cornstalks yet standing, the spot
Like a wound rubbed raw in the vast pelt of the forest. There
Is the cabin, a huddle of logs with no calculation or craft:
The human filth, the human hope.

                              Smoke,
From the mud-and-stick chimney, in that air, greasily
Brims, cannot lift, bellies the ridgepole, ravels
White, thin, down the shakes, like sputum.

                              He stands,
Leans on his gun, stares at the smoke, thinks: "Punk-wood."
Thinks: "Dead-fall half-rotten." Too sloven,
That is, to even set axe to clean wood.

                                    His foot,
On the trod mire by the door, crackles
The night-ice already there forming. His hand
Lifts, hangs. In imagination, his nostrils already
Know the stench of that lair beyond
The door-puncheons. The dog
Presses its head against his knee. The hand
Strikes wood. No answer. He halloos. Then the voice.

        [B]
What should he recognize? The nameless face
In the dream of some pre-dawn cock-crow—about to say what,
Do what? The dregs
Of all nightmare are the same, and we call it
Life. He knows that much, being a man,
And knows that the dregs of all life are nightmare.

Unless.

Unless what?

        [C]
The face, in the air, hangs. Large,
Raw-hewn, strong-beaked, the haired mole
Near the nose, to the left, and the left side by firelight
Glazed red, the right in shadow, and under the tumble and tangle
Of dark hair on that head, and under the coarse eyebrows,
The eyes, dark, glint as from the unspecifiable
Darkness of a cave. It is a woman.

She is tall, taller than he.
Against the gray skirt, her hands hang.

"Ye wants to spend the night? Kin ye pay?
Well, mought as well stay then, done got one a-ready,
And leastwise, ye don't stink like no Injun."

[D]
The Indian,
Hunched by the hearth, lifts his head, looks up, but
From one eye only, the other
An aperture below which blood and mucus hang, thickening slow.

"Yeah, a arrow jounced back off his bowstring.
Durn fool—and him a Injun." She laughs.

                                    The Indian's head sinks.
So he turns, drops his pack in a corner on bearskin, props
The gun there. Comes back to the fire. Takes his watch out.
Draws it bright, on the thong-loop, from under his hunter's-frock.
It is gold, it lives in his hand in the firelight, and the woman's
Hand reaches out. She wants it. She hangs it about her neck.

And near it the great hands hover delicately
As though it might fall, they quiver like moth-wings, her eyes
Are fixed downward, as though in shyness, on that gleam, and her face
Is sweet in an outrage of sweetness, so that
His gut twists cold. He cannot bear what he sees.

Her body sways like a willow in spring wind. Like a girl.

The time comes to take back the watch. He takes it.
And as she, sullen and sunken, fixes the food, he becomes aware
That the live eye of the Indian is secretly on him, and soundlessly
The lips move, and when her back is turned, the Indian
Draws a finger, in delicious retardation, across his own throat.

After food, and scraps for his dog, he lies down:
In the corner, on bearskins, which are not well cured,
And stink, the gun by his side, primed and cocked.

Under his hand he feels the breathing of the dog.

The woman hulks by the fire. He hears the jug slosh.

[E]
The sons come in from the night, two, and are
The sons she would have. Through slit lids
He watches. Thinks: "Now."

The sons
Hunker down by the fire, block the firelight, cram food
Into their large mouths, where teeth
Grind in the hot darkness, their breathing
Is heavy like sleep, he wants to sleep, but
The head of the woman leans at them. The heads
Are together in firelight.

He hears the jug slosh.

Then hears,
Like the whisper and *whish* of silk, that other
Sound, like a sound of sleep, but he does not
Know what it is. Then knows, for,
Against firelight, he sees the face of the woman
Lean over, and the lips purse sweet as to bestow a kiss, but
This is not true, and the great glob of spit
Hangs there, glittering, before she lets it fall.

The spit is what softens like silk the passage of steel
On the fine-grained stone. It whispers.

When she rises, she will hold it in her hand.

[F]
With no sound, she rises. She holds it in her hand.
Behind her the sons rise like shadow. The Indian
Snores. Or pretends to.

He thinks: "Now."
And knows

He has entered the tale, knows
He has entered the dark hovel

In the forest where trees have eyes, knows it is the tale
They told him when he was a child, knows it
Is the dream he had in childhood but never
Knew the end of, only
The scream.

      [G]
But no scream now, and under his hand
The dog lies taut, waiting. And he, too, knows
What he must do, do soon, and therefore
Does not understand why now a lassitude
Sweetens his limbs, or why, even in this moment
Of fear—or is it fear?—the saliva
In his mouth tastes sweet.

"Now, now!" the voice in his head cries out, but
Everything seems far away, and small.

He cannot think what guilt unmans him, or
Why he should find the punishment so precious.

It is too late. Oh, oh, the world!

Tell me the name of the world.

      [H]
The door bursts open, and the travelers enter:
Three men, alert, strong, armed. And the Indian
Is on his feet, pointing.

              He thinks
That now he will never know the dream's ending.

      [I]
Trussed up with thongs, all night they lie on the floor there.
The woman is gagged, for she had reviled them.

All night he hears the woman's difficult breath.

Dawn comes. It is gray. When he eats,
The cold corn pone grinds in his throat, like sand. It sticks there.

Even whiskey fails to remove it. It sticks there.

The leg-thongs are cut off the tied-ones. They are made to stand up.
The woman refuses the whiskey. Says: "What fer?"
The first son drinks. The other
Takes it into his mouth, but it will not go down.

The liquid drains, slow, from the slack side of the mouth.

                    [J]
They stand there under the long, low bough of the great oak.
Eastward, low over the forest, the sun is nothing
But a circular blur of no irradiation, somewhat paler
Then the general grayness. Their legs
Are again bound with thongs.

They are asked if they want to pray now. But the woman:
"If'n it's God made folks, then who's to pray to?"
And then: "Or fer?" And bursts into laughing.

For a time it seems that she can never stop laughing.

But as for the sons, one prays, or tries to. And one
Merely blubbers. If the woman
Gives either a look, it is not
Pity, nor even contempt, only distance. She waits,

And is what she is,

And in the gray light of morning, he sees her face. Under
The tumbled darkness of hair, the face
Is white. Out of that whiteness
The dark eyes stare at nothing, or at

The nothingness that the gray sky, like Time, is, for
There is no Time, and the face
Is, he suddenly sees, beautiful as stone, and

So becomes aware that he is in the manly state.

      [K]
The affair was not tidy: bough low, no drop, with the clients
Simply hung up, feet not much clear of the ground, but not
Quite close enough to permit any dancing.
The affair was not quick: both sons long jerking and farting, but she,
From the first, without motion, frozen
In a rage of will, an ecstasy of iron, as though
This was the dream that, lifelong, she had dreamed toward.

                                        The face,
Eyes a-glare, jaws clenched, now glowing black with congestion
Like a plum, had achieved,
It seemed to him, a new dimension of beauty.

      [L]
There are tears in his eyes.
He tries to remember his childhood.
He tries to remember his wife.
He can remember nothing.

His throat is parched. His right hand,
Under the deerskin frock, has been clutching the gold watch.

The magic of that object had been,
In the secret order of the world, denied her who now hangs there.

He thinks: "What has been denied me?"
Thinks: "There is never an answer."

Thinks: "The question is the only answer."

He yearns to be able to frame a definition of joy.

[M]
And so stood alone, for the travelers
Had disappeared into the forest and into
Whatever selves they were, and the Indian,
Now bearing the gift of a gun that had belonged to the hanged-ones,
Was long since gone, like smoke fading into the forest,
And below the blank and unforgiving eye-hole
The blood and mucus had long since dried.

He thought: "I must go."

But could not, staring
At the face, and stood for a time even after
The first snowflakes, in idiotic benignity,
Had fallen. Far off, in the forest and falling snow,
A crow was calling.

So stirs, knowing now
He will not be here when snow
Drifts into the open door of the cabin, or,
Descending the chimney, mantles thinly
Dead ashes on the hearth, nor when snow thatches
These heads with white, like wisdom, nor ever will he
Hear the infinitesimal stridor of the frozen rope
As wind shifts its burden, or when

The weight of the crow first comes to rest on a rigid shoulder.

III
WE ARE ONLY OURSELVES

We never know what we have lost, or what we have found.
We are only ourselves, and that promise.
Continue to walk in the world. Yes, love it!

He continued to walk in the world.

IV
THE SIGN WHEREBY HE KNEW

[A]
His life, at the end, seemed—even the anguish—simple.
Simple, at least, in that it had to be,
Simply, what it was, as he was,
In the end, himself and not what
He had known he ought to be. The blessedness!—

To wake in some dawn and see,
As though down a rifle barrel, lined up
Like sights, the self that was, the self that is, and there,
Far off but in range, completing that alignment, your fate.

Hold your breath, let the trigger-squeeze be slow and steady.

The quarry lifts, in the halo of gold leaves, its noble head.

This is not a dimension of Time.

[B]
In this season the waters shrink.

The spring is circular and surrounded by gold leaves
Which are fallen from the beech tree.

Not even a skitter-bug disturbs the gloss
Of the surface tension. The sky

Is reflected below in absolute clarity.
If you stare into the water you may know

That nothing disturbs the infinite blue of the sky.

[C]
Keep store, dandle babies, and at night nuzzle
The hazelnut-shaped sweet tits of Lucy, and
With the piratical mark-up of the frontier, get rich.

But you did not, being of weak character.

You saw, from the forest pond, already dark, the great trumpeter swan
Rise, in clangor, and fight up the steep air where,
At the height of last light, it glimmered, like white flame.

The definition of love being, as we know, complex,
We may say that he, after all, loved his wife.

The letter, from campfire, keelboat, or slum room in
New Orleans,
Always ended, "God bless you, dear Lucy." After sunset,

Alone, he played his flute in the forest.

[D]
Listen! Stand very still and,
Far off, where shadow
Is undappled, you may hear

The tusked boar grumble in his ivy-slick.

Afterward, there is silence until
The jay, sudden as conscience, calls.

The call, in the infinite sunlight, is like
The thrill of the taste of—on the tongue—brass.

[E]
The world declares itself. That voice
Is vaulted in—oh, arch on arch—redundancy of joy, its end
Is its beginning, necessity

Blooms like a rose. Why,

Therefore, is truth the only thing that cannot
Be spoken?

It can only be enacted, and that in dream,
Or in the dream become, as though unconsciously, action,
       and he stood,

At dusk, in the street of the raw settlement, and saw
The first lamp lit behind a window, and did not know
What he was. Thought: "I do not know my own name."

He walked in the world. He was sometimes seen to stand
In perfect stillness, when no leaf stirred.

Tell us, dear God—tell us the sign
Whereby we may know the time has come.

V

THE SOUND OF THAT WIND

[A]
He walked in the world. Knew the lust of the eye.

Wrote: "Ever since a Boy I have had an astonishing desire
      to see Much of the World and particularly
      to acquire a true knowledge of the Birds of North America."

He dreamed of hunting with Boone, from imagination painted
      his portrait.
He proved that the buzzard does not scent its repast, but sights it.
He looked in the eye of the wounded white-headed eagle.

Wrote: "... the Noble Fellow looked at his Ennemies
      with a Contemptible Eye."

At dusk he stood on a bluff, and the bellowing of buffalo
Was like distant ocean. He saw
Bones whiten the plain in the hot daylight.

He saw the Indian, and felt the splendor of God.

Wrote: ". . . for there I see the Man Naked from his
        hand and yet free from acquired Sorrow."

Below the salt, in rich houses, he sat, and knew insult.
In the lobbies and couloirs of greatness he dangled,
And was not unacquainted with contumely.

Wrote: "My Lovely Miss Pirrie of Oackley Passed by Me
        this Morning, but did not remember how beautifull
        I had rendered her face once by Painting it
        at her Request with Pastelles."

Wrote: ". . . but thanks to My humble talents I can run
        the gantlet throu this World without her help."

And ran it, and ran undistracted by promise of ease,
Nor even the kind condescension of Daniel Webster.

Wrote: ".. . would give me a fat place was I willing to
        have one; but I love indepenn and piece more
        than humbug and money."

And proved same, but in the end, entered
On honor. Far, over the ocean, in the silken salons,
With hair worn long like a hunter's, eyes shining,
He whistled the bird-calls of his distant forest.

Wrote: ". . . in my sleep I continually dream of birds."

And in the end, entered into his earned house,
And slept in a bed, and with Lucy.

But the fiddle
Soon lay on the shelf untouched, the mouthpiece
Of the flute was dry, and his brushes.

His mind
Was darkened, and his last joy
Was in the lullaby they sang him, in Spanish, at sunset.

He died, and was mourned, who had loved the world.

Who had written: "... a world which though wicked
                enough
                in all conscience is *perhaps* as good
                as worlds unknown."

[B]
So died in his bed, and
Night leaned, and now leans,
Off the Atlantic, and is on schedule.
Grass does not bend beneath that enormous weight
That with no sound sweeps westward. In the Mississippi,
On a mud bank, the wreck of a great tree, left
By flood, lies, the root-system and now-stubbed boughs
Lifting in darkness. It
Is white as bone. That whiteness
Is reflected in dark water, and a star
Thereby.

Later,
In the shack of a sheep-herder, high above the Bitterroot,
The light goes out. No other
Light is visible.

The Northwest Orient plane, New York to Seattle, has passed,
        winking westward.

[C]
For everything there is a season.

But there is the dream
Of a season past all seasons.

In such a dream the wild-grape cluster,
High-hung, exposed in the gold light,
Unripening, ripens.

Stained, the lip with wetness gleams.

I see your lip, undrying, gleam in the bright wind.

I cannot hear the sound of that wind.

VI
LOVE AND KNOWLEDGE

Their footless dance
Is of the beautiful liability of their nature.
Their eyes are round, boldly convex, bright as a jewel,
And merciless. They do not know
Compassion, and if they did,
We should not be worthy of it. They fly
In air that glitters like fluent crystal
And is hard as perfectly transparent iron, they cleave it
With no effort. They cry
In a tongue multitudinous, often like music.

He slew them, at surprising distances, with his gun.
Over a body held in his hand, his head was bowed low,
But not in grief.

He put them where they are, and there we see them:
In our imagination.

What is love?

One name for it is knowledge.

VII
TELL ME A STORY

[A]
Long ago, in Kentucky, I, a boy, stood
By a dirt road, in first dark, and heard
The great geese hoot northward.

I could not see them, there being no moon
And the stars sparse. I heard them.

I did not know what was happening in my heart.

It was the season before the elderberry blooms,
Therefore they were going north.

The sound was passing northward.

[B]
Tell me a story.

In this century, and moment, of mania,
Tell me a story.

Make it a story of great distances, and starlight.

The name of the story will be Time,
But you must not pronounce its name.

Tell me a story of deep delight.

Elizabeth Bishop (1911–1979)

The Moose

For Grace Bulmer Bowers

From narrow provinces
of fish and bread and tea,
home of the long tides
where the bay leaves the sea
twice a day and takes
the herrings long rides,

where if the river
enters or retreats
in a wall of brown foam
depends on if it meets
the bay coming in,
the bay not at home;

where, silted red,
sometimes the sun sets
facing a red sea,
and others, veins the flats'
lavender, rich mud
in burning rivulets,

on red, gravelly roads,
down rows of sugar maples,
past clapboard farmhouses
and neat, clapboard churches,
bleached, ridged as clamshells,
past twin silver birches,

through late afternoon

a bus journeys west,
the windshield flashing pink,
pink glancing off of metal,
brushing the dented flank
of blue, beat-up enamel;

down hollows, up rises,
and waits, patient, while
a lone traveller gives
kisses and embraces
to seven relatives
and a collie supervises.

Goodbye to the elms,
to the farm, to the dog.
The bus starts. The light
grows richer; the fog,
shifting, salty, thin,
comes closing in.

Its cold, round crystals
form and slide and settle
in the white hens' feathers,
in gray glazed cabbages,
on the cabbage roses
and lupins like apostles;

the sweet peas cling
to their wet white string
on the whitewashed fences;
bumblebees creep
inside the foxgloves,
and evening commences.
One stop at Bass River.
Then the Economies—
Lower, Middle, Upper;
Five Islands, Five Houses,
where a woman shakes a tablecloth
out after supper.

A pale flickering. Gone.
The Tantramar marshes
and the smell of salt hay.
An iron bridge trembles
and a loose plank rattles
but doesn't give way.

On the left, a red light
swims through the dark:
a ship's port lantern.
Two rubber boots show,
illuminated, solemn.
A dog gives one bark.

A woman climbs in
with two market bags,
brisk, freckled, elderly.
"A grand night. Yes, sir,
all the way to Boston."
She regards us amicably.

Moonlight as we enter
the New Brunswick woods,
hairy, scratchy, splintery;
moonlight and mist
caught in them like lamb's wool
on bushes in a pasture.

The passengers lie back.
Snores. Some long sighs.
A dreamy divagation
begins in the night,
a gentle, auditory,
slow hallucination....

In the creakings and noises,
an old conversation

—not concerning us,
but recognizable, somewhere,
back in the bus:
Grandparents' voices

uninterruptedly
talking, in Eternity:
names being mentioned,
things cleared up finally;
what he said, what she said,
who got pensioned;

deaths, deaths and sicknesses;
the year he remarried;
the year (something) happened.
She died in childbirth.
That was the son lost
when the schooner foundered.

He took to drink. Yes.
She went to the bad.
When Amos began to pray
even in the store and
finally the family had
to put him away.

"Yes..." that peculiar
affirmative. "Yes..."
A sharp, indrawn breath,
half groan, half acceptance,
that means "Life's like that.
We know *it* (also death)."

Talking the way they talked
in the old featherbed,
peacefully, on and on,
dim lamplight in the hall,
down in the kitchen,
the dog tucked in her shawl.

Now, it's all right now
even to fall asleep
just as on all those nights.
—Suddenly the bus driver
stops with a jolt,
turns off his lights.

A moose has come out of
the impenetrable wood
and stands there, looms, rather,
in the middle of the road.
It approaches; it sniffs at
the bus's hot hood.

Towering, antlerless,
high as a church,
homely as a house
(or, safe as houses).
A man's voice assures us
"Perfectly harmless...."

Some of the passengers
exclaim in whispers,
childishly, softly,
"Sure are big creatures."
"It's awful plain."
"Look! It's a she!"

Taking her time,
she looks the bus over,
grand, otherworldly.
Why, why do we feel
(we all feel) this sweet
sensation of joy?

"Curious creatures,"
says our quiet driver,

rolling his *r*'s.
"Look at that, would you."
Then he shifts gears.
For a moment longer,

by craning backward,
the moose can be seen
on the moonlit macadam;
then there's a dim
smell of moose, an acrid
smell of gasoline.

3

Gwendolyn Brooks (1917–2000)

In the Mecca

Sit where the light corrupts your face.
Mies Van der Rohe retires from grace.
And the fair fables fall.

S. Smith is Mrs. Sallie. Mrs. Sallie
hies home to Mecca, hies to marvelous rest;
ascends the sick and influential stair.
The eye unrinsed, the mouth absurd
with the last sourings of the master's Feast.

She plans
to set severity apart,
to unclench the heavy folly of the fist.
Infirm booms
and suns that have not spoken die behind this
low-brown butterball. Our prudent partridge.
A fragmentary attar and armed coma.
A fugitive attar and a district hymn.

Sees old St. Julia Jones, who has had prayer,
and who is rising from amenable knees
inside the wide-flung door of 215.
"Isn't He wonderfulwonderful!" cries St. Julia.
"Isn't our Lord the greatest to the brim?
The light of my life. And I lie late
past the still pastures. And meadows. He's the comfort
and wine and piccalilli for my soul.
He hunts me up the coffee for my cup.
Oh how I love that Lord."
                              And Mrs. Sallie,
all innocent of saints and signatures,
nods and consents, content to endorse
Lord as an incense and a vintage. Speaks
to Prophet Williams, young beyond St. Julia,
and rich with Bible, pimples, pout: who reeks
with lust for his disciple, is an engine
of candid steel hugging combustibles.
His wife she was a skeleton.
His wife she was a bone.
Ida died in self-defense.
(Kinswomen!
Kinswomen!)
Ida died alone.

Out of her dusty threshold bursts Hyena.
The striking debutante. A fancier of firsts.
One of the first, and to the tune of hate,
in all the Mecca to paint her hair sun-gold.
                              And Mrs.

Sallie sees Alfred. Ah, his God!—
To create! To create! To bend with the tight intentness
over the neat detail, come to
a terrified standstill of the heart, then shiver,
then rush—successfully—
at that rebuking thing, that obstinate and
recalcitrant little beast, the phrase!
To have the joy of deciding—successfully—
how stuffs can be compounded or sifted out
and emphasized; what the importances are;
what coats in which to wrap things. Alfred is un-
talented. Knows. Marks time and themes at Phillips,
stares, glares, of mornings, at a smear
which does not care what he may claim or doubt
or probe or clear or want, or what he might have been.
He "fails" no one; at faculty lunch hour
allows the zoology teacher, who has great legs,
to fondle him and curse his pretty hair. He
reads Shakespeare in the evenings or reads Joyce
or James or Horace, Huxley, Hemingway.
Later, he goes to bed with Telly Bell
in 309, or with that golden girl,
or thinks, or drinks until the Everything
is vaguely a part of One thing and the One thing
delightfully anonymous
and undiscoverable. So he is weak,
is weak, is no good. Never mind.
It is a decent enough no-goodness. And it is
a talkative, curly, charitable, spiced weakness
which makes a woman in charge of zoology
dream furiously at night.
When there were all those gods
administering to panthers,
jumping over mountains,
and lighting stars and comets and a moon,
what was their one Belief?
what was their joining thing?

A boy breaks glass and Mrs. Sallie
rises to the final and fourth floor.

Children, what she has brought you is hock of ham.
She puts the pieces to boil in white enamel, right
already with water of many seasonings, at the back
of the cruel stove. And mustard mesmerized by
eldest daughter, the Undaunted (she who once
pushed her thumbs in the eyes of a Thief), awaits
the clever hand. Six ruddy yams abide, and
cornbread made with water.

> Now Mrs. Sallie
> confers her bird-hat to her kitchen table,
> and sees her kitchen. It is bad, is bad,
> her eyes say, and My soft antagonist,
> her eyes say, and My headlong tax and mote,
> her eyes say, and My maniac default,
> my least light.
> "But all my lights are little!"
> Her denunciation
> slaps savagely not only this sick kitchen but
> her Lord's annulment of the main event.
> "I want to decorate!" But what is that? A
> pomade atop a sewage. An offense.
> First comes correctness, *then* embellishment!
> And music, mode, and mixed philosophy
> may follow fitly on propriety
> to tame the whiskey of our discontent!
> "What can I do?"
> But World (a sheep)
> wants to be Told.
> If you ask a question, you
> can't stop there.
> You must keep going.
> You can't stop there: World will
> waive; will be
> facetious, angry. You can't stop there.
> You have to keep on going.

Doublemint as a protective device. Yvonne
prepares for her lover.
Gum is something he can certify.
Gum is something he can understand.
A tough girl gets it. A rough
Ruthie or Sue. It is unembarrassable,
and will seem likely. It is very bad,
but in its badness it is nearly grand,
and is a crown that tops bald innocence
and gentle fright.
It is not necessary, says Yvonne,
to have every day him whom
to the end thereof you will love.
Because it is tasty to remember
he is alive, and laughs
in somebody else's room,
or is slicing a cold cucumber,
or is buttoning his cuffs,
or is signing with his pen
and will plan
to touch you again.

Melodie Mary hates everything pretty and plump.
And Melodie, Cap and Casey
and Thomas Earl, Tennessee, Emmett and Briggs
hate sewn suburbs;
hate everything combed and strong; hate people who
have balls, dolls, mittens and dimity frocks and trains
and boxing gloves, picture books, bonnets for Easter.
Lace handkerchief owners are enemies of Smithkind.

Melodie Mary likes roaches,
and pities the gray rat.
To delicate Melodie Mary
headlines are secondary.
It is interesting that in China
the children blanch and scream,
and that blood runs like a ragged wound
through the ancient flesh of the land.

It matters, mildly,
that the Chinese girls are grim,
and that hurried are the seizures
of yellow hand on hand....
What if they drop like the tumbling tears
of the old and intelligent sky?
Where are the frantic bulletins
when other importances die?
Trapped in his privacy of pain
the worried rat expires,
and smashed in the grind of a rapid heel
last night's roaches lie.

Briggs is adult as a stone
(who if he cries cries alone).
The Gangs are out, but he must go
to and fro,
appease what reticences move
across the intemperate range.
Immunity is forfeit, love
is luggage, hope is heresy.
Gang
is health and mange.
Gang
is a bunch of ones and a singlicity.
Please pity Briggs. But there is a central height in pity
past which man's hand and sympathy cannot go;
past which the little hurt dog
descends to mass—no longer Joe,
not Bucky, not Cap'n, not Rex,
not Briggs—and is all self-employed,
concerned with Other,
not with Us.
Briggs, how "easy," finally, to accept (after the shriek and
                              repulsion)
the unacceptable evil. To proceed with some eclat;
some salvation of the face;
awake! to choke the chickens, file their blood.

One reason cats are happier than people
is that they have no newspapers ... I must be,
culls Tennessee,
like my cat, content to gaze
at men and women spurting here and there.
I must sit, let
them stroke me as and when they will;
must drink their milk and cry
for meat. At other times I must be still.
Who tingles in
and mixes with affairs and others met
comes out with scratches and is very thin
and rides the red possession of regret.

          In the midst
of hells and gruels and little halloweens
tense Thomas Earl loves Johnny Appleseed.
"I, Johnny Appleseed."
It is hard to be Johnny Appleseed.
The ground shudders.
The ground springs up;
hits you with gnarls and rust,
derangement and fever, or blare and clerical treasons.

Emmett and Cap and Casey
are skin wiped over bones
for lack of chub and chocolate
and ice cream cones,
for lack of English muffins
and boysenberry jam.
What shall their redeemer be?
Greens and hock of ham.
For each his greens and hock of ham
and a spoon of sweet potato.

Alfred says:
The faithless world!
betraying yet again

trinities!
My chaste displeasure
is not enough;
the brilliant British of the new command
is not enough;
the counsels of division, the hot counsels,
the scuffle and short pout
are not enough, are only
a pressure of clankings and affinities
against
the durable fictions of a Charming Trash.
Mrs. Sallie
evokes and loves and loathes a pink-lit image
of the toy-child. Her Lady's.
Her Lady's pink convulsion, toy-child dances
in stiff wide pink through Mrs. Sallie. Stiff pink is
on toy-child's poverty of cream
under a shiny tended warp of gold.
What shiny tended gold is an aubade
for toy-child's head! Has ribbons too!
Ribbons. Not Woolworth cotton comedy,
not rubber band, not string. . . .
"And that would be my baby be my baby. . . .
And I would be my lady I my lady...."

What else is there to say but everything?

SUDDENLY, COUNTING NOSES, MRS. SALLIE
SEES NO PEPITA. "WHERE PEPITA BE?"

. .. Cap, where Pepita? Casey, where Pepita?
Emmett and Melodle Mary, where Pepita?
Briggs, Tennessee, Yvonne, and Thomas Earl,
where may our Pepita be?—
our Woman with her terrible eye,
with iron and feathers in her feet,
with all her songs so lemon-sweet,
with lightning and a candle too
and junk and jewels too?

My heart begins to race.
I fear the end of Peace.

Ain seen er I ain seen er I ain seen er
Ain seen er I ain seen er I ain seen er

Yvonne up-ends her iron. And is constrained.
Cannot now conjure love-within-the-park.
Cannot now conjure spice and soft explosion
mixing with miffed mosquitoes where the dark
defines and re-defines.

       And Melodic Mary
and Thomas Earl and Tennessee and Briggs
yield cat-contentment gangs rats Appleseed.

Emmett and Cap and Casey
yield visions of vice and veal,
dimes and windy carnival,
candied orange peel,
peppermint in a pickle;
and where the ladybug
glistens in her leaf-hammock; *light*
lasses to hiss and hug.

And they are constrained. All are constrained.
      And there is no thinking of grapes or gold
      or of any wicked sweetness and they ride
      upon fright and remorse and their stomachs
      are rags or grit.
In twos!
In threes! Knock-knocking down the martyred halls
at doors behind whose yelling oak or pine
      many flowers start, choke, reach up,
      want help, get it, do not get it,
      rally, bloom, or die on the wasting vine.

"One of my children is missing. One of my children is gone."

Great-great Gram hobbles, fumbles at the knob,
mumbles, "I ain seen no Pepita. But
I remember our cabin. The floor was dirt.
And something crawled in it. That is the thought
stays in my mind. I do not recollect
what 'twas. But something. Something creebled in that dirt
for we wee ones to pop. Kept popping at it.
Something that squishied. *Then* your heel come down!
I hear them squishies now. . . . *Pop,* Pernie May!
That's sister Pernie. That's my sister Pernie.
Squish. .. . Out would jump her little heel.
And that was the end of Something. Sister Pernie
was our best popper. Pern and me and all,
we had no beds. Some slaves had beds of hay
or straw, with cover-cloth. We six-uns curled
in corners of the dirt, and closed our eyes,
and went to sleep—or listened to the rain
fall inside, felt the drops
big on our noses, bummies and turn-turns. . . ."

Although he has not seen Pepita, Loam
Norton considers Belsen and Dachau,
regrets all old unkindnesses and harms.
. . . The Lord was their shepherd.
Yet did they want.
Joyfully would they have lain in jungles or pastures,
walked beside waters. Their gaunt
souls were not restored, their souls were banished.
In the shadow valley
they feared the evil, whether with or without God.
They were comforted by no Rod,
no Staff, but flayed by, 0 besieged by, shot a-plenty.
The prepared table was the rot or curd of the day.
Anointings were of lice. Blood was the spillage of cups.
Goodness and mercy should follow them
            all the days of their death.
They should dwell in the house of the Lord forever
and, dwelling, save a place for me.
I am not remote,

not unconcerned....

Boonisie De Broe has
not seen Pepita Smith: but is
a Lady
among Last Ladies.
Erect. Direct.
An engraving on the crowd, the blurred crowd.
She is away and fond.
Her clear voice tells you life may be controlled.
Her clear mind is the extract
of massive literatures, of lores,
transactions of old ocean; suffrages.

Yvonne
recovers to aver
despite the stomp of the stupor.
        She will not go
in Hudson's hashhouse. And the Tivoli
is a muffler of Love.
In the blasé park,
that winks and mocks but is at all times tolerant
of the virtuous defect, of audit,
        and of mangle and of wile, he
may permit perusal of their ground,
its rubble-over-rose: may look to rainbow:
may sanction bridal tulle, white flowers,
may allow a mention of a minister and twins. . . .

        But *other* Smiths are twitching. They recall
vain vagrants, recall old peddlers, young fine bumlets,
The Man Who Sells The Peaches Plums Bananas.
They recall the Fuller Brush Man,
oblique and delicate, who tries on
the very fit and feature of despair.
"Pepita's smart," says Sallie; her stretched eyes
reject the exact despatches of a mind turned boiler,
epithet, toiler, guillotine. *What*
of the Bad Old Man? the lover-like young man? the

half-mad boy who put his hand across Pepita's knee?
"Pepita's smart," says Sallie.
Knowing the ham hocks are burning at the bottom of the pan.

S. and eight of her children reach their door. The
door says, "What are you doing here? and where
is Pepita the puny—the halted, glad-sad child?"
They pet themselves, subdue
the legislation of their yoke and devils.
>   *Has just wandered!*
>   Has just blundered
>   away
>   from her own.
>   And there's no worry
>   that's necessary.
>   She
>   comes soon alone.
Comes soon alone or will be brought by neighbor.
Kind neighbor.

"Kind neighbor." They consider.
Suddenly
every one in the world is Mean.
Could that old woman, passively passing, mash a child?
Has she a tot's head in that shiny bag?
And that lank fellow looking furtive.
What
cold poison could he spew, what stench commit
upon a little girl, a little lost girl,
lone and languid in the world, wanting
her ma, her glad-sad, her Yvonne?

Emmett runs down the hall.
Emmett seizes John Tom's telephone.
(Despite the terror and the derivation,
despite the not avuncular frontier,
John Tom, twice forty in 420, claims
Life sits or blazes in this Mecca.
>   And thereby—tenable.

And thereby beautiful.)

Provoking calm and dalliance of the Law.
How shall the Law allow for littleness!
How shall the Law enchief the chapters of
wee brown-black chime, wee brown-black chastity?

The Law arrives—and does not quickly go
to fetch a Female of the Negro Race.
A lariat of questions.
The mother screams and wants her baby. Wants her baby,
and wants her baby wants her baby.

Law leaves, with likeness of a "southern" belle. Sheriffs,
South State Street is a Postulate!
Until you look. You look—and you discover
the paper dolls are terrible. You touch.
You look and touch.
The paper dolls are terrible and cold.

Aunt Dill arrives to help them. "Little gal got
raped and choked to death last week. Her gingham
was tied around her neck and it was red
but had been green before with pearls and dots
of rhinestone on the collar, and her tongue
was hanging out (a little to the side);
her eye was all a-pop, one was; was one
all gone. Part of her little nose was gone
(bit off, the Officer said). The Officer said
that something not quite right been done that girl.
Livid Langley: 'round the corner from my house."
Aunt Dill extends
sinister pianissimos and apples,
and at that moment of the Thousand Souls is
a Christ-like creature, Doing Good.

The Law returns. It trots about the Mecca.
It pounds a dozen doors.

No, Alfred has not seen Pepita Smith.
But he (who might have been an architect)
can speak of Mecca: firm arms surround
disorders, bruising ruses and small hells,
small semiheavens: hug barbarous rhetoric
built of buzz, coma and petite pell-mells.
No, Alfred has not seen Pepita Smith.
But he (who might have been a poet-king)
can speak superbly of the line of Leopold.
The line of Leopold is thick with blackness
        and Scriptural drops and rises.
The line of Leopold is busy with betrothals of royal rage
        and conditional pardon and with
refusal of mothballs for outmoded love.
Senghor will not shred
love,
gargantuan gardens careful in the sun,
fairy story gold, thrones, feasts, the three princesses,
summer sailboats
like cartoon ghosts or Klansmen, pointing up
white questions, in blue air....
No.
Believes in beauty.
But believes that blackness is among the fit filters.
Old cobra
coughs and curdles in his lungs,
spits spite, spits exquisite spite, and cries, "Ignoble!"
Needs "negritude."
Senghor (in Europe rootless and lonely) sings in art-lines of
        Black Woman.
Senghor sighs and, "negritude" needing,
speaks for others, for brothers. Alfred can tell of
Poet, and muller, and President of Senegal, who
in voice and body
loves sun,
listens
to the rich pound in and beneath the black feet of Africa.

Hyena, the striking debutante, is back;

bathed, used by special oils and fumes, will be
off to the Ball tonight. She has not seen
Pepita—"a puny and a putrid little child."

Death is easy.
It may come quickly.
It may come when nobody is ready.
Death may come at any time. Mazola
has never known Pepita S. but knows
the strangest thing is when the stretcher goes!—
the elegant hucksters bearing the body when the body
leaves its late lair the last time leaves.
With no plans for return.

Don Lee wants
not a various America.
Don Lee wants
a new nation
under nothing;
a physical light that waxes; he does not want to
be exorcised, adjoining and revered;
he does not like a local garniture
nor any impish onus in the vogue;
is not candlelit
but stands out in the auspices of fire
and rock and jungle-flail;
wants
new art and anthem; will
want a new music screaming in the sun.

Says Alfred:
To be a red bush!
In the West Virginia autumn.
To flame out red.
"Crimson" is not word enough,
although close to what I mean.
How proud.
How proud.
(But the bush does not know it flames.)

"Takes time," grated the gradualist.
"Starting from when?" asked Amos.
Amos (not Alfred) says,
"Shall we sit on ourselves; shall we wait behind roses and veils
for monsters to maul us,
      for bulls to come butt us forever and ever,
shall we scratch in our blood,
      point air-powered hands at our wounds,
reflect on the aim of our bulls? "And Amos
(not Alfred) prays, for America prays:
"Bathe her in her beautiful blood.
A long blood bath will wash her pure.
Her skin needs special care.
Let this good rage continue out beyond
her power to believe or to surmise.
Slap the false sweetness from that face.
Great-nailed boots
must kick her prostrate, heel-grind that soft breast,
outrage her saucy pride,
remove her fair fine mask.
Let her lie there, panting and wild, her pain
red, running roughly through the illustrious ruin—
with nothing to do but think, think
of how she was so long grand,
flogging her dark one with her own hand,
watching in meek amusement while he bled.
Then shall she rise, recover.
Never to forget."

The ballad of Edie Barrow:
      I fell in love with a Gentile boy,
All creamy-and-golden fair.
He looked deep and long in my long black eyes,
And he played with my long black hair.
He took me away to his summertime house.
He was wondrous wealthy, was he.
And there in the hot black drapes of night
he whispered, "Good lovers are we."
Close was our flesh through the winking hours,

closely and sweetly entwined.
Love did not guess in the tight-packed dark
it was flesh of varying kind.
Scarletly back when the hateful sun
came bragging across the town.
And I could have killed the gentle Gentile
who waited to strap him down.
He will wed her come fall, come falling of fall.
And she will be queen of his rest.
I shall be queen of his summerhouse storm.
A hungry tooth in my breast.

"Pepita who?" And Prophet Williams yawns.
Prophet Williams' office in the Mecca
has a soiled window and a torn front sign.
His suit is shabby and slick.
He is not poor (clothes do *not* make the man).
He has a lawyer named Enrico Jason,
who talks. The Prophet advertises
in every Colored journal in the world....
An old woman wants
from the most reverend Prophet of all prophets
a piece of cloth, licked by his Second Tongue,
to wrap around her paralytic leg.
Men with malicious sweethearts, evil sweethearts—
bringers of bad, bringers of tedium—
want Holy Thunderbolts, and Love Balls too.
And all want lucky numbers all the time.
Mallie (the Superintendent of six secretaries)
types. Mallie alone may know
the Combinations:
14-15-16
and 13-14-15. . . .
(magic is Cut-out Number Forty-three).
Prophet will help you hold your Job, solve problems,
and, like a Sister Stella in Blue Island,
"can call your friends and enemies by name
without a single clue."
There is no need to visit in Blue Island.

Prophet will give you trading stamps and kisses,
or a cigar.
One visit will convince you.
Lucky days
and Lucky Hands. Lifts you
from Sorrow and the Shadows. Heals the body.
A Sister Marlo on east Sixty-third
announces One
Visit Can Keep You Out of the Insane Asylum,
but
she stocks no Special Holiday Blessings for
Columbus Day and Christmas, nor keeps off
green devils and orange witches with striped fangs.
Prophet
has Drawing and Holding Powder, Attraction Powder, Black
Cat Powder, Powerful Serum,
"Marvelous Potency Number Ninety-one"
(which stoppeth husbands and lovers from dastardy),
Pay-check Fluid, Running-around Elixir,
Policy Number Compeller, Voodoo Potion.
Enrico Jason, a glossy circular blackness, who
sees Lawmen and enhances Lawmen, soon
will lie beside his Prophet in bright blood,
a rhythm of stillness
above the nuances.

How many care, Pepita?—
Staley and Lara,
the victim grasped, the harlot had and gone?
Eunie, the intimate tornado?
Simpson, the peasant king, Bixby and June,
the hollowed, the scant, the
played-out deformities? the margins?
Not those.
Not these three Maries
with warm unwary mouths and asking eyes
wide open, full of vagueness and surprise;
the limp ladies
(two in awful combat now:

a terrible battle of the Old:
speechless and physical: oh horrible
the obscene gruntings
the dull outwittings
the flabby semi-rhythmic shufflings
the blear starings
the small spittings).
Not Great-uncle Beer, white-headed twinkly man!—
laugher joker gambler killer too.
Great-uncle Beer says, "Casey Jones.
Yes, Casey Jones is still alive,
a chicken on his head."
Not Weziyn, the wandering woman, the woman who wanders
the halls of the Mecca at night, in search
of Lawrence and Love.
            Not Insane Sophie! If
you scream, you're marked "insane."
But silence is a *place* in which to scream!
Hush.
An agitation in the bush.
Occluded trees.
Mad life heralding the blue heat of God
snickers in a corner of the west windowsill.
"What have I done, and to the world,
        and to the love I promised Mother?"
An agitation in occluded trees.
The fires run up. Things slant.
The pillow's wet.
The fires run down and flatten.
(The grilles will dance over glass!)
You're marked "insane."
You cower.
Suddenly you're no longer
well-dressed. You're not
pretty in halls.
Like the others you want love, but
a cage is imminent.
Your doll is near. And will go with you.
Your doll, whom none will stun.

. . . How many care, Pepita?
Does Darkara?
Darkara looks at *Vogue*. Darkara sees
a mischievous impromptu and a sheen.
(In Palm Beach, Florida, Laddie Sanford says:
"I call it My Ocean. Of course, it's the Atlantic.")
The painter, butcher, stockyards man, the Typist,
Aunt Tipple, Zombie Bell,
Mr. Kelly with long gray hair who begs
subtly from door to door, Gas Cady
the man who robbed J. Harrison's grave of mums
and left the peony bush only because
it was too big (said Mama), the janitor
who is a Political Person, Queenie King who
is an old poem silvering the noise,
and Wallace Williams who knows the
Way the Thing Is Supposed To Be Done—
these little care, Pepita, what befalls a
nullified saint or forfeiture (or child).
Alfred's Impression—his Apologie—
his Invocation—and his Ecstasie:
"Not Baudelaire, Bob Browning, not Neruda.
Giants over Steeples
are wanted in this Crazy-eyes, this Scar.
A violent reverse.
We part from all we thought we knew of love
and of dismay-with-flags-on. What we know
is that there are confusion and conclusion.
Rending.
Even the hardest parting is a contribution....
What shall we say?
Farewell. And Hail! Until Farewell again."

Officers!—
do you nearly wish you had not come into this room?
The sixtyish sisters, the twins with the floured faces,
who dress in long stiff blackness,
who exit stiffly together and enter together stiffly,
muffle their Mahler, finish their tea,

stare at the lips of the Law—
but have not seen Pepita anywhere.
They pull on their long white gloves,
they flour their floured faces,
and stiffly leave Law and the Mecca.

Way-out Morgan is collecting guns
in a tiny fourth-floor room.
He is not hungry, ever, though sinfully lean.
He flourishes, ever, on porridge or pat of bean
pudding or wiener soup—fills fearsomely
on visions of Death-to-the-Hordes-of-the-White-Men!
Death!
(This is the Maxim painted in big black
above a bed bought at a Champlain rummage sale.)
Remembering three local-and-legal bearings, he
rubs his hands in glee,
does Way-out Morgan. Remembering his Sister
mob-raped in Mississippi, Way-out Morgan
smacks sweet his lips and adds another gun
and listens to Blackness stern and blunt and beautiful,
organ-rich Blackness telling a terrible story.
Way-out Morgan
predicts the Day of Debt-pay shall begin,
the Day of Demon-diamond,
of blood in mouths and body-mouths,
of flesh-rip in the Forum of Justice at last!
Remembering mates in the Mississippi River,
mates with black bodies once majestic, Way-out
postpones a yellow woman in his bed, postpones
wetnesses and little cries and stomachings—
to consider Ruin.

"Pepita? No."
Marian is mixing.
Take Marian mixing. Gumbo File or roux.
At iron: at ire with faucet, husband, young.
Knows no
gold hour.

Sings
but sparsely, and subscribes to axioms
atop her gargoyles and tamed foam. Good axioms.
Craves crime: her murder, her deep wounding, or
a leprosy so lovely as to pop
the slights and sleep of her community,
her Mecca.
A Thing. To make the people heel and stop
and See her.
Never strides
about, up!
Never alters earth or air!
Her children cannot quake, be proud.
Her husband never Saw her, never said
her single silver certain Self aloud.

Pops Pinkham, forgetting Pepita,
is somewhat doubtful of a specific right
to inherit the earth or to partake of it now. . . .

Old women should not seek to be perfumed, said Plutarch.
But Dill, the kind of woman you
peek at in passing and thank your God or zodiac you
may never have to know, puts on *Tabu,*
Aunt Dill is happy. Nine years Little Papa
has been completely at rest in Lincoln Cemetery.
Children were stillbirths all. Aunt Dill
has bits of brass and marble, and Franciscan
china; has crocheted doilies; has old mahogany,
polished till it burns with a smothered glow; has
antimacassars, spreads, silk draperies,
her silver creamer and her iron lamp,
her piece of porcelain, her seventeen
Really Nice handkerchiefs pressed in cedar. Dill
is woman-in-love-with-God.
Is not
true-child-of-God—for are we ever to
be children?—are we never to mature,
be lovely lovely? be soft Woman

rounded and darling. . . almost caressable . . .
and certainly wearing *Tabu* in the name of the Lord.
Dill straightens—tries to forget the hand of God
(. . . which would be skillful. . . would be flattering . . .)

      I hate it.
      Yet, murmurs Alfred—
who is lean at the balcony, leaning—
something, something in Mecca
continues to call! Substanceless; yet like mountains,
like rivers and oceans too; and like trees
with wind whistling through them. And steadily
an essential sanity, black and electric,
builds to a reportage and redemption.
      A hot estrangement.
      A material collapse
that is Construction.

Hateful things sometimes befall the hateful
but the hateful are not rendered lovable thereby.
The murderer of Pepita
looks at the Law unlovably. Jamaican
Edward denies and thrice denies a dealing
of any dimension with Mrs. Sallie's daughter.
      Beneath his cot
a little woman lies in dust with roaches.
She never went to kindergarten.
She never learned that black is not beloved.
Was royalty when poised,
sly, at the A and P's fly-open door.
Will be royalty no more.
"I touch"—she said once—"petals of a rose.
A silky feeling through me goes!"
Her mother will try for roses.

She whose little stomach fought the world had
wriggled, like a robin!
Odd were the little wrigglings
and the chopped chirpings oddly rising.

4

Richard Wilbur (1921–)

The Mind-Reader

Lui parla.
For Charles and Eula

Some things are truly lost. Think of a sun-hat
Laid for the moment on a parapet
While three young women—one, perhaps, in mourning—
Talk in the crenellate shade. A slight wind plucks
And budges it; it scuffs to the edge and cartwheels
Into a giant view of some description:
Haggard escarpments, if you like, plunge down
Through mica shimmer to a moss of pines
Amidst which, here or there, a half-seen river
Lobs up a blink of light. The sun-hat falls,
With what free flirts and stoops you can imagine,
Down through that reeling vista or another,
Unseen by any, even by you or me.
It is as when a pipe-wrench, catapulted
From the jounced back of a pick-up truck, dives headlong
Into a bushy culvert; or a book
Whose reader is asleep, garbling the story,
Glides from beneath a steamer chair and yields
Its flurried pages to the printless sea.

It is one thing to escape from consciousness
As such things do, another to be pent
In the dream-cache or stony oubliette
Of someone's head.
                              They found, when I was little,
That I could tell the place of missing objects.
I stood by the bed of a girl, or the frayed knee
Of an old man whose face was lost in shadow.

When did you miss it?, people would be saying,
Where did you see it last? And then those voices,
Querying or replying, came to sound
Like cries of birds when the leaves race and whiten
And a black overcast is shelving over.
The mind is not a landscape, but if it were
There would in such case be a tilted moon
Wheeling beyond the wood through which you groped,
Its fine spokes breaking in the tangled thickets.
There would be obfuscations, paths which turned
To dried-up stream-beds, hemlocks which invited
Through shiny clearings to a groundless shade;
And yet in a sure stupor you would come
At once upon dilapidated cairns,
Abraded moss, and half-healed blazes leading
To where, around the turning of a fear,
The lost thing shone.
                        Imagine a railway platform—
The long cars come to a cloudy halt beside it,
And the fogged windows offering a view
Neither to those within nor those without.
Now, in the crowd—forgive my predilection—
Is a young woman standing amidst her luggage,
Expecting to be met by you, a stranger.
See how she turns her head, the eyes engaging
And disengaging, pausing and shying away.
It is like that with things put out of mind,
As the queer saying goes: a lost key hangs
Trammeled by threads in what you come to see
As the webbed darkness of a sewing-basket,
Flashing a little; or a photograph,
Misplaced in an old ledger, turns its bled
Oblivious profile to rebuff your vision,
Yet glistens with the fixative of thought.
What can be wiped from memory? Not the least
Meanness, obscenity, humiliation,
Terror which made you clench your eyes, or pulse
Of happiness which quickened your despair.
Nothing can be forgotten, as I am not

Permitted to forget.
                    It was not far
From that to this—this corner café table
Where, with my lank grey hair and vatic gaze,
I sit and drink at the receipt of custom.
They come here, day and night, so many people:
Sad women of the quarter, dressed in black,
As to a black confession; blinking clerks
Who half-suppose that Taurus ruminates
Upon their destinies; men of affairs
Down from Milan to clear it with the magus
Before they buy or sell some stock or other;
My fellow-drunkards; fashionable folk,
Mocking and ravenously credulous,
And skeptics bent on proving me a fraud
For fear that some small wonder, unexplained,
Should leave a fissure in the world, and all
Saint Michael's host come flapping back.
                                I give them
Paper and pencil, turn away and light
A cigarette, as you have seen me do;
They write their questions; fold them up; I lay
My hand on theirs and go into my frenzy,
Raising my eyes to heaven, snorting smoke,
Lolling my head as in the fumes of Delphi,
And then, with shaken, spirit-guided fingers,
Set down the oracle. All that, of course,
Is trumpery, since nine times out of ten
What words float up within another's thought
Surface as soon in mine, unfolding there
Like paper flowers in a water-glass.
In the tenth case, I sometimes cheat a little.
That shocks you? But consider: what I do
Cannot, so most conceive, be done at all,
And when I fail, I am a charlatan
Even to such as I have once astounded—
Whereas a tailor can mis-cut my coat
And be a tailor still. I tell you this
Because you know that I have the gift, the burden.

Whether or not I put my mind to it,
The world usurps me ceaselessly; my sixth
And never-resting sense is a cheap room
Black with the anger of insomnia,
Whose wall-boards vibrate with the mutters, plaints,
And flushings of the race.

What should I tell them?

I have no answers. *Set your fears at rest,*
I scribble when I must. *Your paramour*
Is faithful, and your spouse is unsuspecting.
You were not seen, that day, beneath the fig-tree.
Still, be more cautious. When the time is ripe,
Expect promotion. I foresee a message
From a far person who is rich and dying.
You are admired in secret. If, in your judgment,
Profit is in it, you should take the gamble.
As for these fits of weeping, they will pass.

It makes no difference that my lies are bald
And my evasions casual. It contents them
Not to have spoken, yet to have been heard.
What more do they deserve, if I could give it,
Mute breathers as they are of selfish hopes
And small anxieties? Faith, justice, valor,
All those reputed rarities of soul
Confirmed in marble by our public statues—
You may be sure that they are rare indeed
Where the soul mopes in private, and I listen.
Sometimes I wonder if the blame is mine,
If through a sullen fault of the mind's ear
I miss a resonance in all their fretting.
Is there some huge attention, do you think,
Which suffers us and is inviolate,
To which all hearts are open, which remarks
The sparrow's weighty fall, and overhears
In the worst rancor a deflected sweetness?
I should be glad to know it.

Meanwhile, saved

By the shrewd habit of concupiscence,

Which, like a visor, narrows my regard,
And drinking studiously until my thought
Is a blind lowered almost to the sill,
I hanker for that place beyond the sparrow
Where the wrench beds in mud, the sun-hat hangs
In densest branches, and the book is drowned.
Ah, you have read my mind. One more, perhaps . . .
A mezzo-litro. Grazie, professore.

5

Frederick Morgan (1922–2004)

Captain Blaze

He told me to come around midnight, unobserved,
by the back way through the garden—so I parked the car
off the ocean side of the road, a little way down,
and walked twenty yards through the fog to his gray stone wall.
I saw no one else on foot, no cars, no lights.

That tall gate of white ash—all covered with pictures
he'd carved himself, of Pacific deities—
had been left unlatched as he'd promised: it made no sound
as I passed on through it and up the long flagstone path
between flower beds damply swept by billowing fog.

. . . You never knew him? I think no one knew him well,
and of course he had no friends: they were long since dead.
He was tall and stooped, very old but very strong,
leather-skinned, white-haired, clean-shaven, with

yellowish eyes
(from atabrine maybe? He had sailed many years in the tropics)

and a fixed evil grin. But perhaps you've seen him in town, moving slow
and stately, leaning on a black knotted cane
and all the while wickedly smirking and smacking his lips? Well, he
wanted to consult me on a legal point, he said—
trusted me because I was of old New England stock

like himself, not some goddamn dago, mick, or jew,
the new base breed that has sucked all the juice from
    our land
and rotted our northern strength with its vile weak ways
(those were his words)—it was something to do with
    his Will.
I admit I was curious: said I'd be over that night. . . .

There were steps to his kitchen porch. While I paused
    just outside,
trying to adjust, as it were, to the feel of the place,
I heard a low laugh sounding deep from within the dimness.
It wasn't repeated, but I'm certain I didn't mistake it—
so easy and strong, and full of a dark satisfaction.

I told myself not to be frightened, and went up the steps.
Once again a door gave: I entered and crossed to the kitchen,
a clean empty space dimly lit from its farther end.
"Captain Blaze!" I called out. "I'm here. I've kept to
    my promise."
No reply—so I moved softly on to where the light shone—

his dining room, I presumed. A single brass lamp
set high on a shelf near some books shed a feeble glow
over massed dark cupboards and chests and a huge oak table from whose
farther shore a seated figure glared. . . .
It was he—with a heart-shaking grin on his hideous face.

There were shadows all round, and it seemed as though

something had moved—
which made me at first uncertain of what I was seeing,
of just what it was that confronted me there. Was he
   breathing?
Would he speak? Was there someone in hiding? It came to
   me then
he was dead, or caught up in a trance. I didn't dare touch him.

On the table before him were bottles—blue, amber, and
   purple
in various shapes, twelve in all. Could this be the secret?
Had he drunk himself strangely to death? No—they were
   bone dry.
What's more, from the cap of each one I found deftly
   suspended
a small piece of metal hung pendulumwise from a string.

I squinted and stared at them, wondering if here was a clue
to the vestige of movement I'd sensed a moment before
on entering the room: had these little ambiguous nuggets
been swinging, and winking, and ticking their messages up
to that old obscene horror who gloated and laughed in
   his chair?

Call me insane if you like. I don't care two straws
what word you finally hit on to help yourself through
your awareness of what may be deeper awareness in me—
for it's not very pleasant, I know, to come up against fear
of the kind that compels you to question your sense of
   yourself!

What had happened, and what was the point? Well may
   you ask,
but you won't get an answer from me: I can't comprehend
   it—
except in this sense I've kept of an evil communion
into which I blamelessly stumbled, or rather, was tricked.
—For I have this bad feeling I'm caught now, with lots worse
   to come!

You know all the rest. He was dead, they took him away,
and vandals (they say) burned his house down the very
    next night.
Because of the corpse's condition, bloat-bellied and dry,
the coroner found he'd been dead at least forty-eight hours.
I mentioned to no one I'd taken his call that same morning.

6

James Dickey (1923–1997)

The Lifeguard

In a stable of boats I lie still,
From all sleeping children hidden.
The leap of a fish from its shadow
Makes the whole lake instantly tremble.
With my foot on the water, I feel
The moon outside

Take on the utmost of its power.
I rise and go out through the boats.
I set my broad sole upon silver,
On the skin of the sky, on the moonlight,
Stepping outward from earth onto water
In quest of the miracle

This village of children believed
That I could perform as I dived
For one who had sunk from my sight.
I saw his cropped haircut go under.
I leapt, and my steep body flashed
Once, in the sun.

Dark drew all the light from my eyes.
Like a man who explores his death
By the pull of his slow-moving shoulders,
I hung head down in the cold,
Wide-eyed, contained, and alone
Among the weeds,

And my fingertips turned into stone
From clutching immovable blackness.
Time after time I leapt upward
Exploding in breath, and fell back
From the change in the children's faces
At my defeat.

Beneath them I swam to the boathouse
With only my life in my arms
To wait for the lake to shine back
At the risen moon with such power
That my steps on the light of the ripples
Might be sustained.

Beneath me is nothing but brightness
Like the ghost of a snowfield in summer.
As I move toward the center of the lake,
Which is also the center of the moon,
I am thinking of how I may be
The savior of one

Who has already died in my care.
The dark trees fade from around me.
The moon's dust hovers together.
I call softly out, and the child's
Voice answers through blinding water.
Patiently, slowly,

He rises, dilating to break
The surface of stone with his forehead.
He is one I do not remember

Having ever seen in his life.
The ground I stand on is trembling
Upon his smile.

I wash the black mud from my hands.
On a light given off by the grave
I kneel in the quick of the moon
At the heart of a distant forest
And hold in my arms a child
Of water, water, water.

7

Anthony Hecht (1923–)

Behold the Lilies of the Field

for Leonard Baskin

And now. An attempt.
Don't tense yourself; take it easy.
Look at the flowers there in the glass bowl.
Yes, they are lovely and fresh. I remember
Giving my mother flowers once, rather like those
(Are they narcissus or jonquils?)
and I hoped she would show some pleasure in them
but got that mechanical enthusiastic show
she used on the telephone once in praising some friend
for thoughtfulness or good taste or whatever it was,
and when she hung up, turned to us all and said,

"God, what a bore she is!"
I think she was trying to show us how honest she was,
At least with us. But the effect
Was just the opposite, and now I don't think
She knows what honesty is. "Your mother's a whore,"
Someone said, not meaning she slept around,
Though perhaps this was part of it, but
Meaning she had lost all sense of honor,
And I think this is true.

But that's not what I wanted to say.
What was it I wanted to say?
When he said that about Mother, I had to laugh,
I really did, it was so amazingly true.
Where was I?
Lie back. Relax.
Oh yes. I remember now what it was.
It was what I saw them do to the emperor.
They captured him, you know. Eagles and all.
They stripped him, and made an iron collar for his neck,
And they made a cage out of our captured spears,
And they put him inside, naked and collared,
And exposed to the view of the whole enemy camp.
And I was tied to a post and made to watch
When he was taken out and flogged by one of their generals
And then forced to offer his ripped back
As a mounting block for the barbarian king
To get on his horse;
And one time to get down on all fours to be the royal throne
When the king received our ambassadors
To discuss the question of ransom.
Of course, he didn't want ransom.
And I was tied to a post and made to watch.
That's enough for now. Lie back. Try to relax.
No, that's not all.
They kept it up for two months.
We were taken to their outmost provinces.
It was always the same, and we were always made to watch,
The others and I. How he stood it, I don't know.

And then suddenly
There were no more floggings or humiliations,
The king's personal doctor saw to his back,
He was given decent clothing, and the collar was taken off,
And they treated us all with a special courtesy.
By the time we reached their capital city
His back was completely healed.
They had taken the cage apart—
But of course they didn't give us back our spears.
Then later that month, it was a warm afternoon in May,
The rest of us were marched out to the central square.
The crowds were there already, and the posts were set up,
To which we were tied in the old watching positions.
And he was brought out in the old way, and stripped,
And then tied flat on a big rectangular table
So that only his head could move.
Then the king made a short speech to the crowds,
To which they responded with gasps of wild excitement,
And which was then translated for the rest of us.
It was the sentence. He was to be flayed alive,
As slowly as possible, to drag out the pain.
And we were made to watch. The king's personal doctor,
The one who had tended his back,
Came forward with a tray of surgical knives.
They began at the feet.
And we were not allowed to close our eyes
Or to look away. When they were done, hours later,
The skin was turned over to one of their saddle-makers
To be tanned and stuffed and sewn. And for what?
A hideous life-sized doll, filled out with straw,
In the skin of the Roman Emperor, Valerian,
With blanks of mother-of-pearl under the eyelids,
And painted shells that had been prepared beforehand
For the fingernails and toenails,
Roughly cross-stitched on the inseam of the legs
And up the back to the center of the head,
Swung in the wind on a rope from the palace flag-pole;
And young girls were brought there by their mothers
To be told about the male anatomy.

His death had taken hours.
They were very patient.
And with him passed away the honor of Rome.

In the end, I was ransomed. Mother paid for me.
You must rest now. You must. Lean back.
Look at the flowers.
Yes. I am looking. I wish I could be like them.

8

Louis Simpson (1923–)

The Previous Tenant

1

All that winter it snowed.
The sides of roads were heaped with it.
The nights were quiet. If you stepped outside,
above the dark woods and fields
hung glittering stars and constellations.

My landlord, Stanley, came by now and then
to see how things were going.
I reminded him that the previous tenant
had left boxes full of clothes,
a pair of skis, a rifle,
three shelves of books, and a fishing pole.

All right, he said, he'd get in touch with him.

I said, he must have left in a hurry.
A hurry? Stanley considered.
His eyes gleamed under bushy eyebrows.
Satanic. But I happened to know that Stanley
wouldn't hurt a fly. All that fall
I'd seen him trying to think of something
to persuade some raccoons to quit the premises—
everything short of a gun.

"McNeil was a bit disorganized,"
he said with a smile.

I asked if he'd like some coffee,
and he said yes. While I was making it
he talked about the previous tenant.

2

A doctor named Hugh McNeil
came on the staff at Mercy Hospital
and bought a house in Point Mercy.

Hugh and Nancy fitted right in ...
people liked them.
Helen Knox, whose husband was vice-president
of the National Maritime Bank,
called on Nancy and invited her
to join the Garden Club.
Then they were asked to join the Golf Club.
(The Levines, on the other hand, hadn't been invited.
After two years of Point Mercy
they sold their house and moved back to Queens.)

The McNeils had children: Tom, fourteen,
and Laurie, nine and a half, nearly ten.
McNeil was one of the fathers on Saturday
dashing about. He drove a green Land Rover
as though he were always on safari
with the children and an Irish setter.

Nancy was nice . . . blonde,
and intelligent—she'd been to Wellesley.
She took on the job of secretary
of the Garden Club, that nobody wanted,
and helped organize the dance at the Yacht Club
on July the Fourth, for Hugh had joined that too.
He bought a "Cal" Thirty Martini-rigged sloop,
and with Tom as crew went sailing.
They came in fifth in the Martha Woodbury
Perpetual Trophy.

                          Nancy didn't sail,
it made her seasick. She sat on the patio
with her knitting till the boats hove in sight,
then went down to the basin.
McNeil spoke at village meetings
with moderation and common sense.
Once he argued for retaining
the Latin teacher at the high school.
Latin, he explained, was still useful
for medicine and law, and a foundation
for good English. They heard him out
and voted to let the Latin teacher go
and remodel the gymnasium.
McNeil accepted defeat gracefully.
That was one of the things they liked about him.

The residents of Point Mercy
are proud of their village
with its beautiful homes and gardens
and bird sanctuary.
Contrary to what people say
about the suburbs, they appreciate culture.
Hugh McNeil was an example . . .
doing the shopping, going to the club,
a man in no way different from themselves,
husband and family man
and good neighbor, who nevertheless spoke Latin.

3

Her name was Irene Davis.
Before she married it was Cristiano.
"I met her once," said Helen Knox.
"Harry introduced her to me
at the bank. A dark woman . . .
I think, a touch of the tar brush."

There is no accounting for tastes
observed Sandie Bishop.

The woman's husband was an invalid
and patient of Dr. McNeil.
The green Land Rover had been seen
parked outside the Davises' house
in the afternoon, in the evening,
and once—this was hilarious—the doctor
ran out of gas in that part of town
at three in the morning. He didn't have cash
or credit cards on him, and had to walk
to the nearest open service station.
The attendant let him have a gallon.
"I've been in the same fix," he told McNeil,
"you can pay me some other time."

The attendant talked, and the story
got back to Point Mercy.
"It's a scandal," said Sandie.
"Do you think Nancy knows?"

Helen said, "I'm sure she does."

"Someone should have a talk with him,
Sandie said. She remembered
with some excitement, the occasion
when a resident of Point Mercy
had been thinking of selling his house
to a family that was black.

Every morning he would find garbage
dumped on his lawn. The prospective buyer
received an anonymous letter,
and that was the end of that.

"Let's not be hasty," said Helen
who was president of the Garden Club
and had more experience.
"These things have a way of working themselves out."

4

One day there was a sensation:
Dr. McNeil had been mugged,
beaten and left by the road.

"Mugged?" said the service station attendant.
This was long after the event.
He looked around, but there was no one
in hearing distance, only the dog,
a hound that wandered around
with an infected ear, snapping at flies.
All at once it perked up its ears
and went running. It must have smelled something
mixed with the odor of gasoline
and dust ... a delirious
fragrance of sensual life.

The attendant leaned closer
and said in a conspiratorial voice,
"He was never mugged.
It was Irene Davis's brothers,
the Cristianos. They had him beat up."

He knew about gangsters. They would beat up a guy
to warn him. The next time it was curtains.

5

So McNeil was in the hospital
with two broken ribs, black eyes,
and a missing tooth.

At the next meeting of the Garden Club
the president said she was as broad-minded
as anyone, but this . . .
here she paused as though it were beneath her
to find words for such low behavior . . .
had brought violence into their midst.

Sandie moved they send a delegation
to the hospital, to demand McNeil's
immediate resignation.

The next day four of the members
called on Dr. Abrahams, chief of staff,
and told him what they wanted.
A short man, with hair on his face,
all the time they were talking he kept turning
from one to the other, and grinning,
like some sort of monkey, Sandie said afterwards.

He thanked them for their concern.
But McNeil's private life—
not that he knew anything about it—
had nothing to do with his work
or his position here at the hospital.
If they would take his advice
they would be careful what they said—
they might find themselves charged
with libel. Speaking, he was sure,
for the entire staff, they were fortunate
to have a surgeon of Hugh McNeil's caliber.

Could he be of service in anything else?
No? Then would they please excuse him . . .

it looked like a busy day.

They were halfway to the parking lot.
"What can you expect?" said Helen.
"It was bad enough letting them in,
but to make one chief of staff!"

She knew how to put what they were feeling
into words. This was why
she was president—elected not once
or twice . . . this was her third term in office.

6

Then Nancy sued for divorce.
She had all the evidence she needed:
her husband had been with Irene Davis
in Providence, Rhode Island.
when he was supposed to be in Boston
attending a medical conference.

This was when he moved into the cottage.
It consisted of a small bedroom,
living room, bathroom, kitchen.
Thoreau, who recommends sleeping in the box
railroad workers keep their tools in,
would have found this house commodious.

I could imagine him coming home . . .
putting some fries on a metal sheet
and sliding it into the oven
set at 350 degrees.
Sprinkling a couple of chops
with pepper and garlic.
Deciding which frozen vegetable . . .
say, spinach. Putting the block
in a saucer with water and salt.
Making a salad . . . but this would mean
slicing tomatoes, radishes, scallions,

and washing lettuce. There would be times
when he just couldn't be bothered.

He would have a drink, then a second.
You have to be careful not to make it three
and four. On the other hand
you shouldn't be too careful,
or like Robinson Crusoe you may find yourself
taking pride in the neatness and efficiency
of your domestic arrangements:
all your bowls made out of gourds
lined up on a shelf according to size.
Ditto your spoons.
"A place for everything," you say to the parrot,
"and everything in its place."

Bake the French fries,
boil the frozen vegetable, broil the lamb chops.
You can prepare a nourishing dinner
in twenty minutes, and eat it in five
while reading the *Times* or watching *Charlie's Angels.*

He would watch TV again after dinner.
My God, he'd say to the walls,
it can't be this bad. But it was.
He'd turn it off and pick up a book.
Now that he had plenty of time
he could catch up on the ones he'd missed
when they came out: titles like *Future Shock*
and *The Greening of America,*

Then he was on an express train
racing to the end of the line,
a flash and a moment of excruciating
pain. He was paralyzed,
helpless to move a leg or an arm.

And woke, having fallen asleep
in his chair, to hear the dripping

of snow melting on the roof.

On nights when he couldn't sleep
he'd watch the late late show.
In the dark night of the soul,
says F. Scott Fitzgerald,
it is always three in the morning.
Hemingway says, it isn't so bad . . .
in fact, the best hour of the night
once you've reconciled yourself to insomnia
and stopped worrying about your sins.
And I say that insomnia can be
a positive joy if you're tuned in to *Dames*
or *Gold Diggers of 1933*.
I remember seeing *The Producers*
at three in the morning, and practically
falling out of bed. There are pleasures
known to none but late late movie-goers,
moments of the purest absurdity,
such as, in an otherwise boring movie
starring the Marx Brothers, the "Tenement Symphony"
as sung by Tony Martin.

So there he was, watching Busby Berkeley's
electrically lighted waterfalls,
and the Warner Brothers cuties
viewed from underneath, treading water.

"Ain't we got fun!" shrieked the parrot,
and the goat gave a great bound.

7

Behind the Perry Masons and Agatha Christies
I came across a packet of letters.
It was like being a detective.

When Irene's husband came home
from the hospital, he was confined

to his bed, by doctor's orders.
And McNeil was the doctor.
"Call me at home," said Irene.
"There is no problem about telephone calls."

I copied some of the passages.
They might come in useful. There was an idea for a novel
I'd had for years: *A Bovary of the Sierras* . . .
The Bovary of Evanston . . . *The Bovary of Green Harbor.*

There was a paragraph about some flowers
and his cock that might have been conceived
by the author of *Lady Chatterley's Lover.*
It went to show that when an idea
has genuine merit, individuals
far removed in space and time
come upon it independently.

She even knew her Bible:
"When my beloved slipped his hand through the latch-hole
my bowels stirred within me."

Rumor was right. It was her brothers
who had McNeil beaten up.
She told him that he wasn't to see her
ever again. She feared for his life.
"Irene . . . signing off."
But she didn't sign off. Here she was again.
"If you have a new woman in your life
or you've gone back to your wife
I don't want to muck things up.
This is just a peacepipe, kid—
send me a smoke signal
if I'm getting in the way of anything.
Cheerio, Irene."

Then they picked up again where they'd left off.

They had been with each other

yesterday. She could still feel him inside her.
I was beginning to be afraid
for him. For her. For both of them.

8

Stanley telephoned to say that McNeil
was coming to pick up his things.

I put the books in cartons,
and piled the cartons and the rest of his things
next to the door: the boxes of clothes,
the skis, the fishing pole,
and the rifle—I was loath to part with it,
the way America was greening.

The next day my predecessor
arrived. A man of forty
with red hair . . . looking slightly angry.
Suspicious. I couldn't put my finger on it.

He was accompanied by a young woman
wearing jeans and a sweater.
She was fair, and had a friendly smile.
"It was good of you to take care
of Hugh's things," she said. "Wasn't it, Hugh?"
"O yes," he said. "Thanks."

I helped them carry things out
to the station wagon. It was snowing again . . .
not flakes, but particles, coming down fast
at an angle, like rain or hail.

They drove away.
She waved. He looked straight ahead.
It appeared he was back on the track
once more, after his derailment.
With a woman of the right kind at his side
to give him a nudge. "Say thanks!"

9

It is always that famous day and year
at the Colony Inn ... a brick fireplace,
rough-hewn beams, and pewter candlesticks.
From the ceiling hang the flags
of the thirteen original colonies.

The waitresses wear bonnets and muslin gowns
that hang straight from the shoulder
to the floor, leaving their arms and elbows
exposed. Some of the older waitresses
seem to resent being made to dress
like children. Their movements are slow.

One of them arrived finally
to take our order, and departed
moving with slow steps
as befitted an early American.

Maggie said, "Don't look now!
By the window . . . that's Irene Davis,
the woman McNeil had the affair with."

I looked around the room casually
and let my gaze come to rest
on Irene.

They said she was dark. What they hadn't said
was that the darkness, jet-black hair,
was set off by a skin like snow,
like moonlight in a dark field glimmering.
Her features were . . . fine. She wouldn't have been
out of place in an Italian villa
with walls five feet thick, and chickens
roosting on the furniture . . . the family
crowded into three rooms upstairs . . .
a *contessa,* married to the invalid son
of impoverished aristocracy.

I wondered what she would have thought
if she'd known I'd read her letters.

There were two people with her:
an old woman with white hair
who looked as though she'd just got off
the boat from Palermo . . .
and a man, he must be Irene's brother . . .
the same black hair and white complexion.
But what in her looked romantic,
in him spelled murder. He was thin
and sinewy . . . wearing a green jacket,
dark green shirt, white tie.

I imagined he was being tolerant
of the restaurant . . . these assholes
with their consommés and casseroles,
their salads consisting of lettuce
and cottage cheese . . . And what was this
for chrissake? Sweet potato
with marshmallow on top . . . you call this food?

But he was on his best behavior.
He didn't pull an automatic
and blow holes through the flags
of the thirteen original colonies.

Irene must have felt me staring.

She turned . . . her eyes met mine
for a few seconds. I had an impression
of . . . defiance. "What do you want?"

I quickly looked away.

10

Maggie was meeting a friend
at three. It was now two-thirty.

So we walked around Island Bay.
The village has been reconstructed
to preserve a Colonial atmosphere.
At the crest of a slope facing the bay
stands the post office. This at least
is authentic. It has four columns,
white of course, and a big golden eagle
above the entrance. On either side
in a crescent, there are shops
with signs lettered in gold:
Optometrist, Pharmacy, Antiques . . .
There's a shop selling Irish linen
and wool. Another selling jewelry
and notions . . . Royal Doulton . . .
little statues of Colonial women
in hoopskirts and wigs,
and the figure of a young girl
in shorts, taking a swing at a golf ball.

The slope goes down to a road.
Between this and the bay
stands a gazebo, an open dome
housing a bust of Hercules.
This, they say, was a ship's figurehead.
All but the bearded head
is a reconstruction . . . some local artist
has added a muscular torso
and draped over one shoulder
the skin of the Nemean lion.
A sillier, more pathetic monster
it would be hard to imagine,
with his doggy nose and wide-open eyes
that seem to say, Look at me.
I never did any harm.

This monument to our culture,
believe it or not, had been vandalized . . .
battered and gashed.
Whoever did it must have used a hammer

or an axe.

I said, "Boys will be boys."

"I'm sure," Maggie said, "it wasn't anyone
from around here."

I wasn't so sure. Our high schools
every year turn out their quota of vandals
and thieves. Not to mention illiterates.
You don't have to go into New York City . . .

How, she said, could I be so cynical?

I said, why was it
that when you told the truth
people accused you of being cynical?

We were on our way to having a quarrel.
I didn't want to. I liked Maggie,
with her quizzical way of looking at me,
her air of calm, unclouded judgment,
her mouth that turned down at one corner
when she smiled.

But now she wasn't smiling.
She said, "It's your attitude.
Like what you said in the restaurant
about Hugh McNeil and the Davis woman
being better than the rest of us."

She had her back to the post office.
The wings of the golden eagle
seemed to spring out of her shoulders.
I was filled with a sense of the ridiculous.

She sensed it, and became really angry.
"I know, you prefer vulgar people.

Anyone who tries to be decent and respectable
is either a hypocrite or a fool."

So we had our quarrel.
Then a car drove up and stopped.
It was Helen Knox. She leaned over
and opened the door for Maggie.

"Good afternoon," she said to me,
very cool. I knew what she thought of me
and my writing. A friend told me—
for writers have such friends.

She said, "I thought I ought to read
one of his novels. But I couldn't bring myself
to finish it. Why write about
such ordinary things?

What with chauffeuring the children
and entertaining Harry's friends,
if I find time to read, it has to be something
that takes me out of myself.

You have to be selective—
this is why I read the *New Yorker,* and *Time,*
and subscribe to the Book of the Month."

Sway

Swing and sway with Sammy Kaye

Everyone at Lake Kearney had a nickname:
there was a Bumstead, a Tonto, a Tex,
and, from the slogan of a popular orchestra,
two sisters, Swing and Sway.

Swing jitterbugged, hopping around

on the dance floor, working up a sweat.
Sway was beautiful. My heart went out to her
when she lifted her heavy rack of dishes
and passed through the swinging door.

She was engaged, to an enlisted man
who was stationed at Fort Dix.
He came once or twice on weekends
to see her. I tried talking to him,
but he didn't answer…out of stupidity
or dislike, I could not tell which.
In real life he was a furniture salesman.
This was the hero on whom she had chosen
to bestow her affections.

I told her of my ambition:
to write novels conveying the excitement
of life . . . the main building lit up
like a liner on Saturday night;
the sound of the band . . . clarinet,
saxophone, snare drum, piano.
He who would know your heart (America)
must seek it in your songs.

And the contents of your purse . . .
among Kleenex, aspirin,
chewing gum wrappers, combs, et cetera.

"Don't stop," she said, "I'm listening.
Here it is!" flourishing her lighter.

*

In the afternoon when the dishes were washed
and tables wiped, we rowed out on the lake.
I read aloud . . . *The Duino Elegies*,
while she reclined, one shapely knee up,
trailing a hand in the water.

She had chestnut-colored hair.
Her eyes were changing like the surface
with ripples and the shadows of clouds.

"Beauty," I read to her, "is nothing
but beginning of Terror we're still just able to bear."

*

She came from Jersey, the industrial wasteland
behind which Manhattan suddenly rises.
I could visualize the street where she lived,
and see her muffled against the cold,
in galoshes, trudging to school.
Running about in tennis shoes
all through the summer . . .
I could hear the porch swing squeak
and see into the parlor.
It was divided by a curtain or screen...

"That's it," she said, "all but the screen.
There isn't any."

When she or her sister had a boyfriend
their mother used to stay in the parlor,
pretending to sew, and keeping an eye on them
like Fate.

At night she would lie awake
looking at the sky, spangled over.
Her thoughts were as deep and wide as the sky.
As time went by she had a feeling
of missing out . . . that everything
was happening somewhere else.

Some of the kids she grew up with
went crazy . . . like a car turning over and over.

One of her friends had been beaten
by the police. Some vital fluid
seemed to have gone out of him.
His arms and legs shook. Busted springs.

*

She said, "When you're a famous novelist
will you write about me?"

I promised . . . and tried to keep my promise.

Recently, looking for a toolbox,
I came upon some typewritten pages,
all about her. There she is
in a canoe . . . a gust of wind
rustling the leaves along the shore.
Playing tennis, running up and down the baseline.
Down by the boathouse, listening to the orchestra
playing "Sleepy Lagoon."

Then the trouble begins. I can never think of anything
to make the characters do.
We are still sitting in the moonlight
while she finishes her cigarette.
Two people go by, talking in low voices.
A car door slams. Driving off . . .

"I suppose we ought to go,"
I say.
                    And she says, "Not yet."

Edward Field (1924–)

The Bride Of Frankenstein

The Baron has decided to mate the monster,
to breed him perhaps,
in the interests of pure science, his only god.

So he goes up into his laboratory
which he has built in the tower of the castle
to be as near the interplanetary forces as possible,
and puts together the prettiest monster-woman you ever saw
with a body like a pin-up girl
and hardly any stitching at all
where he sewed on the head of a raped and murdered beauty
       queen.

He sets his liquids burping, and coils blinking and buzzing,
and waits for an electric storm to send through the equipment
the spark vital for life.
The storm breaks over the castle
and the equipment really goes crazy
like a kitchen full of modern appliances
as the lightning juice starts oozing right into that pretty corpse.

He goes to get the monster
so he will be right there when she opens her eyes,
for she might fall in love with the first thing she sees as ducklings
       do.
That monster is already straining at his chains and slurping,
ready to go right to it:
he has been well prepared for coupling
by his pinching leering keeper, who's been saying for weeks,
"Ya gonna get a little nookie, kid,"
or "How do you go for some poontang, baby?"

All the evil in him is focused on this one thing now
as he is led into her very presence.

She awakens slowly,
she bats her eyes,
she gets up out of the equipment,
and finally she stands in all her seamed glory,
a monster princess with a hairdo like a fright wig,
lightning flashing in the background
like a halo and a wedding veil,
like a photographer snapping pictures of great moments.

She stands and stares with her electric eyes,
beginning to understand that in this life too
she was just another body to be raped.
The monster is ready to go:
he roars with joy at the sight of her,
so they let him loose and he goes right for those knockers.
And she starts screaming to break your heart
and you realize that she was just born:
in spite of her big tits she was just a baby.

But her instincts are right—
rather death than that green slobber:
she jumps off the parapet.
And then the monster's sex drive goes wild.
Thwarted, it turns to violence, demonstrating sublimation crudely;
and he wrecks the lab, those burping acids and buzzing coils,
overturning the control panel so the equipment goes off like a
          bomb,
the stone castle crumbling and crashing in the storm,
destroying them all ... perhaps.

Perhaps somehow the Baron got out of that wreckage of his
          dreams
with his evil intact, if not his good looks,
and more wicked than ever went on with his thrilling career.
And perhaps even the monster lived
to roam the earth, his desire still ungratified;

and lovers out walking in shadowy and deserted places
will see his shape loom up over them, their doom—
and children sleeping in their beds
will wake up in the dark night screaming
as his hideous body grabs them.

Curse Of The Cat Woman

It sometimes happens
that the woman you meet and fall in love with
is of that strange Transylvanian people
with an affinity for cats.

You take her to a restaurant, say, or a show,
on an ordinary date, being attracted
by the glitter in her slitty eyes and her catlike walk,
and afterwards of course you take her in your arms
and she turns into a black panther
and bites you to death.

Or perhaps you are saved in the nick of time
and she is tormented by the knowledge of her tendency:
that she daren't hug a man
unless she wants to risk clawing him up.

This puts you both in a difficult position—
panting lovers who are prevented from touching
not by bars but by circumstance:
you have terrible fights and say cruel things
for having the hots does not give you a sweet temper.

One night you are walking down a dark street
and hear the pad-pad of a panther following you,
but when you turn around there are only shadows,
or perhaps one shadow too many.

You approach, calling, "Who's there?"

and it leaps on you.
Luckily you have brought along your sword
and you stab it to death.

And before your eyes it turns into the woman you love,
her breast impaled on your sword,
her mouth dribbling blood saying she loved you
but couldn't help her tendency.

So death released her from the curse at last,
and you knew from the angelic smile on her dead face
that in spite of a life the devil owned,
love had won, and heaven pardoned her.

10

Donald Justice (1925–2004)

Ralph: A Love Story

In what had been a failing music store
A man named Flowers opened the first cinema
In Moultrie. Ralph was the projectionist,
At seventeen the first projectionist.
And there was a piano from the store
On which the wife accompanied the action
With little bursts of von Suppé and Wagner.

Ralph liked the dark of the projection booth;
He liked the flickering images of the screen.
And yet because he liked it all so well,
He feared expulsion from this Eden,

Not so much feared as knew the day must come,
Given his luck, when it would all run out,
Which made the days more paradisal still.

Margot, the daughter, twenty and unmarried—
To tell it all quickly—seduced Ralph.
She let him think he was seducing her.
They used to meet in the projection booth,
Embracing wordlessly but laughing too,
Unable to suppress their self-delight.
Time after time they had almost been caught.
Then, as in novels, Margot became pregnant.

The cinema closed on Sundays. What Ralph did
Was slip off to the depot about dusk
To wait among the shadows for the train;
That night he watched with a sudden hurt nostalgia
The sparse pale farmlights passing from his life—
And he understood nothing, only that he was young.
Within a week or two he joined the navy.

Not that he could have guessed it at the time,
But those quick laughing grapplings in the dark
Would be the great romance his life would know,
Though there would be more women, more than he wanted
Really, before it was all finished for him.
And even in the last few years, working
His final job, night watchman at a warehouse,
He might be resting on a stack of lumber
Toward morning, say, and there would come to him
The faces of the stars before the stars
Had names, only dark-painted eyes, and hands
That spoke the sign-language of the secret heart.
(Oh, not that he remembered. He did not.)

She wrote him over the first months two letters
In care of his parents in another town.
The envelopes were decorated boldly
With home-drawn hearts, some broken, pierced by arrows,

From which the mother understood enough
To save the letters but not forward them.
And when his tour of duty ended finally
He opened them and read them and was sorry.
It had been the happiness of his life.
But he could not go back to it. He could not.

So it was gone, the way a thing does go
Yet keep a sort of phantom presence always.
He would be drinking with some woman, lying
Beside her on a tourist cabin bed,
When something would come ghosting back to him,
Some little thing. Such paradise it had been!

And when it *was* all finished for him, at the end,
In the small bedroom of his sister's house,
Surrounded by his shelves of paperbacks—
Westerns mostly, and a few private-eyes—
Lying there on the single bed, half gone
On Echo Springs, he could not call it back.
Or if it came back it was in the form
Of images in the dark, shifting and flashing,
Badly projected, spooling out crazily
In darkness, in a little room, and he
Could not control it. It was like dying.
No, it *was* dying, and he let it go.

Maxine Kumin (1925–)

The Selling of the Slaves

Lexington, Kentucky

The brood mares on the block at Tipton Pavilion
have ears as delicate as wineglass stems.
Their eyes roll up and out like china dolls'.
Dark red petals flutter in their nostrils.
They are a strenuous ballet, the thrust and suck
of those flanks, and meanwhile the bags of foals
joggle, each pushing against its knapsack.

They are brought on one at a time, worked over
in the confines of a chain-link silver tether
by respectful attendants in white jackets
and blackface. The stage manager hovers
in the background with a gleaming shovel
and the air ripens with the droppings he dips up.

In the velvet pews a white-tie congregation
fans itself with the order of the service.
Among them pass the prep-school deacons
in blazers and the emblems of their districts.
Their hymnals are clipboards. The minister
in an Old Testament voice recites
a liturgy of bloodlines. Ladies and Gentlemen:

Hip Number 20 is Rich and Rare
a consistent and highclass producer.
She is now in foal to that good horse, Brazen.
Candy Dish slipped twins on January one
and it is with genuine regret I must announce
that Roundabout, half sister to a champion,
herself a dam of winners, is barren this season.

She is knocked down at eleven thousand dollars
to the man from Paris with a diamond in his tooth,
the man from Paris with a snake eye in his collar.

When money changes hands among men of worth
it is all done with sliding doors and decorum
but snake whips slither behind the curtain.
In the vestry flasks go round. The gavel's
report is a hollow gunshot:
sold, old lady! and the hot
manure of fear perfumes God's chapel.

12

James Merrill (1926–1995)

Days of 1935

Ladder horned against moonlight,
Window hoisted stealthily—
That's what I'd steel myself at night
To see, or sleep to see.

My parents were out partying,
My nurse was old and deaf and slow.
Way off in the servants' wing
Cackled a radio.

On the Lindbergh baby's small
Cold features lay a spell, a swoon.
It seemed entirely plausible
For my turn to come soon,

For a masked and crouching form
Lithe as tiger, light as moth,
To glide towards me, clap a firm
Hand across my mouth,

Then sheer imagination ride
Off with us in its old jalopy,
Trailing bedclothes like a bride
Timorous but happy.

A hundred tenuous dirt roads
Dew spangles, lead to the web's heart.
That whole pale night my captor reads
His brow's unwrinkling chart.

Dawn. A hovel in the treeless
Trembling middle of nowhere,
Hidden from the world by palace
Walls of dust and glare.

A lady out of *Silver Screen*,
Her careful rosebud chewing gum,
Seems to expect us, lets us in,
Nods her platinum

Spit curls deadpan (I will wait
Days to learn what makes her smile)
At a blue enamel plate
Of cold greens I can smell—

But swallow? Never. The man's face
Rivets me, a lightning bolt.
Lean, sallow, lantern-jawed, he lays
Pistol and cartridge belt

Between us on the oilskin (I
Will relive some things he did
Until I die, until I die)
And clears his throat: "Well, Kid,

You've figured out what's happening.
We don't mean to hurt you none
Unless we have to. Everything
Depends on, number one,

How much you're worth to your old man,
And, number two, no more of this—"
Meaning my toothprints on his hand,
Indenture of a kiss.

With which he fell upon the bed
And splendidly began to snore.
"Please, I'm sleepy too," I said.
She pointed to the floor.

The rag rug, a rainbow threadbare,
Was soft as down. For good or bad
I felt her watching from her chair
As no one ever had.

Their names were Floyd and Jean. I guess
They lived in what my parents meant
By sin: unceremoniousness
Or common discontent.

"Gimme—Wait—Hey, watch that gun—
Why don't these dumb matches work—
See you later—Yeah, have fun—
Wise guy—Floozie—Jerk—"

Or else he bragged of bygone glories,
Stores robbed, cars stolen, dolls betrayed,
Escape from two reformatories.
Said Jean, "Wish you'd of stayed."

To me they hardly spoke, just watched
Or gave directions in dumb show.
I nodded back like one bewitched
By a violent glow.

Each morning Floyd went for a ride
To post another penciled note.
Indignation nationwide
Greeted what he wrote.

Each afternoon, brought papers back.
One tabloid's whole front page was spanned
By the headline bold and black:
FIEND ASKS 200 GRAND.

Photographs too. My mother gloved,
Hatted, bepearled, chin deep in fur.
Dad glowering—was it true he loved
Others besides her?

Eerie, speaking likenesses.
One positively heard her mild
Voice temper some slow burn of his,
"Not before the child."

The child. That population map's
Blanknesses and dots were me!
Mine, those swarming eyes and lips,
Centers of industry

Italics under which would say
(And still do now and then, I fear)
Is This Child Alive Today?
Last Hopes Disappear.

Toy ukelele, terrorstruck
Chord, the strings so taut, so few—
Tingling I hugged my pillow. *Pluck*
Some deep nerve went. I knew

That life was fiction in disguise.
My teeth said, chattering in Morse,
"Are you a healthy wealthy wise
Red-blooded boy? Of course?

Then face the music. Stay. Outwit
Everyone. Captivity
Is beckoning—make a dash for it!
It will set you free."

Sometimes as if I were not there
He put his lips against her neck.
Her head lolled sideways, just like Claire
Coe in "Tehuantepec."

Then both would send me looks so heaped
With a lazy, scornful mirth,
This was growing up, I hoped,
The first flushed fruits of earth.

One night I woke to hear the room
Filled with crickets—no, bedsprings.
My eyes dilated in the gloom,
My ears made out things.

Jean: The kid, he's still awake . . .
Floyd: Time he learned . . . Oh baby . . . God . . .
Their prone tango, for my sake,
Grew intense and proud.

And one night—pure "Belshazzar's Feast"
When the slave-girl is found out—
She cowered, face a white blaze ("Beast!")
From his royal clout.

Mornings, though, she came and went,
Buffed her nails and plucked her brows.
What had those dark doings meant?
Less than the fresh bruise

Powdered over on her cheek.
I couldn't take my eyes away.
Let hers meet them! Let her speak!
She put down *Photoplay:*

"Do you know any stories, Kid?
Real stories—but not real, I mean.
Not just dumb things people did.
Wouldja tell one to Jean?"

I stared at her—*she* was the child!—
And a tale came back to me.
Bluebeard. At its end she smiled
Half incredulously.

I spun them out all afternoon.
Wunspontime, I said and said . . .
The smile became a dainty yawn
Rose-white and rose-red.

The little mermaid danced on knives,
The beauty slept in her thorn bower.
Who knows but that our very lives
Depend on such an hour?

The fisherman's hut became Versailles
Because he let the dolphin go ...
Jean's lids have shut. I'm lonely. I
Am pausing on tiptoe

To marvel at the shimmer breath
Inspires along your radii,
Spider lightly running forth
To kiss the simple fly

Asleep. A chance to slip the net,
Wriggle down the dry stream bed,
Now or never! This child cannot.
An iridescent thread

Binds him to her slumber deep
Within a golden haze made plain
Precisely where his fingertip
Writes on the dusty pane

In spit his name, address, age nine
—Which the newspapers and such
Will shortly point to as a fine
Realistic touch.

Grown up, he thinks how S, T, you—
Second childhood's alphabet
Still unmastered, it is true,
Though letters come—have yet

Touched his heart, occasioned words
Not quickened by design alone,
Responses weekly winging towards
Your distance from his own,

Distance that much more complex
For its haunting ritornel:
*Things happen to a child who speaks
To strangers, mark it well!*

Thinks how you or V—where does
It end, will *any*one have done?—
Taking the wheel (cf. those "Days
Of 1971")

Have driven, till his mother's Grade
A controls took charge, or handsome
Provisions which his father made
Served once again as ransom,

Driven your captive far enough
For the swift needle on the gauge
To stitch with delicate kid stuff
His shoddy middle age.

Here was Floyd. The evening sun
Filled his eyes with funny light.
"Junior, you'll be home real soon."
To Jean, "Tomorrow night."

What was happening? Had my parents
Paid? pulled strings? Or maybe I
Had failed in manners, or appearance?
Must this be goodbye?

I'd hoped I was worth more than crime
Itself, which never paid, could pay.
Worth more than my own father's time
Or mother's negligée

Undone where dim ends barely met,
This being a Depression year . . .
I'd hoped, I guess, that they would let
Floyd and Jean keep me here.

We ate in silence. He would stop
Munching and gaze into the lamp.
She wandered out on the dark stoop.
The night turned chill and damp.

When she came in, she'd caught a bug.
She tossed alone in the iron bed.
Floyd dropped beside me on the rug;
Growled, "Sleep." I disobeyed.

Commenced a wary, mortal heat
Run neck by nose. Small fingers felt,
Sore point of all that wiry meat,
A nipple's tender fault.

Time stopped. His arm somnambulist
Had circled me, warm, salt as blood.
Mine was the future in his fist
To get at if I could,

While his heart beat like a drum
And *Oh baby* faint and hoarse
Echoed from within his dream . . .
The next day Jean was worse

—Or I was. Dawn discovered me
Sweating on my bedroom floor.
Was there no curbing fantasy
When one had a flair?

Came those nights to end the tale.
I shrank to see the money tumble,
All in 20s, from a teal
Blue Studebaker's rumble

Down a slope of starlit brush.
Sensed with anguish the foreseen
Net of G-men, heard the hush
Deepen, then Floyd's voice ("Jean,

Baby, we've been doublecrossed!")
Drowned out by punctual crossfire
That left the pillow hot and creased.
By three o'clock, by four,

They stood in handcuffs where the hunt
Was over among blood-smeared rocks
—Whom I should not again confront
Till from the witness-box

I met their stupid, speechless gaze.
How empty they appeared, how weak
By contrast with my opening phrase
As I began to speak:

"You I adored I now accuse ..."
Would imagination dare
Follow that sentence like a fuse
Sizzling towards the Chair?

See their bodies raw and swollen
Sagging in a skein of smoke?
The floor was reeling where I'd fallen.
Even my old nurse woke

And took me in her arms. I pressed
My guilty face against the void
Warmed and scented by her breast.
Jean, I whispered, Floyd.

A rainy day. The child is bored.
While Emma bakes he sits, half-grown.
The kitchen dado is of board
Painted like board. Its grain

Shiny buff on cinnamon
Mimics the real, the finer grain.
He watches icing sugar spin
Its thread. He licks in vain

Heavenly flavors from a spoon.
Left in the metallic bowl
Is a twenty-five watt moon.
Somewhere rings a bell.

Wet walks from the East porch lead
Down levels manicured and rolled
To a small grove where pets are laid
In shallow emerald.

The den lights up. A Sazerac
Helps his father face the *Wall
Street Journal.* Jules the colored (black)
Butler guards the hall.

Tel & Tel executives,
Heads of Cellophane or Tin,
With their animated wives
Are due on the 6:10.

Upstairs in miles of spangled blue
His mother puts her make-up on.
She kisses him sweet dreams, but who—
Floyd and Jean are gone—

Who will he dream of? True to life
He's played them false. A golden haze
Past belief, past disbelief . . .
Well. Those were the days.

13

Donald Hall (1928–)

Wolf Knife

from The Journals of CF Hoyt, USN, 1826–1889

"In mid August, in the second year
of my First Polar Expedition, the snow and ice of winter
almost upon us, Kantiuk and I
attempted to dash by sledge
along Crispin Bay, searching again for relics
of the Franklin Expedition. Now a storm blew,
and we turned back, and we struggled slowly
in snow, lest we depart land and venture onto ice
from which a sudden fog and thaw
would abandon us to the Providence
of the sea.

                              "Near nightfall
I thought I heard snarling behind us.
Kantiuk told me
that two wolves, lean as the bones
of a wrecked ship,
had followed us the last hour, and snapped their teeth
as if already feasting.
I carried but the one charge

in my rifle, since, approaching the second winter,
we rationed stores.

        "As it turned dark,
we could push no further, and made
camp in a corner
of ice hummocks,
and the wolves stopped also, growling
just past the limits of vision,
coming closer, until I could hear
the click of their feet on ice. Kantiuk laughed
and remarked that the wolves appeared to be most hungry.
I raised my rifle, prepared to shoot the first
that ventured close, hoping
to frighten the other.

        "Kantiuk struck my rifle
down, and said again
that the wolves were hungry, and laughed.
I feared that my old companion
was mad, here in the storm, among ice-hummocks,
stalked by wolves. Now Kantiuk searched
in his pack, and extracted
two knives—*turnoks*, the Innuits called them—
which by great labor were sharpened, on both sides,
to the sharpness like the edge of a barber's razor,
and approached our dogs
and plunged both knives
into the body of our youngest dog
who had limped all day.

        "I remember
that I considered turning my rifle on Kantiuk
as he approached, then passed me,
carrying knives red with the gore of our dog—
who had yowled, moaned, and now lay
expiring, surrounded

by curious cousins and uncles,
possibly hungry—and thrust the knives
handle-down in the snow.

                     "Immediately
he left the knives, the vague, gray
shape of the wolves
turned solid, out of the darkness and the snow,
and set ravenously
to licking blood from the honed steel.
The double edge of the knives
so lacerated the tongues of the starved beasts
that their own blood poured
copiously forth
to replenish the dog's blood, and they ate
more furiously than before, while Kantiuk laughed,
and held his sides
laughing.

                     "And I laughed also,
perhaps in relief that Providence had delivered us
yet again, or perhaps—under conditions of extremity,
far from Connecticut—finding these creatures
acutely ridiculous, so avid
to swallow their own blood. First one, and then the other
collapsed, dying,
bloodless in the snow black with their own blood,
and Kantiuk retrieved
his *turnoks*, and hacked lean meat
from the thigh of the larger wolf,
which we ate
gratefully, blessing the Creator, for we were hungry."

14

Anne Sexton (1928–1974)

The Moss of His Skin

Young girls in old Arabia were often buried
alive next to their dead fathers, apparently as
sacrifice to the goddesses of the tribes...
> Harold Feldman, "Children of the Desert"
> *Psychoanalysis and Psychoanalytic Review,*
> Fall 1958

It was only important
to smile and hold still,
to lie down beside him
and to rest awhile,
to be folded up together
as if we were silk,
to sink from the eyes of mother
and not to talk.
The black room took us
like a cave or a mouth
or an indoor belly.
I held my breath
and daddy was there,
his thumbs, his fat skull,
his teeth, his hair growing
like a field or a shawl.
I lay by the moss
of his skin until
it grew strange. My sisters
will never know that I fall
out of myself and pretend
that Allah will not see
how I hold my daddy
like an old stone tree.

15

X. J. Kennedy (1929–)

What She Told the Sheriff

Hot nights out in the cornshocks,
  Snakelike they'd go
Bashing about in pickup trucks,
  Headlights on low,
Staking out soft beds in Hell,
  Giggling. Till morning,
Safe on my windowsill,
  I'd do the darning,
Three-way lamp all the way up,
  Hymns turned on louder,
Knees tight locked, china cup
  Of headache powder
Running over. I'd kiss Christ
  (My own right arm)
Or read till, my eyes crossed,
  Red words would squirm.
I'd pray: Change places. Lord,
  Stroke by stroke the corn
Watches You nailed back on Your board
  Sure as You're born.
Lend me the power to damn
  Those lipsticked, caving
Doors to man's battering-ram.
  What one's worth saving?—
No sign. Only the moon's gleam,
  Monotonous tick talk
From the wall clock, shine of ice cream
  Bowls from the dish rack,
Four years locked in a frame
  Instead of marriage:
The sheepskin bearing my name
  Like some miscarriage.

Paul said. *Our days in earth*
  Are as a shadow . . .
Father no doubt slept with
  His plump grass-widow
While Mother courted sleep,
  As ever ailing,
Spending life's ocean trip
  Hugged to the railing.
Next noon, out choosing ears
  For the lunch pot,
I'd come on sin's arrears
  Still body-hot:
There in the scrambled dirt
  The telltale pressings
Of buttocks, a torn-off shirt,
  Love's smelly passings.
Father, how could Your Hand
  Deign to forgive?
Smite them! Don't understand,
  Don't just let live!
I'd weep, the sun's broadsword
  Carving my bonnet,
For this blood-handed world
  And all here on it.
Then one noon, my Maker's ways
  Laid themselves bare.
Scabs fell down from my eyes,
  All stood forth clear:
Worms, worms in leaf and ear,
  Kernel and tassel,
Gnawing the Wurlitzer
  In Burger Castle!
Hell peered through surgeon's slits,
  Burst out of faucets—
Babies chopped off at the root,
  Crushed flat in corsets!
My heart caught fire in me,
  Fire hard to cover—
How endlessly time marks time

When God's your lover—
And it was all I could do
Till my right hour
To hold a lid over my glow,
Sifting cake flour.
Midnight. Led by my sword,
Ripe for reborning,
I strode in where Dad snored,
Mother lay turning:
Two old and swollen sheep
Stretched out for slaughter,
Teeth set adrift to keep
In mineral water,
They were like chopping wood.
Drunk, uncomplaining,
And wondering Dad stood
A long while draining.
Mother half raised her, coughed,
Said—for once painless—
Girl, wipe that cleaver off,
That one's not stainless.
Next, blazing kerosene
Smote the brown oily
Head-shaped time-honored stain
From Dad's chair doily.
Along the henhouse path,
Dry faggots crackled.
At each step I shook earth with
The bantam cackled.
Saint Michael goaded me,
Grass fire his halo,
Render unto Your Father on high
Your father's silo!
Wrath roared in my right hand,
How soon it catched
Where, like deceivers' tents,
Hay sat pitched.
Creatures of hoof and horn,
Sheol's lumps of tallow,

Struck at the walls of their barn
  That soon grew hollow.
Far as earth led the eye,
  Smoke bloomed, burnt stubble
Crawled legless. It was I
  Cast down the Devil.
Why do you handcuff me?
  Let go! By morning
All Iowa could be
  One high bush, burning.

16

Etheridge Knight (1931–)

Hard Rock Returns to Prison from the Hospital for the Criminal Insane

Hard Rock / was / "known not to take no shit
From nobody," and he had the scars to prove it:
Split purple lips, lumbed ears, welts above
His yellow eyes, and one long scar that cut
Across his temple and plowed through a thick
Canopy of kinky hair.

The WORD / was / that Hard Rock wasn't a mean nigger
Anymore, that the doctors had bored a hole in his head,
Cut out part of his brain, and shot electricity
Through the rest. When they brought Hard Rock back,
Handcuffed and chained, he was turned loose,
Like a freshly gelded stallion, to try his new status.

And we all waited and watched, like a herd of sheep,
To see if the WORD was true.

As we waited we wrapped ourselves in the cloak
Of his exploits: "Man, the last time, it took eight
Screws to put him in the Hole." "Yeah, remember when he
Smacked the captain with his dinner tray?" "He set
The record for time in the Hole—67 straight days!"
"Ol Hard Rock! man, that's one crazy nigger."
And then the jewel of a myth that Hard Rock had once bit
A screw on the thumb and poisoned him with syphilitic spit.

The testing came, to see if Hard Rock was really tame.
A hillbilly called him a black son of a bitch
And didn't lose his teeth, a screw who knew Hard Rock
From before shook him down and barked in his face.
And Hard Rock did *nothing*. Just grinned and looked silly,
His eyes empty like knot holes in a fence.

And even after we discovered that it took Hard Rock
Exactly 3 minutes to tell you his first name,
We told ourselves that he had just wised up,
Was being cool; but we could not fool ourselves for long,
And we turned away, our eyes on the ground. Crushed.
He had been our Destroyer, the doer of things
We dreamed of doing but could not bring ourselves to do,
The fears of years, like a biting whip,
Had cut deep bloody grooves
Across our backs.

A Poem for Black Relocation Centers

Flukum couldn't stand the strain.
Flukum wanted inner and outer order, so
he joined the army where U.S. Manuals made
everything plain—even how to button his shirt,
and how to kill yellow men. (If Flukum

ever felt hurt or doubt about who his enemy
was, the Troop Information Officer or the *Stars
and Stripes* straightened him out.)
And, we must not forget
that Flukum was paid well to let the Red
Blood. And sin? If Flukum ever thought about sin
or Hell for squashing the yellow men, the good Chaplain
(Holy by God and by Congress) pointed out with
Devilish skill that to kill the colored men was not
altogether a sin.

Flukum marched back from the war, straight and tall,
and with presents for all: a water pipe for daddy,
teeny teacups for mama, sheer silk for tittee, and
a jade inlaid dagger for me. But, with a smile
on his face in a place just across the bay,
Flukum, the patriot, got shot that same day,
got shot in his great wide chest, bedecked with good
conduct ribbons. He died surprised, he had thought
the enemy far away on the other side of the sea.

17

Russell Edson (1935–)

The Terrible Angel

In a nursery a mother can't get her baby out of its cradle. The baby, it
has turned to wood, it has become part of its own cradle.

The mother, she cries, tilting, one foot raised, as if in flight for the
front door, just hearing her husband's car in the driveway; but can't, the
carpet holds her . . .

Her husband, he hears her, he wants to rush to her, but can't, the door of the car won't open . . .

The wife, she no longer calls, she has been taken into the carpet, and is part of it; a piece of carpet in the shape of a woman tilted, one foot raised as if to flight.

The husband, he no longer struggles toward his wife. As if he sleeps he has been drawn into the seat of his car; a man sculptured in upholstery.

In the nursery the wooden baby stares with wooden eyes into the last red of the setting sun, even as the darkness that forms in the east begins to join the shadows of the house; the darkness that rises out of the cellar, seeping out from under furniture, oozing from the cracks in the floor . . . The shadow that suddenly collects in the corner of the nursery like the presence of something that was always there . . .

Ape

You haven't finished your ape, said mother to father, who had monkey hair and blood on his whiskers.
I've had enough monkey, cried father.
You didn't eat the hands, and I went to all the trouble to make onion rings for its fingers, said mother.
I'll just nibble on its forehead, and then I've had enough, said father.
I stuffed its nose with garlic, just like you like it, said mother.

Why don't you have the butcher cut these apes up? You lay the whole thing on the table every night; the same fractured skull, the same singed fur; like someone who died horribly. These aren't dinners, these are post-mortem dissections.

Try a piece of its gum, I've stuffed its mouth with bread, said mother.
Ugh, it looks like a mouth full of vomit. How can I bite into its cheek with bread spilling out of its mouth? cried father.
Break one of the ears off, they're so crispy, said mother.

I wish to hell you'd put underpants on these apes; even a jockstrap, screamed father.

Father, how dare you insinuate that I see the ape as anything more than simple meat, screamed mother.

Well, what's with this ribbon tied in a bow on its privates? screamed father.

Are you saying that I am in love with this vicious creature? That I would submit my female opening to this brute? That after we had love on
the kitchen floor I would put him in the oven, after breaking his head
with a frying pan; and then serve him to my husband, that my husband
might eat the evidence of my infidelity . . . ?

I'm just saying that I'm damn sick of ape every night, cried father.

18

George Keithley (1935–)

Silver

Over the frozen lake the wind shines.
Over the prairie it shivers
the migrant camp: Foxes, Sioux,
Winnebagos left behind when the buses rolled
south after harvest. All night
they drift into the Dry Dock Inn. Growers, too,

and their white wives. Over the tavern road
the moon spills its blood
in the wind. Fretfully, as the glow
of scarlet candles warms
her eyes. Erica sheds
her coat of wool and snow.

The jukebox wails blues. Her husband orders
corn whiskey, clips
his tobacco. Tucks the sleek
blade in his boot. She drains her glass and roams
the dance floor. When he calls
Erica shakes her yellow hair—

He hears her laughter as the rhythms stir
her skirt. Wabashaw, a fieldhand
half Sioux, walks her way
and grins. Wicks in tin cups
fling at their feet the shadows
hawks cast on summer hay—

Shadow wings which circle
the couple as they spin
in slow time. They turn, stare.
Twice the steel gleam strikes—
Breathless in each other's arms
they cling, falling to the floor.

Two off-duty deputies handcuff
her husband, phone the coroner:
Mueller's battered Buick arrives.
The bartender obliges, helps carry
both bodies. "So damn quick—
One dance. It cost two lives!"

Mueller blows on his fingers,
fumbles for the keys.
His ancient stationwagon, broad
as a hearse, wallows toward town

like a boat too low in the water—
A black boat sinking in the road.

The wolf whose thirst has lured her
onto the lake, watches
the wagon crawl out of sight.
When her raw tongue lolls
over the ice unsatisfied,
her throat opens to the night—

The wind, pure silver, howls.

19

Nancy Willard (1936–)

Pish, Posh, said Hieronymous Bosch

Once upon a time there was an artist
named Hieronymous Bosch who loved odd creatures.
Not a day passed that the good woman who looked
after his house didn't find a new creature
lurking in a corner or sleeping in a cupboard.
To her fell the job of
      feeding them,
      weeding them,
      walking them,
      stalking them,

calming them,
combing them,
scrubbing and tucking in all of them—
until one day…

"I'm quitting your service, I've had quite enough
of your three-legged thistles asleep in my wash,
of scrubbing the millstone you use for a dish,
and riding to shops on pickle-winged fish."

"Pish, posh,"
said Hieronymous Bosch.

"How can I cook for you? How can I bake
when the oven keeps turning itself to a rake,
and a beehive in boots and a pear-headed priest
call monkeys to order and lizards to feast?

"The nuns were quiet. I'd rather be bored
and hang out their laundry in sight of the Lord,

"Than wrestle with dragons to get to my sink
while the cats chase the cucumbers, slickity-slink."

"They go slippity-slosh,"
said Hieronymous Bosch.

"I don't mind the ferret, I do like the bee.
All witches' familiars are friendly to me.
I'd share my last crust with a pigeon-toed rat,
And some of my closest relations are cats."

"My aunt was a squash,"
said Hieronymous Bosch.

She packed her fur tippet, her second-best hat.
(The first was devoured by a two-headed bat.)

With a pain in her back and a fog in her head,
she walked twenty-two miles and collapsed into bed.

That night she awoke to a terrible roar.
Her suitcase yawned and unleashed on the floor
a mole in a habit,
      a thistle-down rabbit,
           a troop of jackdaws,
                A three-legged dish,
the pickle-winged fish, and a head wearing claws.

"Take us under your wing, take us up on your back,"
they howled, while the claws murmured, "clickety-clack."

"They're not what I wished for. When women are young
they want curly-haired daughters and raven-haired sons.
In this vale of tears we must take what we're sent,
Feathery, leathery, lovely, or bent."

With her suitcase and tippet secure on the dish,
she clambered aboard the pickle-winged fish.

Hieronymous rose from a harrowing night,
saw salvation approaching, and crowed with delight.

"My lovey, my dear, have you come back to stay?
Let the crickets rejoice and the mantises pray,
let the lizards do laundry, the cucumbers cook.
I shall set down new rules in my gingerbread book.

"The dragon shall wear a gold ring in his nose
and the daws stoke the fire and the larks mend our clothes
forever and ever, my nibble, my nosh,
till death do us part," said Hieronymous Bosch.

20

Lawson Inada (1938–)

Legends from Camp

PROLOGUE

It began as truth, as fact.
That is, at least the numbers, the statistics,
are there for verification:

10 camps, 7 state,
120,113 residents.

Still, figures can lie: people are born, die.
And as for the names of the places themselves,
these, too, were subject to change:

Denson or Jerome, Arkansas;
Gila or Canal, Arizona;
Tule Lake or Newell, California;
Amache or Granada, Colorado.

As was the War Relocation Authority
with its mention of "camps" or "centers" for:

Assembly,
Concentration,
Detention,
Evacuation,
Internment,
Relocation,—
among others.

"Among others"—that's important also. Therefore, let's not forget
contractors, carpenters, plumbers, electricians and architects, sewage

engineers, and all the untold thousands who provided the materials, decisions, energy, and transportation to make the camps a success, including, of course, the administrators, clerks, and families who not only swelled the population but were there to make and keep things shipshape according to D.C. directives and people deploying coffee in the various offices of the WRA, overlooking, overseeing rivers, city-scapes, bays, whereas in actual camp the troops—excluding, of course, our aunts and uncles and sisters and brothers and fathers and mothers serving stateside, in the South Pacific, the European theater—pretty much had things in order; finally, there were the grandparents, who since the turn of the century, simply assumed they were living in America "among others."

The situation, obviously, was rather confusing.
It obviously confused simple people
who had simply assumed they were friends, neighbors,
colleagues, partners, patients, customers, students,
teachers, of, not so much "aliens" or "non-aliens,"
but likewise simple, unassuming people
who paid taxes as fellow citizens and populated
pews and desks and fields and places
of ordinary American society and commerce.

Rumors flew. Landed. What's what? Who's next?

And then, "Just like that," it happened.
And then, "Just like that," it was over.
Sun, moon, stars—they came, and went.

And then, and then, things happened,
and as they ended they kept happening,
and as they happened they ended
and began again, happening, happening,

until the event, the experience, the history,
slowly began to lose its memory,
gradually drifting into a kind of fiction—

a "true story based on fact,"
but nevertheless with "all the elements of fiction"—
and then, and then, sun, moon, stars,
we come, we come, to where we are:
Legend.

I. THE LEGEND OF PEARL HARBOR

"Aloha or Bust!"

We got here first!

II. THE LEGEND OF THE HUMANE SOCIETY

This is as
simple
as it gets:

In a pinch,
dispose
of your pets.

III. THE LEGEND OF PROTEST

The F.B.I. swooped in early,
taking our elders in the process—

for "subversive" that and this.

People ask: "Why didn't you protest?"
Well, you might say: "They had *hostages.*"

IV. THE LEGEND OF LOST BOY

Lost Boy was not his name.

He had another name, a given name—
at another, given time and place—
but those were taken away.
The road was taken away.
The dog was taken away.
The food was taken away.
The house was taken away.

The boy was taken away—
but he was not lost.
Oh, no—he knew exactly where he was—

and if someone had asked
or needed directions,
he could have told them:

"This is the fairgrounds.
That's Ventura Avenue over there.
See those buildings? That's town!"

This place also had buildings—
but they were all black, the same.
There were no houses, no trees,
no hedges, no streets, no homes.

But, every afternoon, a big truck
came rolling down the rows.
It was full of water, cool,
and the boy would follow it, cool.
It smelled like rain,
and even made some rainbows!

So on this hot, hot day,
the boy followed and followed,
and when the truck stopped,
then sped off in the dust,
the boy didn't know where he was.

He knew, but he didn't know

which barrack was what.
And so he cried. A lot.
He looked like the truck.
Until Old Man Ikeda
found him, bawled him out.
Until Old Man Ikeda
laughed and called him
"Lost Boy."
Until Old Man Ikeda
walked him through
the rows, and rows,
the people, the people,
the crowd.

Until his mother
cried and laughed
and called him
"Lost Boy."

Until Lost Boy
thought he was found.

V. THE LEGEND OF FLYING BOY

This only happened once,
but once is enough—
so listen carefully.

There was a boy
who had nothing to do.
No toys, no nothing.
Plus, it was hot
in the empty room.

Well, the room was full
of sleeping parents
and an empty cot.
The boy was bored.

He needed something to do.
A hairpin on the floor
needed picking up.

It, too, needed
something to do—
like the wire, the socket
over there on the wall.

You know the rest
of the story—
but not the best
of the story:

the feel of power,
the empowering act
of being the air!

You had to be there.
Including the activity
that followed.

Flying Boy—
where are you?

Flying Boy—
you flew!

VI. THE LEGEND OF THE GREAT ESCAPE

The people were passive:
Even when a train paused
in the Great Plains, even
when soldiers were eating,
they didn't try to escape.

VII. THE LEGEND OF TALKS-WITH-HANDS

Actually, this was a whole,
intact family who lived
way over there at the edge
of our Arkansas camp.

Their name? I don't know.
Ask my mother—such ladies
were friends from "church camp."

Also, the family didn't just
talk with their hands.
The man made toys with his,
the woman knitted, and the boy
could fold his paper airplanes.

And, back in those days,
a smile could go a long ways
toward saying something.

And we were all ears.
Talking, and during prayers.

VIII. THE LEGEND OF THE HAKUJIN WOMAN

This legend is about legendary
freedom of choice, options—

because this Hakujin woman
chose to be there.

She could have been anywhere—
New York City, Fresno, or over
with the administration.
Instead, she selected an ordinary

barracks room to share
with her husband.

IX. THE LEGEND OF COYOTE

Buddy was his name. And, yes, he was a Trickster.
He claimed he wasn't even one of us.
He claimed he had some kind of "tribe" somewhere.

He claimed he "talked with spirits."
He claimed he could "see God in the stars."
He claimed the "spirits are everywhere."

He was just a kid. We were just barracks neighbors.
And the one thing Buddy did was make paper airplanes
out of any catalog page or major announcement—

and I mean to tell you, those things could fly!
Those things would go zipping off over barbed wire,
swirl by amazed soldiers in guard towers,

and, sometimes in the swamp, they didn't seem to land.
That was when another claim came in—they went
"all the way to Alaska" and also "back to the tribe."

Buddy. If I had smarts like that, I'd be an engineer.
Buddy. His dreams, his visions. He simply disappeared.

X. THE LEGEND OF THE MAGIC MARBLES

My uncle was going overseas.
He was heading to the European theater,
and we were all going to miss him.

He had been stationed by Cheyenne,
and when he came to say good-bye

he brought me a little bag of marbles.
But the best one, an agate, cracked.
It just broke, like bone, like flesh—
so my uncle comforted me with this story:

> *"When we get home to Fresno,*
> *I will take you into the basement*
> *and give you my box of magic marbles.*
>
> *These marbles are marbles—*
> *so they can break and crack and chip—*
> *but they are also magic*
>
> *so they can always be fixed:*
> *all you have to do is leave them*
> *overnight in a can of Crisco*
>
> *next day they're good as new."*

Uncle. Uncle. Uncle. What happened to *you*?

XI. THE LEGEND OF SHOYU

Legend had it that, even in Arkansas,
some people had soy sauce.
Well, not exactly *our* soy sauce,
which we were starved for,
but some related kind of dark
and definitive liquid
to flavor you through the day.

That camp was in the Delta,
where the Muddy Waters lay.

Black shoyu. Black shoyu.
Let me taste the blues!

XII. THE LEGEND OF THE JEROME SMOKESTACK

There is no legend.
It just stands there
in a grassy field,
the brush of swampland,
soaring up to the sky.

It's just the tallest
thing around for miles.
Pilots fly by it.

Some might say it's
a tribute, a monument,
a memorial to something.
But no, not really.

It's just a massive
stack of skills, labor,
a multitude of bricks.
And what it expressed
was exhaust, and waste.

It's just a pile of past.
Home of the wind, rain,
residence of bodies, nests.
I suppose it even sings.

But no, it's not legend.
It just stands, withstands.

XIII. THE LEGEND OF BAD BOY

Bad Boy wasn't his name.
And as a matter of fact,
there were a lot of them.

Bad Boy watched. He saw
soldiers shoot rats, snakes;
they even shot a dog.

Bad Boy learned. He did
what he could to insects—
whatever it took to be a Man.

XIV. THE LEGEND OF GOOD GIRL

Good Girl was good. She really was.
She never complained; she helped others.
She worked hard; she played until tired.
Good Girl, as you guessed, was Grandmother.

XV. THE LEGEND OF THE FULL MOON OVER AMACHE

As it turned out,
Amache is said to have been named
for an Indian princess—

not a regular squaw—

who perished upstream,
in the draw,
of the Sand Creek Massacre.

Her bones floated down
to where the camp was now.

The full moon?
It doesn't have anything to do
with this. It's just there,

illuminating, is all.

XVI. THE LEGEND OF AMATERASU

The Sun Goddess ruled the Plain of Heaven.
She did this for eons and eons, forever
and ever, before anyone could remember.

Amaterasu, as a Goddess, could always do
exactly as She wanted; thus, She haunted
Colorado like the myth She was, causing

wrinkles in the heat, always watching You.

XVII. THE LEGEND OF GROUCHO

Hey, come on now, let's hear it for Groucho!
Groucho was a florist by profession
and the doggone best natural-born comedian.

It was said by some, with tears in their eyes,
that ol' Groucho could make a delivery to a funeral
and have everyone just a-rollin' in the aisles,

Even on the worst of bad days, he was worth a smile.

Groucho was Groucho—before, during, after.
Wherever he was, there was bound to be laughter.

And the thing is, he really wasn't all that witty.
He was actually serious, which made it really funny—

him and that broken English and the gimpy leg.
He was a reserved bachelor too, a devoted son
who sent whatever he had to his mother in Japan.

Still, he had that something that tickled people
pink and red and white and blue and even had
the lizards lapping it up, basking in it, happy!

Maybe that was the magic—he was "seriously happy."
And not only legend has it, but I was there,
when a whole mess of pheasants came trekking clear
from Denver, just for Groucho and the heck of it,
and proceeded to make themselves into sukiyaki—

with the rest of us yukking and yakking it up all the while!

Ah, yes, Groucho! He brought joy out in people!
And when he finally got back home to Sacramento
and the news, he threw his flowers in the air,

toward Hiroshima—and of course he died laughing!

XVIII. THE LEGEND OF SUPERMAN

Superman, being Superman,
had his headquarters out there
somewhere between Gotham City
and Battle Creek, Michigan.

Superman, being Superman,
even knew my address:

  Block 6G, 5C
  Amache, Colorado
  America

And Superman, being Superman,
sent me his Secret Code,
based on all the Planets—

with explicit instructions
to keep it hidden from others,
like "under a bed, a sofa,
or under stockings in a drawer."

Superman, being Superman,
didn't seem to understand.
Where could anything hide?

And, since we all spoke code
on a regular basis, day to day,

Superman, being Superman,
gathered up his Planets
and simply flew away!

XIX. THE LEGEND OF OTHER CAMPS

They were out there, all right,
but nobody knew what they were up to.
It was tough enough deciphering
what was going on right here.

Still, even barracks have ears:
so-and-so shot and killed;
so-and-so shot and lived;
infants, elders, dying of heat;
epidemics, with so little care.

It was tough enough deciphering
what was going on anywhere.

XX. THE LEGEND OF HOME

Home, too, was out there.
It had names like
Marysville, Placerville,
Watsonville, and Lodi—

and they were all big cities
or at least bigger than camp.

And they were full of trees,
and grass, with fruit
for the picking, dogs
to chase, cats to catch

on streets and roads
where Joey and Judy lived.

Imagine that!
The blue tricycle
left in the weeds somewhere!
And when you came to a fence,
you went around it!

And one of those homes
not only had a tunnel
but an overpass
that, when you went over,

revealed everything
going on forever up to
a gleaming bridge
leading into neon lights
and ice cream leaning
double-decker.

Imagine that!

XXI. THE LEGEND OF THE BLOCK 6G OBAKE

I still don't mention his name in public.
And I'm sure he's long since passed on.
As a matter of fact, he may have died in camp.

He was that old. And he was also slow—
slow and loud enough to frighten
grown men out of their wits.

And all he did was go around our block
banging a stick on a garbage can lid
and chanting, droning, *"Block 6G Obake."*

He did that every evening, when the ghost
to him appeared—his personal ghost,
or whatever it was that haunted the camp.
He was punctual, persistent, specific.
And then I guess he either moved or died
Whatever it was, we never spoke of him.

Because, the thing is, he was right.
Amache really was haunted. As it still is.
Amache was, is, are: Nightly, on television.

XXII. THE LEGEND OF BURNING THE WORLD

It got so cold in Colorado we would burn the world.
That is, the rocks, the coal, that trucks would dump in a pile.
Come on, children! Everybody! Bundle up! Let's go!
But then, in the warmth, you remembered how everything goes up
In smoke.

XXIII. THE LEGEND OF TARGETS

It got so hot in Colorado we would start to go crazy.
This included, of course, soldiers in uniform, on patrol.
So, once a week, just for relief, they went out for target practice.
We could hear them shooting hundreds of rounds, shouting
        like crazy.
It sounded like a New Year's celebration! Such fun is not to
        be missed!
So someone cut a deal, just for the kids, and we went out past the
        fence.
The soldiers shot, and between rounds, we dug in the dunes for
        bullets.
It was great fun! They would aim at us, go *"Pow!"* and we'd
        shout *"Missed!"*

XXIV. THE LEGEND OF BUDDHA

Buddha said we are all buddhas,

XXV. THE LEGEND OF LEAVING

Let's have one more turn
around the barracks.
Let's have one more go
down the rows, rows, rows.
Let's have one last chance
at the length of the fence—

slow, slow, slow,
dust, dust, dust,
billowing behind
the emperor's caravan,
king of the walled city.

Head of State.
Head of Fence.
Head of Towers.
Head of Gate.

Length, height, weight,
corners and corrections
duly dedicated
to my dimensions
and directions.

It's early, it's late.
I'm in no hurry.
An Amache evening.
an Amache morning.
Slowly, this date
came dusty, approaching.
One more turn,
another go,

one last chance—

fast and slow—
before I go.

Who would have known.
Who would have guessed
the twists, the turn
of such events
combined in this
calligraphy of echoes
as inevitable,
as inscrutable
as nostalgia

jangling the nerves,
jangling the keys
of my own release.
Let's have one more turn
of the lock, the key.
Let's have one last look
as I leave
this morning, evening.

All my belongings
are gathered.
All my connections
are scattered.

What's over the horizon?
What's left to abandon?
What's left to administer?
Will anyone ever need
another Camp Director?

21

Dick Allen (1939–)

Cliff Painting

The girls who asked you to do it were the kind who leaned
Against you and no more. I don't think they knew the danger
Up there, at dawn when the cops wouldn't spot you.

I know I was scared. But I was also in love,
So deeply in love my hair would stand on end
Whenever I thought of her. That's why, one morning,

Brush and a can of paint in my old Boy Scout knapsack,
I started to climb. I was so crazy, I'd planned
To paint the biggest heart ever, and fill it with our names,

So the whole valley could see it, and every driver
On the Interstate—maybe even someone looking down
From a low-flying plane. . . . At first it was easy

As I passed the names of junior high school kids,
A few peace signs, a "Black is Beautiful," a "Stop the War,"
Several Bob Dylans and three Rolling Stones—

No pun intended. But then I began to come upon
The highest names, the ones from boys in college
On athletic scholarships, names of the weirdos

Who'd dare anything, and I realized I hadn't thought
This whole thing out enough. Every accessible place
Was taken with a name or heart, or both, and I knew

They must have used ropes, teams of boys with ropes
Had climbed before me, swinging out into space
To declare their love, allegiance, or obsession

At some risk of death. . . . I clung for a long time up there,
Looking down at the valley, thinking of my love, and hearing
What she would say if I failed. It started to drizzle

And a few small pebbles tumbled from the crevice
Where I was wedged. Pieces of moss came loose.
The valley darkened slightly. I closed my eyes and imagined

Falling, and my girl and parents at my funeral,
Then who she would marry instead. . . . And yet, you know,
I wanted fame and immortality right then—so if

Later I failed, wherever I was I could think of someone
Looking up at the cliff and seeing what I'd done, and maybe
For a moment I'd be someone other than a man

With a beer belly, sitting at a bar like this and reminiscing
Over what? Over love, that's what. I kept on climbing
And I found a place, 1 almost killed myself, but should

You look up now you'll see us, though the letters
Are somewhat faded and the heart looks like a kidney,
And later someone wrote above me even larger.
Still, I didn't marry her. At the end, we really fought
One night at the revival drive-in, Dean and Wood and Mineo
Together in the dark. She even wanted me

To climb again, to paint us over, and I laughed.
No way, I told her. Often I think of her trundling with her kids
And husband through the valley, and she glances

Up and there she is, with me again, forever
Linked with me upon the mountainside. . . . I'm glad I did it.
That's love for you. And also, that's revenge.

22

Frank Bidart (1939–)

Herbert White

"When I hit her on the head, it was good,

and then I did it to her a couple of times,—
but it was funny,—afterwards,
it was as if somebody else did it...

Everything flat, without sharpness, richness or line.

Still, I liked to drive past the woods where she lay,
tell the old lady and the kids I had to take a piss,
hop out and do it to her . . .

The whole buggy of them waiting for me
                                        made me feel good;
but still, just like I knew all along,
                        she didn't move.

When the body got too discomposed,
I'd just jack off, letting it fall on her . . .

—It sounds crazy, but I tell you
sometimes it was *beautiful*—; I don't know how
to say it, but for a minute, *everything* was possible—;
and then,
then,—
        well, like I said, she didn't move: and I saw,
under me, a little girl was Just lying there in the mud:

and I knew I couldn't have done that,—
somebody *else* had to have done that,—

standing above her there,

in those ordinary, shitty leaves . . .

—One time, I went to see Dad in a motel where he was
staying with a woman; but she was gone;
you could smell the wine in the air; and he started,
real embarrassing, to cry . . .
                              He was still a little drunk,
and asked me to forgive him for
all he hadn't done—; but, What the shit?
Who would have wanted to stay with Mom? with bastards
not even his own kids?

                    I got in the truck, and started to drive,
and saw a little girl—
who I picked up, hit on the head, and
screwed, and screwed, and screwed, and screwed, then

buried,
          in the garden of the motel . . .

—You see, ever since I was a kid I wanted
to *feel* things make sense: I remember

looking out the window of my room back home,—
and being almost suffocated by the asphalt;
and grass; and trees; and glass;
just *there,* just *there,* doing nothing!
not saying anything! filling me up—
but also being a wall; dead, and stopping me;
—how I wanted to see beneath it, cut

beneath it, and make it
somehow, come alive . . .

                    The salt of the earth;
Mom once said, 'Man's spunk is the salt of the earth . . .'

—That night, at that Twenty-nine Palms Motel
I had passed a million times on the road, everything

fit together; was alright;
it seemed like
                    everything *had* to be there, like I had spent years
trying, and at last finally finished drawing this
                                        huge circle . . .

—But then, suddenly I knew
somebody *else* did it, some bastard
had hurt a little girl—; the motel
                              I could see again, it had been
itself all the time, a lousy
pile of bricks, plaster, that didn't seem to
have to be there,—but *was,* just by chance . . .

—Once, on the farm, when I was a kid,
I was screwing a goat; and the rope around his neck
when he tried to get away
pulled tight;—and Just when I came,
he *died* .. .
              I came back the next day; jacked off over his body;
but it didn't do any good . . .

Mom once said:
'Man's spunk is the salt of the earth, and grows kids.'

I tried so hard to come; more *pain* than anything else;
but didn't do any good . . .

—About six months ago, I heard Dad remarried,
so I drove over to Connecticut to see him and see
if he was happy.
                    She was twenty-five years younger than him:
she had lots of little kids, and I don't know why,
I felt shaky . . .

              I stopped in front of the address; and
snuck up to the window to look in ...
                              —There he was, a kid
six months old on his lap, laughing

and bouncing the kid, happy in his old age
to play the papa after years of sleeping around,—
it twisted me up ...

                    To think that what he wouldn't give me,
                        he *wanted* to give them . . .

        I could have killed the bastard . . .

—Naturally, I just got right back in the car,
and believe me, was determined, determined,
to head straight for home . . .

                        but the more I drove,
I kept thinking about getting a girl,
and the more I thought I shouldn't do it,
the more I had to—

                I saw her coming out of the movies,
saw she was alone, and
kept circling the blocks as she walked along them,
saying, 'You're going to leave her alone.'
'You're going to leave her alone.'

                        —The woods were scary!
As the seasons changed, and you saw more and more
of the skull show through, the nights became clearer,
and the buds,—erect, like nipples . . .

—But then, one night,
nothing *worked* . . .
                Nothing in the sky
would blur like I wanted it to;
and I couldn't, *couldn't,*

get it to seem to me
that somebody *else* did it ...

I tried, and tried, but there was just me there,
and her, and the sharp trees

saying, That's you standing there.
                              You're . . .
                                        just you.'

                    I hope I fry.

—Hell came when I saw
                    MYSELF...
                              and couldn't stand
what I see .. ."

                              23
                    _____

                    Jared Carter (1939–)

The Measuring

You're sickly pale—a crooked root.
But one last remedy remains:
Before the dawn we'll go on foot
Through grass sleeked down by heavy rains
To the sexton's house. Already he
Takes down his spade, and goes
To walk among the whitened rows.
His wife awaits with lengths of string
Necessary for measuring.

She has no fire alight, nor words
To spare, but bolts the wooden door
And helps you out of clothes that fall
Soundlessly to the floor. Naked,
You mount the table and recline;

She comes, her eight stiff fingers
Trailing bright bits of twine. First
Crown to nose, then mouth to chin,
Pressing against each crevice, in
And down the length of your cold frame—
Whispering unintelligible names.

The feet are last to stretch: from heel
To toe each one must be times seven
The other piece. She nods, and knots
The two together, breathes her spell,
Then turns to go. I leave a pair
Of silver dollars there, and take
The string to tie where it will rot
The winter long: on hinge of gate,
Wheelbarrow shaft, or eave-trough's fall.

Behind us, where the darkness drains,
A blackbird settles on the roof
And calls back to another that rain
Is coming like an awful proof.
The two denounce the scratching sound
The sexton's spade makes on the ground—
Measuring off the careful square
Of someone else expected there.

The Gleaning

All day long they have been threshing
and something breaks: the canvas belt
that drives the separator flies off,
parts explode through the swirl
of smoke and chaff, and he is dead
where he stands—drops the pitchfork
as they turn to look at him—and falls.
They carry him to the house and go on
with the work. Five wagons and their teams
stand waiting, it is still daylight,

there will be time enough for grieving.

When the undertaker comes from town
he brings the barber, who must wait
till the women finish washing the body.
Neighbors arrive from the next farm
to take the children. The machines
shut down, one by one, horses
are led away, the air grows still
and empty, then begins to fill up
with the sounds of cicada and mourning dove.
The men stand along the porch, talking
in low voices, smoking their cigarettes;
the undertaker sits in the kitchen
with the family.
                              In the parlor
the barber throws back the curtains
and talks to this man, whom he has known
all his life, since they were boys
together. As he works up a lather
and brushes it onto his cheeks,
he tells him the latest joke. He strops
the razor, tests it against his thumb,
and scolds him for not being more careful.
Then with darkness coming over the room
he lights a lamp, and begins to scrape
at the curve of the throat, tilting the head
this way and that, stretching the skin,
flinging the soap into a basin, gradually
leaving the face glistening and smooth.

And as though his friend had fallen asleep
and it were time now for him to stand up
and stretch his arms, and look at his face
in the mirror, and feel the closeness
of the shave, and marvel at his dreaming—
the barber trims the lamp, and leans down,
and says, for a last time, his name.

24

Frederick Feirstein (1940–)

The Witch

My right foot punctured by an iron hook,
I hop into the cab. I don't care
About the old woman that I overtook.
She hugs a shopping bag against the hood
To stop the driver: "Do you know the fare
To eighty-third and first?" I know I should
Offer to take her and to split the cost:
She looks poor, my house is close to hers.
But she looks like a witch whose path I crossed
In infant nightmares—her few teeth are hooks,
Her hair is iron gray or a cat's fur.
The driver turns, gives me a pitying look.
"I have to go to eighty-sixth and first,"
I say. "Let's split the fare."
                            She squints, "How much?"
She winces, used to expecting the worst.
"Three bucks," I snap, impatient—I'm the witch:
My foot's too sore by now to even touch
And, having luck like hers, it's started to itch.
I back across the seat against the door:
It's hard for her to enter, she's so huge
She rocks, wriggles, until a kind of snore
Tells us she's in. She grins, her eyebrows raised
As if we were engaged in subterfuge
Against the kindly driver. I'm not fazed
I say by biting on my nail. We go.
"A dollar-fifty each?" She asks.
                            "Yes, yes."
"I guessed it, so I ate no lunch."
                            "Oh no?"
As if rebuking me, my foot goes stiff.

"What brought you to St. Luke's?" I ask her.

                                         "Guess."

"A cold?" She shakes her head. "You wonder if
You're pregnant." She slaps my arm and smiles.
As if she's reading from a shopping list:
"Arthritis, slipped disc, sinus headache, piles."
—She can't stop—"Ulcers, in my left foot: gout,
And in the summer they removed a cyst
From here." She lifts her skirt. To stop her, I shout
"Wow!"

            "And dermatology: my scalp, the flu ..."
I think in Brueghel laughter—"the Kermess"—
But only nod.

                "What's the matter with you?"
"Nothing," I say, thinking she's found me out.
She pinches me: "They make you, don't they, guess
Like they do with me . . . *You* have, hmn, the gout."
I laugh, the driver laughs, and Falstaff roars
  —Each tooth a victory for Hungry Life.
I set the scene: "Death on the bedroom floor ..."
She squints. But not to see, 1 think, to hear.
"A pot-hanger with flattened hooks—my wife
Has left it there. We have just moved." Real fear
Is in her eyes. I want to stop.

                         "Well? Well?"
I am her entertainment.

                     "Fair is fair."
"I call a friend, hoping that he can tell
Me how to make our windows burglar-proof,
Especially in the back bedroom, where
A fire-escape sneaks down from the roof.
I go to check the window's height . . . Bare feet ..."
She feeds on every detail with her eyes. "
And then 1 jump down from the window-seat."
My pain is in her eyes. She grabs my hand.
Her grip says: she wants me to sympathize
With—morse code—her loneliness.

                             "I understand,"
I squeeze back. "My wound knows. Only disease

Relieves the boredom of old age." She winks.
"They cut a twelve-pound tumor, if you please,
From here"—she points—"and one from"—smiling—"Guess."
Each organ that she lists, she says "It stinks"
—False friends. Disease: true friends. The True Prince? Guess.
Her coat is torn in spots, her dress a rag.
She wears a man's white socks: "No one's . . . for the cold."
Her shoes are slippers, terry cloth. Her bag
Is stuffed with a chintz robe: "a dirty mess.
I'm on Medicaid," she says. "Now the old
Are taken care of—don't you think so?"

                                                          "Yes."

She lists the meager prices she would pay
For every operation, every pill:
Each one a victory, her eyes are gay,
Gay as I pay the driver for our fare
  —No pride or thanks: it's from the common till
That pays to thwart the burglar of our air.
The witch grins as I hop away: *Beware.*

25

Tom Disch (1940–)

La Venganza de los Muertos Vivientes

Return to your villages. We won't kill you anymore.
—a Guatemalan general quoted on the evening news

The dead considered whether this promise
could be trusted. They did miss the life
of the village, the cheerful music blasting

from the loudspeaker in the square,
the bustle of the soldiers, the sense
of being part of a drama the whole world
was watching. But they'd grown confused
there in the mass grave, uncertain,
shy. And if they did return,
what could they do, being dead?
Spy on surviving relatives? Live like lizards
in the crevices of walls? *Quien sabe,*
maybe they should just stay planted
where they were, learning ecology.

But the general had summoned them—
they had no choice. They pushed their way up
through the teeming topsoil to emerge
into the Technicolor day, looking exactly
as you'd imagine. And not, of course, able
to repress the natural instinct
of corpses in this classic situation.
Even the withered *abuelita*—"Granny" to us
gringoes—must gnaw at the young corporal's
shinbone; such is the law of retribution.
So what can we do, up here in the north,
to mend matters? I've no idea—
but the President has suggested we send
arms and advisors to help stop the killing.

26

Robert Pinsky (1940–)

The Saving

Though the sky still was partly light
Over the campsite clearing
Where some men and boys sat eating
Gathered near their fire,
It was full dark in the trees,
With somewhere a night-hunter
Up and out already to pad
Unhurried after a spoor,
Pausing maybe to sniff
At the strange, lifeless aura
Of a dropped knife or a coin
Buried in the spongy duff.

Willful, hungry and impatient,
Nose damp in the sudden chill,
One of the smaller,scrawnier boys
Roasting a chunk of meat
Pulled it half-raw from the coals,
Bolted it whole from the skewer
Rubbery gristle and all,
And started to choke and strangle—
Gaping his helpless mouth,
Struggling to retch or to swallow
As he gestured, blacking out,
And felt his father lift him

And turning him upside down
Shake him and shake him by the heels,
Like a woman shaking a jar—
And theblack world upside-down,
The upside-down fire and sky,

Vomited back his life,
And the wet little plug of flesh
Lay under him in the ashes.
Set back on his feet again
In the ring of faces and voices,
He drank the dark air in,
Snuffling and feeling foolish

In the fresh luxury of breath
And the brusque, flattering comfort
Of the communal laughter. Later,
Falling asleep under the stars,
He watched a gray wreath of smoke
Unfurling into the blackness;
And he thought of it as the shape
Of a newborn ghost, the benign
Ghost of his death, that had nearly
Happened: it coiled, as the wind rustled,
And he thought of it as a power,
His luck or his secret name.

27

Stephen Dobyns (1941–)

Black Dog, Red Dog

The boy waits on the top step, his hand on the door
to the screen porch. A green bike lies in the grass,
saddlebags stuffed with folded newspapers. The street
is lined with maples in full green of summer, white houses
set back from the road. The man whom the boy has come

to collect from shuffles onto the porch. As is his custom,
he wears a gray dress with flowers. Long gray hair
covers his shoulders, catches in a week's growth of beard.
The boy opens the door and glancing down he sees yellow
streaks of urine running down the man's legs, snaking
into the gray socks and loafers. For a year, the boy
has delivered the man's papers, mowed and raked his lawn.
He's even been inside the house which stinks of excrement
and garbage, with forgotten bags of groceries on the tables:
rotten fruit, moldy bread, packages of unopened hamburger.
He would wait in the hall as the man counted out pennies
from a paper bag, adding five extra out of kindness.
The boy thinks of when the man's mother was alive.
He would sneak up to the house when the music began
and watch the man and his mother dance cheek to cheek
around the kitchen, slowly, hesitantly, as if each
thought the other could break as simply as a china plate.
The mother had been dead a week when a neighbor found her
and even then her son wouldn't let her go. The boy sat
on the curb watching the man hurl his fat body against
the immaculate state troopers who tried not to touch him
but only keep him from where men from the funeral home
carried out his mother wrapped in red blankets, smelling
like hamburger left for weeks on the umbrella stand.

Today as the boy waits on the top step watching the urine
trickle into the man's socks, he raises his head to see
the pale blue eyes fixed upon him with their wrinkles and
bags and zigzagging red lines. As he stares into them,
he begins to believe he is staring out of those eyes,
looking down at a thin blond boy on his front steps.
Then he lifts his head and still through the man's eyes
he sees the softness of late afternoon light on the street
where the man has spent his entire life, sees the green
of summer, white Victorian houses as through a white fog
so they shimmer and flicker before him. Looking past
the houses, past the first fields, he sees the reddening
sky of sunset, sees the land rushing west as if it wanted
to smash itself as completely as a cup thrown to the floor,

violently pursuing the sky with great spirals of red wind.

Abruptly the boy steps back. When he looks again into
the man's eyes, they appear bottomless and sad; and he
wants to touch his arm , say he's sorry about his mother,
sorry he's crazy, sorry he lets urine run down his leg
and wears a dress. Instead, he gives him his paper
and leaves. As he raises his bike, he looks out toward
red sky and darkening earth, and they seem poised
like two animals that have always hated each other,
each fiercely wanting to tear out the other's throat:
black dog, red dog—now more despairing, more resolved.

28

Linda Hussa (1941–)

Fate's Girl

In memory of Sid Harris

Somewhere between the cuff and the hem
of life's dark coat
there lived a man.
Not a man who as example your father comes to mind
but a father all true of a girl slight and plain to see.
The flat brow of her pale face furrowed for lack of joy
and old eyes with chilling calm
expected no better than they'd seen.

They traveled the low road over the '49 Trail,
the man Fate and his girl.

Now Fate was a man of low ambition
with an eye quick for opportunity,
his habits tasteless, his wits sharp
and guided by a devil plan.
He avoided the symmetry of convention
and if ever right and wrong wrestled an issue in his head
the bout was short and right laid low
blind sided.

On the trail Fate used some greasy ploy
to wrench a weighty pouch from a fellow traveler.
Fate was not a particular man
and whether the traveler laid the night in drunken dreams
and woke a plucked bird
or didn't wake at all
only Fate and his little daughter knew.

The girl and we must call her that for he gave her nothing
not even a name
she followed him
seeking life's need unnoticed, uncared for
a thin, weak shadow he cast in the dark of night.

She followed him
not by design but habit led her
by the balance of abandonment
and hanging like a burr to the hide of a marauding dog
not knowing the path or the choice.

She followed him.
Not knowing right wrong came right for her.

They stopped in an empty shack off the edge of the trail
in a shallow canyon one room
a trellis of moldy blanket roped off the private quarters
and with the stolen bank roll
Fate stocked the shelves with whiskey
—he did not buy the girl a coat or shoes.
Fate knocked together a bar

—he would not make the girl a bed.
In town, he took chairs from behind the church
and a table from the school.

As her father
he took command of her time and service.
She swept up, hauled wood and made meals.
And when buckaroos tied tired horses outside the shack,
Fate's Bar was open for business.

They stopped by
Curiosity and having news to tell forced them to.
They reported a sorry place
but others went to see for themselves.

Fate set out a bottle
as he measured each man with his black eyes.
He slid shaved cards from his pocket
and planned how to take their money.
When he saw their mood turn sour and feared of losing their gold
to places in town
he pushed *her* toward them.

She watched gold's glint pass from palm to palm
and found that *she* changed hands.

No horse could outrun this tale of madness.
No shame ever bore could stand beside.
The wooden shack might well be made of daggers
sharpened points thrust outward
or pox or witch's sign
for the only ones to turn their horse to Fate's Bar
were uncut strangers on the '49.

Among them was a horseman
slightly built and young of heart.
of life his tastes were not full taught for chance was slim
He was fond of God and God of he as his smile was well at hand.
Troubles few beset this lad and troubles few he gave.

On an early morning in the cool of Fall's last dance
he came upon Fate's girl on the spine of a barren hill.

Caped by blowing hair and leaving barefoot tracks
in earth softened by dew
she went fast as if to outrun her own skin.
As weeks went by
he left his cattle grazing free to find her in the hills.
He took a kitten from the woman at the general store
—yellow with white mitts—
rode to the ridge near the bar and waited.

He meant the kitten as a kindness
but she shied from him like a colt
so he tucked it beneath his heart and rode away

On another day she took it from his hands
scarcely touched him as her fingers curled in yellow fur.
Muted by circumstance
her eyes gave back the gift of blueness and tears.

His own eyes held her strong to reappear in dreams.

On a certain icy day with a gun swung from a leather
the bold boy pressed by anger rode direct to Fate's Bar.
There he was witness to the fate of Fate
and it rides him heavy still.

Horses waited around the shack
the door was thrown back wide.
The room was full of rowdy men hoisting bottles
shooting guns and shouting fit to bust.

They grabbed him by the collar, dragged him to the bar
—Drink up, old son,
don't lift your purse the drinks are on the house!

The boy jerked free his purpose not for fun
'til they showed him Fate

eyes as cold in death as in life
belly up across the poker table
six round burns gathered where his heart would be.
The kitten sprawled on the bloodied floor
yellow head bent back wrong.

Nobody knew who did it.
Nobody seemed to care.
They raged the party on and on
'til they wrung the bottles dry
broke the last for Fate
flared a match across a thumbnail
and watched the flame take life.

Cold wind brought snow along the '49
wiped tracks from sight
sputtered as it hit the embers.

When he tired of staring into the fire
he took himself away
rode through a curtain of snow to a silence
where he hoped to forget
what he had seen and what he knew.

And so
did she consider life and death
and that hairline of purpose that separates the two?

If she stood near enough
to smell Fate's biled contempt

to hear his heart give one last tick
to see the awful surprise in his eyes when winged truth
of what he was and what he was to be
settled on him like death birds at dark

we will not know
for she is gone.

29

B. H. Fairchild (1942–)

The Welder, Visited by the Angel of Mercy

Something strange is the soul on the earth.
—George Trakl

Spilled melons rotting on the highway's shoulder sweeten
the air, their bruised rinds silvering under the half-moon.
A blown tire makes the pickup list into the shoulder
like a swamped boat, and the trailer that was torn loose

has a twisted tongue and hitch that he has cut away,
trimmed, and wants to weld back on. Beyond lie fields
of short grass where cattle moan and drift like clouds, hunks
of dark looming behind barbed wire. The welder, crooning

along with a Patsy Cline tune from the truck's radio,
smokes his third joint, and a cracked bottle of Haig and Haig
glitters among the weeds, the rank and swollen melons.
Back at St Benedict's they're studying Augustine now,

the great rake in his moment sobbing beneath the fig trees,
the child somewhere singing, take and read, take and read.
What they are not doing is fucking around in a ditch
on the road to El Paso ass-deep in mushmelons

and a lame pickup packed with books that are scattered now
from hell to breakfast. Jesus. Flipping the black mask up,
he reaches into the can for a fresh rod, clamps it,
then stares into the evening sky. Stars. The blackened moon.

The red dust of the city at night. Roy Garcia,
a man in a landscape, tries to weld his truck and his life
back together, but forgetting to drop the mask back down,
he touches rod to iron, and the arc's flash hammers

his eyes as he stumbles, blind, among the fruit of the earth.
The flame raging through his brain spreads its scorched wings
in a dazzle of embers, lowering the welder, the good student,
into his grass bed, where the world lies down to sleep

until it wakes once more into the dream of Being:
Roy and Maria at breakfast, white cups of black coffee,
fresh melons in blue bowls, the books in leather bindings
standing like silent children along the western wall.

30

Sydney Lea (1942–)

The Feud

I don't know your stories. This one here
is the meanest one I've got or ever hope to.
Less than a year ago. Last of November,
but hot by God! I saw the Walker gang,

lugging a little buck. (A sandwich size.
It *would* be. That bunch doesn't have the patience.
I'd passed up two no smaller, and in the end
the family had no venison that fall.)

I waved to them from the porch—they just looked up—
and turned away. I try to keep good terms
with everyone, but with a crowd like that
I don't do any more than necessary.

It wasn't too much cooler back inside.

A note from my wife on the table said the heat
had driven her and the kids to the town pond beach
to sit. That made some sense. It's the last that will.

I peeked out quick through the window as the Walkers'
truck ripped past, and said out loud, "Damn fools!"
The old man, Sanitary Jim they call him,
at the wheel, the rifles piled between

him and Step-and-a-Half, the crippled son.
In back, all smiles and sucking down his beer,
Short Jim and the deer. Now Short Jim seems all right.
To see his eyes, in fact, you'd call him shy.

He doesn't talk quite plain. Each word sounds like
a noise you'd hear from under shallow water.
I didn't give it too much thought till later,
when the wife and kids came home, and wanted to know

what in Jesus' name that awful smell was,
over the road? Turns out that Walker crew
had left their deer guts cooking in the sun.
And wasn't that just like them? Swear to God,

to leave that mess beside a neighbor's house
for stink, and for his dogs to gobble up?
And there was one thing more that puzzled me:
why wouldn't they take home that pile of guts

to feed *their* dogs? A worthless bunch—
the dogs, I mean, as well as them. You'd think
they wouldn't be above it. Every decent
dog they ever had was bullshit luck,

since every one they run is one they stole
or mooched out of the pound. You'll see them all,
hitched to one lone post, dung to the elbows,
and every time they get themselves a new one,

he'll have to fight it out until the others
either chew him up or give him up.
I guessed I'd do this feeding for them, so
I raked up all the lights into a bag

and after nightfall strewed them in their dooryard
with a note: "Since I'm not eating any deer meat,
I'd just as quick your guts rot somewhere else
as by my house." And signed my actual name.

The whole thing's clear as judgment in my mind:
the sky was orange, the air so thick it burned
a man out of his senses. I'm the one.
And evening never seemed to cool me off,

though I'm a man whose aim is not to truck
in such a thing. I've lost most of my churching,
but don't believe in taking up with feuds.
I usually let the Good Lord have His vengeance.

Nothing any good has ever grown
out of revenge. So I was told in school
when I slapped up Lemmie Watson, because he broke
the little mill I built down on the brook.

And so I learned. I spent the afternoons
that week indoors, and I've been different since,
till this one day. Then something else took over.
There passed a week: they stove my mailbox up.

At least I don't know who in hell beside them
would have done it. I had a spare. (The Lord
knows why.) I cut a post and put it up,
and could have left the blessed fracas there,

and would have, as my wife advised me to.
And I agreed. I told myself all night,
my eyes wide open, lying there and chewing,
"Let it go." And would have, as I claim,

but two days passed, and they came hunting coons
on this side of the ridge. I heard their hounds.
(God knows what *they* were running. Hedgehogs? Skunks?
It could have been.) Out on the porch

I heard *tick-tick*. Dog paws, and all *my* dogs
began to yap and whine. I made a light.
Shaky, thin as Satan, a docktail bitch,
a black-and-tan (almost), was looking in.

I made other. She followed me as if
I'd owned her all my life out to the kennel.
I stuck her in the empty run that was
Old Joe's before I had to put him down.

I filled a dish with meal. She was a wolf!
The first square feed she'd had in quite a time.
My wife kept asking what I could be up to.
Likes to worry. Next day I drove clear

to Axtonbury, to the county pound.
"This dogs been hanging round my house all week.
Don't know who she belongs to." Lies, of course.
I had her collar locked in the Chevy's glovebox.

I wouldn't harm a dog unless I had to,
and figured this one stood a better show
to make out at the pound than at the Walkers'.
But the Walkers didn't know that. Driving home,

I flung the collar in their dooryard. After dark,
and spitting snow, six inches by next day,
late in December now, toward Christmastime.
Things shifted into higher gear despite me.

Or on account of me. Why not be honest?
I know that nowadays it's not the fashion
to think a person's born what he becomes;
but Sanitary Jim, his wife and family:

I never gave it too much thought but must
have figured right along that they belonged
to that great crowd of folks who *don't* belong.
Their children wear their marks right on them: speech

you hardly understand, a rock and sway
where a normal boy would take an easy stride.
And in and out of jail. If they can't find
another bunch to fight with, why, they'll fight

with one another. (Sleep with one another
too, if talk can be believed. There are
two homely sisters in the mix as well.)
Short Jim beat an uncle or a cousin

—I disremember—beat him right to death.
(It's not the fashion either nowadays
to keep a violent man in jail. A month, no more,
goes by, and Short Jim's on the town again.)

But back to what I just began. The Walkers
are as bad as banty roosters, and I figured
they were meant somehow to be. Where most of
us are meant to eat one little peck of dirt,

they eat a truckload. Is it any wonder,
then, I didn't make a special point
of mixing with them? No more than I would
with any crowd that filthed itself that way.

But mix with them I did. It seemed as if
their style of working things reached up and grabbed me.
I was in the game so quick it turned my head.
The snow came on, the first big storm of winter,

that night I pulled the trick with the docktail's collar.
In the morning, barely rilled, I saw their tracks
around my kennel. But *my* runs both are solid
chain-link, and the doors are padlocked shut.

They mean a thing or two to me, those dogs.
I keep the keys right on me. No one else
—no family, no good friend—can spring a dog
of mine. That way, I know they're there, or *with* me.

I'm only puzzled that they never growled. They do
as a rule. I was surely glad the Walkers hadn't
had the sense to bring along some poison.
A dog's a dog, which means he's five-eighths stomach.

Thinking on this gave me bad ideas.
But I'll get to that when time is right. For now,
I called myself a lucky fool, out loud,
and bolted both dogs shut inside their houses

nights. I judged this thing would soon blow over.
I burned a yardlight too, which I'd never done.
And that (I guessed) was the last they'd come past dark.
You know, the funny part of this whole battle

up to now, when you consider who
I'd got myself involved with, was that neither
side had come right out into the open.
The only thing I knew for sure they'd done

was leave a mess of guts out on my lawn.
The only thing for sure they knew of me—
that I returned that mess to its right home.
The mailbox and the collar and the tracks . . .

For all we either knew, the Boss was making
visions in our eyes which, feeling righteous,
we took upon our *selves* to figure out.
And since, between the parties, I guessed *I*

had better claim to righteousness than they did,
I'm the one who—thinking back—began
to read the signs according to my will.
How many times have village hoodlums stove

a mailbox up? Or just plain village kids?
How many times, to mention what comes next,
has one old drunk shitkicker or another
raised some hell outside Ray Lawson's Auction

and Commission Sales on Friday night? And still,
I judged it was the Walkers who had slashed
all four of my new pickup's summer tires.
(Four months had passed.) And judged it quick as God.

The pickup spraddled like a hog on ice. It cost me
two hundred dollars just to run it home.
Next day I passed Short Jim as he came out
of Brandon's store and sized him up, and looked

at him: a man who'd killed another man,
but shyness in his eyes. He looked away.
And if *I'd* looked away just then . . . Instead,
I saw a basket full of winter apples,

Baldwins mostly, full of slush and holes.
No wonder Brandon had that crop on sale!
Four cents each was asking more than enough
for winter apples still unsold in April.

If the top one hadn't had a hole as big,
almost, as half a dollar ... By God, where
would we be now? But there it was, the hole,
and I got notions. Maybe fate is notions

that you might have left alone, but took instead.
I did. I bought that apple, and another
just for show. And a box of pellets, too—
more rat pellets than I ever needed,

more than I could stuff into that hole
and still have stay enough in the rotten skin
to hold them in enough to fool a hog
that he *had* an apple. Walkers' hog, I mean.

They penned her on the far side of the road
from where that firetrap shack of theirs was built.
I didn't set right out. That apple sat
as much as seven days up on a post

of metal in the shed, where even rats
—Lord! let alone my kids—could never reach it.
And it sat inside my mind. Especially nights.
Or say it burned, the while I cooled myself

—or tried to do, with every nerve and muscle—
in bed, and said the same thing over and over:
"Nothing good will ever grow from feuds."
And just to get the apple *out* of mind,

spoke such damn foolishness you never heard:
"Old Mother Hubbard," "Stars and Stripes Forever"
(tried to get the words of one to go
along with the rhymes and rhythms of the other).

Then went down that seventh night, as if it was
another person who was going down
inside the shed (because the person I
believed I was kept up the sermon: "Nothing

any good from any feud," and so on),
picked the apple down, and put it in
my pocket, and—the moon was full—began
the uphill climb across the ridge. To Walkers'.

Stopped for breath at height of land, I turned
to see the house, where everyone was sleeping,
wondered what they dreamed, and if their dreams
were wild as mine become when moon's like that—

they say there's nothing in it, but as God
will witness me, a full moon fills my head,
asleep or not, with every bad idea.
One spring, the moon that big, a skunk came calling

in the shed, and my fool tomcat gave a rush.
The smell was worse than death. It woke me up,
if I was sleeping (I'd been trying to),
and till the dawn arrived, for hours I felt

the stink was like a judgment: every sin
from when I was a child till then flew back
and played itself again before my eyes.
High on the ridge, I felt I might reach out

and touch that moon, it was so close, but felt
that if I reached it, somehow it would burn.
It was a copper color, almost orange,
like a fire that's just beginning to take hold.

Your mind plays tricks. You live a certain while
and all the spooky stories that you read
or hear become a part of memory,
and you can't help it, grown or not, sometimes

the damnedest foolishness can haunt you. Owls,
for instance. I know owls. How many nights
do they take up outside, and I don't think
a thing about it? *That* night, though,

a pair began close by me. I'd have run,
the Devil take me, if the light had been
just one shade brighter, I'd have run right home
to get out of the woods or else to guard

the house, the wife, the kids. I don't know which.
A rat or mouse would shuffle in the leaves
and I would circle twenty yards around it.
I was close to lost until I found the brook

and waded it on down. It was half past two.
The moon kept working higher till I saw
the hog shed just across the road from Walkers' house.
There wasn't that much difference in the two.

I'm a man can't stand a mess. But they,
the boys and Sanitary Jim. . . . Well, they
can stand it. Seems that that's the way
that they *prefer* it. That hovel for the pig

was made of cardboard, chimney pipe, and wanes.
They'd driven I don't know how many sections
of ladder, side by side, into the mud
for fencing. Come the thaw each year, the ground

will heave that ladder up, and then you'll find
a pig in someone's parsnips. Anyway,
I looked the matter over, and the worry
that I'd felt about the thing that I was doing—

well, it went away. I felt as pure
as any saint or choirboy hunkered there.
I crept up on my knees and clapped the gate
(a box spring from a kid's bed) so the pig

would have a peek. I don't know why, exactly,
but I felt like watching as she took the apple
from my hand. It wouldn't do to leave it.
She just inhaled it, didn't even chew.

I backed up to the brook and watched some more,
then stepped in quick, because that poison sow
began to blow and hoot just like a bear.
The job was done. I hadn't left a track.

I don't know just what you'll make of this:
I fairly marched back up across the ridge
as if I made that climb four times a day.
The air was cold and sweet and clear, the way

it is when you can see the moon so plain.
I walked on to a beat and sang the hymns
—or sang them to myself—I'd got by heart
so many years before: "Old Rugged Cross"

and "Onward Christian Soldiers" and "Amazing
Grace," and never noticed how the cold
had numbed my feet till I was back in bed.
No one woke up. I slept two righteous hours.

You jump into a feud, and every trick's
like one more piece of kindling on the fire.
That's how I think of it, and you'll see why.
Come evening of the next day, I was sick.

You don't go paddling nighttimes in a brook
in April, and expect it's just a trick.
All night it felt like someone had a flatiron
and kept laying it between my shoulder blades.

My feet and legs were colored like old ashes.
My throat was sore enough I couldn't speak.
My wife, who didn't have a small idea
of where I'd been beside beneath the quilts,

lay it all to how I carried on.
"You've heard the old expression, 'sick with worry.'
That's what you've brought yourself, I think, from scheming
on those godforsaken Walkers." She was right,

but not the way she thought she was. In time,
there wasn't any use, I had to go
down to the clinic, twenty miles away.
You know those places: wait there half a day,

then let them pound you, scratch their heads, and scratch
some foolishness on a scrap of paper, wait
the other half while the druggist dubs around
to find the thing he's after. Come home poor.

If it was only poor that I came home!
I drove through town at fifteen miles an hour.
Swear to God I couldn't wheel it faster,
the way I was. It was a job to push

the throttle down, and I could scarcely see,
so blinked my eyes a time or two when I reached
the flat out by the pond. Above the ridge
the sky was copper orange, and thick black smoke

was flying up to heaven, straight as string.
I thought I felt the heat. (But that was fever.)
By Jesus, that was *my* house. "Chimney fire,"
I said out loud, or loud as I could talk,

my throat ached so. The words were just a whisper,
and they sounded wrong the minute they came out.
I felt like I would die from all this sickness.
They called me "walking wounded" at the clinic:

pneumonia, but just barely, in one lung;
but now I felt my blood would burst the skin
and I'd just up and die inside that truck.
I squinched my eyes and lay the throttle on.

I meant to do some good before I died.
My wife was wrestling with a metal ladder
that had sat outside all winter, though I'd meant
to get it under cover every day.

I used it cleaning chimneys. It was stuck
in puddle ice beside the western wall
I jumped out of the truck before it stopped,
and fell, and got back up, sweet Christ,

I tried to run, and every step I took
was like a step you take in dreams, the space
from road to house seemed fifteen thousand miles.
I stumbled to the shed and grabbed an ax

and put it to the ground to free the ladder,
but the ground just wouldn't give the damned thing up,
and every lick was like I swung the ax
from under water. I had no more force

than a kid or cripple. My kid, meanwhile, cried
from behind a big storm window, "Daddy? Daddy?"
It sounded like a question. I gave up
and tried to call back up to him. I couldn't.

My words were nothing more than little squeaks,
and when they did come out, they were not plain.
And so my wife began to call the boy,
"Throw something through the window and jump out!"

He threw a model boat, a book, a drumstick.
He couldn't make a crack. I flung the ax.
It missed by half a mile. I threw again
and broke a hole, and scared the boy back in.

That was the last I saw him. Like a woman
sighing, that old house huffed once and fell.
Out back, beside the kennel, our baby daughter
danced and giggled to hear the howling dogs.

I went into dead faint. And hell could come
for all of me. And that is what has come.
Thirty years gone by since Lemmie Watson
broke my little mill of sticks and weeds

down by the brook, and I kicked the tar from him
and stayed indoors all week when school let out.
And Mrs. What's-Her-Name, I disremember,
fussing at her desk, would shake her head

and ask out loud if one small paddle wheel
was worth all this? I had to answer No.
I had to write it down, "No good can grow
from any feud." I wrote it fifty times

each afternoon. And then one afternoon
the Walker crew laid down a string of guts
across the road . . . The part of life you think
you've got done living lies in wait like Satan.

For me, it was revenge. And what to do
right now? The house is gone, the boy, and I
believe I know just how they came to be.
But do I? Do I know what led to what

or who's to blame? This time I'll let it go.
No man can find revenge for a thing like this.
They say revenge is something for the Lord.
And let Him have it. Him, such as He is.

31

Dave Smith (1942–)

The Colors of Our Age: Pink and Black

That year the war went on, nameless, somewhere,
but I felt no war in my heart,
not even the shotgun's ba-bam
at the brown blur of quail.
I abandoned brothers and fathers,
the slow march through marsh
and soybean nap where
at field's end the black shacks
noiselessly squatted under strings
of smoke. I wore flags of pink:
shirts, cufflinks, belt, stitching.
Black pants noosed my ankles
into scuffed buck shoes.
I whistled Be-Bop-a-Lula
below a hat like Gene Vincent's.
My uniform for the light, and girls.

Or one girl, anyway, whose name I licked
like candy, for it was deliciously
pink as her sweater. Celia,
slow, drawling, and honey-haired,
whose lips hold in the deep mind
our malignant innocence, joy,
and the white scar of being.
Among my children, on the first
of October, I sit for supper,
feet bare, tongue numb with smoke,
to help them sort out my history's
hysterical photographs. In pink
hands they take us up, fearless,
as we are funny and otherworldly.

Just beyond our sill two late hummingbirds,
black and white, fight for the feeder's
red, time-stalled one drop.
They dart in, drink, are gone,
and small hands part before me
an age of look-alikes, images
in time like a truce-wall
I stare over. The hot, warping
smell of concrete comes, fear
bitter as tear gas rakes
a public parking lot. Midtown
Shopping Center, Portsmouth, Va.,
the *Life* caption says, ink
faded only slightly, paper yellowing.

Everyone is here, centered, in horror
like Lee Oswald's stunned Ranger.
A 1958 Ford Victoria, finned,
top down and furred dice hung,
seems ready to leap in the background.
The black teenager, no name given,
glares at the lens in distraction.
Half-crouched, he shows no teeth,
is shirtless, finely muscled,
his arms extended like wings.

White sneakers with red stars
make him pigeon-toed, alert.
His fingers spread by his thighs
like Wilt Chamberlain trying
to know what moves and not look.

Three girls lean behind him, *Norcom H.S.*
stenciled on one who wears a circle
pin, another a ring and chain.
Their soft chocolate faces appear
glazed, cheeks like Almond Joys.
They face the other side, white,
reared the opposite direction,
barbered heads, ears, necks.
In between, a new shiny hammer
towers like an icon lifted
to its highest trajectory.
A Klan ring sinks into flesh,
third finger, left hand,
cuddling the hammer handle.
This man's shirt is white, soiled,
eagle-shaped, and voluminous. Collar up.

Each detail enters my eye like grit
from long nights without sleep.
I might have been this man, risen,
a small-town hero gone gimpy
with hatred of anyone's black eyes.
I watch the hummingbirds feint
and watch my children dismiss them,
focusing hammer and then a woman
tattooed under the man's scarred
and hairless forearm. The scroll
beneath the woman says *Freedom*.
Above her head, in dark letters
shaped like a school name on
my son's team jacket: *Seoul, 1954.*
When our youngest asks, I try
to answer: A soldier, a war . . .

"Was that black man the enemy?"

I watch the feeder's tiny eye-round
drop, perfect as a breast
under the sweater of a girl
I saw go down, scuttling
like a crab, low, hands no use
against whatever had come to beat
into her silky black curls.
Her eyes were like quick birds
when the hammer nailed
her boyfriend's skull. Sick,
she flew against Pennys' wall,
our hands trying to slap her sane
In the Smarte Shop, acidly,
the mannequins smiled
in disbelief. Then I was
yanked from the light, a door

opened. I fell, as in memory I fall
to a time before that time.
Celia and I had gone to a field,
blanket spread, church done,
no one to see, no one expected.
But the black shack door opened,
the man who'd been wordless,
always, spoke, his words intimate
as a brother's, but banging out.
He grinned, he laughed, he wouldn't
stop. I damned his lippy face
but too late. He wiggled
his way inside my head.
He looked out, kept looking
from car window, school mirror,
from face black and tongue
pink as the clothes we wore.

Often enough Celia shrieked for joy,
no place too strange or obscene

for her, a child of the south,
manic for the black inside.
When he fell, she squeezed
my hand and more, her lips came
fragrant at my ear. I see them
near my face, past the hammer.
But what do they say? Why, now,
do I feel the insuck of breath
as I begin to run—and from her?
Children, I lived there and wish
I could tell you this is only
a moment fading and long past.

But in Richmond, Charlotte, God knows
where else, by the ninth green,
at the end of a flagstone pathway
under pine shadow, a Buick waits
and I wait, heart hammering,
bearing the done and the undone,
unforgiven, wondering in what
year, in what terrible hour,
the summons will at last come.
That elegant card in the hand
below the seamless, sealed face—
when it calls whoever I am
will I stand for once and not run?
Or be whistled back, what I was, hers?

In Utah, supper waiting, I watch my son
slip off, jacketed, time, place,
ancestors of no consequence to him,
no more than pictures a man carries
(unless a dunk-shot inscribed).
For him, we are the irrelevance of age.
Who, then, will tell him of wars,
effaces that gather in his face
like shadows? For Christ's sake
look, I call to him, or you will
have to wait, somewhere, with us.

There I am, nearest the stranger
whose hammer moves quicker
than the Lord's own hand. I am
only seventeen. I don't smoke.
That's my friend Celia, kissing me.
We don't know what we're doing.
We're wearing pink and black.
She's dead now, I think.

32

Linda McCarriston (1943-)

Le Coursier de Jeanne D'Arc

You know that they burned her horse
before her. Though it's not recorded,
you know that they burned her Percheron
first, before her eyes, because you

know that story, so old that story,
the routine story, carried to its
extreme, of the cruelty that can make
of what a woman hears *a silence,*

that can make of what a woman sees
a lie. She had no son for them to burn,
for them to take from her in the world
not of her making and put to its pyre,

so they layered a greater one in front of
where she was staked to her own—

as you have seen her pictured sometimes,
her eyes raised to the sky. But they were

not raised. This is yet one of their lies.
They were not closed. Though her hands
were bound behind her, and her feet were
bound deep in what would become fire,

she watched. Of greenwood stakes
head-high and thicker than a man's waist
they laced the narrow corral that would not
burn until flesh had burned, until

bone was burning, and laid it thick
with tinder—fatted wicks and sulphur,
kindling and logs—and ran a ramp
up to its height from where the gray horse

waited, his dapples making of his flesh
a living metal, layers of life
through which the light shone out
in places as it seems to through flesh

of certain fish, a light she knew
as purest, coming, like that, from within.
Not flinching, not praying, she looked
the last time on the body she knew

better than the flesh of any man, or child,
or woman, having long since left the lap
of her mother—the chest with its
perfect plates of muscle, the neck

with its perfect, prow-like curve,
the hindquarters'—pistons—powerful cleft
pennoned with the silk of his tail.
Having ridden as they did together
—those places, that hard, that long—
their eyes found easiest that day

the way to each other, their bodies
wedded in a sacrament unmediated

by man. With fire they drove him
up the ramp and off into the pyre
and tossed the flame in with him.
This was the last chance they gave her

to recant her world, in which their power
came not from God. Unmoved, the Men
of God began watching him burn, and better,
watching her watch him burn, hearing

the long mad godlike trumpet of his terror,
his crashing in the wood, the groan
of stakes that held, the silverblack hide,
the pricked ears catching first

like dryest bark, and the eyes.
And she knew, by this agony, that she
might choose to live still, if she would
but make her sign on the parchment

they would lay before her, which now
would include this new truth: that it
did not happen, this death in the circle,
the rearing, plunging, raging, the splendid

armor-colored head raised one last time
above the flames before they took him
—like any game untended on the spit—into
their yellow-green, their blackening red.

33

Frederick Turner (1943–)

Libbard's Last Case

The last three miles were quiet
and unspeakably fragrant. The scream of
the train, and the crashing gears
of the bus faded out of his ear.

One must walk over the ridge.

The great detective, his last case closed.
This is the village where
he spent his terribly brief honeymoon many years ago.
(They shot her in the gravel pit after
two hours of nervous, distracted bargaining. Libbard
lost her because of an unprofessional mistake.)

The cart track winds between meadows.
There is the strange scent of the dandelion
fresh and dry, like a girl's hair newly washed.
The grass is shiny. Blackberries roll on its blades.

He comes down the hill to the village.
An old man, who must be Zebedee, has just
untied the flat-bottomed punt and is pushing it out
among waterlilies.
Over in the great east field the
barn is almost full. Later
that evening Libbard will walk out there
as he used to, under a moon peeling through
ancient white clouds.
A few drops of rain will patter in the dark.
He will take shelter, sitting on a hay-bale.
He will smell the smoke of the autumn burning.

Earlier that fine evening
he greets Mrs. Shippen with politeness and gallantry.
He can stay as long as he likes, in the loft bedroom
with its big cloth chairs and
mothballs in the wardrobe.
The stairs creak as he comes down for supper. He
limps a little, for it is that time of year.

In the morning he sees someone
among the elms, with a bow, slipping from trunk to trunk.
He thinks nothing of it, for he is retired.
The stairs creak as he goes down to breakfast:
tea, the newspaper, and rashers of bacon.

The country, overnight
has gathered its energies, burst into a still
deeper, more buzzing glow. Like a
golden blush, the fields have ripened and blaze
in the new mist, grain netted with grey.
The birds rise to a shout, and are silent
leaving the lark only, sharpening his juices in the blue.

Fishing in the millpond later that day, Libbard detects two
    figures
gesticulating on the further bank. One is a girl.
He decides to have nothing to do with it.
A dark shade comes over the day, there
is a cello in the flutes, the warbling is timorous of thunder.

The afternoon is rainy. He
goes to his room early, with a good novel and a pint of whisky.

The next day Briscoe, his recent assistant,
comes on a visit, overweight and puffing,
raincoat over his arm. Libbard
never liked Briscoe: the man was ambitious.
He gives him the slip, leaving him
playing at darts in the Seven Stars.

Later he sees the man with the bow again.

On the hill over the village, near the gravel pit,
the girl of the millpond meets him with a message.
She has a lovely wisp of hair over her eyes,
freckles, a short coat. She thinks
someone is trying to kill her brother.
Libbard buckles down. That night
one of the bulldozer men working on the atomic pile
three miles on the far side of the woods, is found
with a grey goose arrow under his second rib.
The old story of Cain, says the detective
to himself; the film flickers for a moment,
going into the next reel.

But the illusion does not waver.
The third day blooms like a nosegay,
a little wind has sprung up and the
air carries the sound of the cock,
the weir changes its note every second,
the sun burns the fine skin under the eyes and
whitens his hair.
All over the fields,
almost throughout the county, a late-blossoming weed
locally known as Lady's Dowry, has come out —
its scent is heady like honey; it forms
echelons of stars, each hedge is a milky way.
The bees are hysterical, one or two children have been stung.

Libbard has been up to the big house
on the rise over the river. He sips
sherry with the master, whom he knew at John's.
He has plenty to go on now, Jessica's
brother is in danger, two men must be watched.
A huge liver-coloured Labrador bitch
lolls in the corner.

The wind drops. Evening odours descend from
the paper-handkerchief-tree, a hundred feet high

as they walk in the grounds.
On a rich hot night, in the rose-garden
the story reaches its climax. There are shots, and a chase.
An arrow transfixes his derby; satanic motives
come to the surface, a cottage is searched
to reveal the psychotic ritual.
In the moonlight the roses appear to swell, there
is a chuckle from a waterbird settling in the pool, black,
with its broken statuary.

In the morning Libbard must leave, for he has
a sick aunt in Highgate. His part was played by himself.
Mrs. Shippen is Mrs. Shippen. Briscoe
who is a loose end, was played by Briscoe.
The Master, who is a real person, has asked
that his name not be used.
Jessica is an actress. Her brother
does not exist for the purposes of the story,
for he never appears.
Any resemblance is purely coincidental.
There is no such plant as Lady's Dowry.
The labrador bitch came from another story altogether.

34

David Lee (1944–)

Back to the Valley

I guess mebbe you better be getting me home
now its getting pretty late
and I'm getting pretty drunk
and tired
I got to get back on that swoker tomorrow
and cut hay the bank
he don't give much of a damn
as to whether I'm having a good time
or not he just wants his money on time
sometimes I think
if I gotta come back and wear out
another life like them Chinermens sez you do
mebbe I be the bank this time
I know it'd be bout my turn
and mebbe his to let me hold the deeds
just oncet
anyways that don't matter now
we got plenty of time
to worry bout that tomorrow
but I better get home and get some sleep tonight
so mebbe we better head on back

you know over yonder in them hills
LaVerne's brother he found a Indin grave oncet
it was a long time ago he wasn't very old yet
and he thot he'd just dig that grave up
to see if there's any jewelry or arrowheads or other
Indin shit in there with that feller
so he come back to it one day
with a shovel and started digging
he wasn't very far along when he sez he felt
sorta nervous like he's about to pee

or something but he knew he didn't need to
he'd arredy had on the way
so's he went on and then got another feeling
like somebody's watching him dig so's he stops
and turns around and there's a Indin standing there
right behind him wearing them Indin clothes
like they don't wear no more
you know them leggings and that thing over
their chest and all and moskins
LaVernes brother he bout shit
cause he never heard nobody walk up
and he sez for a minute he couldn't say nothing
he just set there and finally he sez
what do you want? but that Indin
didn't say nothing just stood looking at him
and he sez I sez what do you want?
do you want me to leave? and when
he sed that that Indin just disappeared
right in front of him and never sed nothing
LaVerne's brother he was ascairt
he got the hell out of there
and won't go back though he told me
about it and it happened up there
somewheres in them hills behind
that old mill I don't know for sure just where
I wouldn't go there for anything
I aint gonna fool around with that stuff

I heard about 2 men out hunting deer
in the hills that got lost
and it started snowing so's they had to
hunt around for a place to get in
and found this cave and when they went in
it's all this Indin stuff
jugs and arrows and jewelry and stuff
and they had to spend the night in there and
they sez it's all haunted cause they heard
noises all night and couldn't sleep
so's when light come they filt their pockets

with all that shit they could carry and left
and finally found their ways home
but later they tried to come back and
get the rest of that stuff in the cave
cause it was worth money
but they looked all over and couldn't find it
again but they sez its out there
and somebody'll find it one day
it aint gonna be me
I aint going in no haunted cave
for all the Indin jewelry in Chiner
it aint worth it to mess around
with no Indin ghosts
you just don't know what they might do

I aint talking about that no more
cause I get ascairt and then feel damn stupid
for doing it a grown man talking
about ghosts and stuff
oh I know they real I aint saying that
they just aint nothing I can do about them
and I aint for sure what they can do
about me so I just leave them alone
they was a haunted house back home
I was in and it made your hair stand up
on your neck when you walked in
didn't nobody have to tell you you
just knew something was wrong when you
walked in and you couldn't get a nigger
to go in that house for money
or whiskey and you couldn't thow
a cat through that house's door
it'd scream like hell and find someways
to keep from going in
cats and niggers they can tell things like that
that's why I won't have no damn cat around
they might just bring that stuff with them
I trapped a cat oncet or he got in my trap
I never planned it I wouldn't set no trap

for a cat and I was ascairt to kill him
he might come back or bring something in
so's I just forgot about that trap for a month
and when I got back surenuff he's dead
but it wasn't my fault
I won't kill no cat but that's how haunted
that house was and I don't
much like thinking about it even now

here I caint get the top screwt off
this beer can you hep?
that's the onliest thing I miss this finger for
I got cut off I just haven't got no grip
to twist off these beer lids
they put them on too tight for me now

they was this guy I heard about
who was a miner or trapper or something
anyways he lived alone up in the hills
he got his finger chopped off
I guess mebbe he's a trapper and got it
caught that happens now and then
so he just picked up his finger and stuck it
in his pocket and went on home
when he got there he took out his needle and thread
and he sewed that finger back on
his hand but it didn't work
2, 3 weeks later it all swoled up
green and the finger fell off
so's he built a fire in the stove
and then held the stump agin it
till he burnt all the green poison out
I think a feller'd have to be
pretty much of a man to do that

I knew this other guy who was loading up
a sow hog and she wouldn't go
so's he was trying to waller her into the truck
and he grabs her by the tail with

one hand and the ear with the other
she's screaming like hell the whole time
and him getting pretty pissed off
so's he does this a time or 2
and then he grabs her again but
gets the one hand in her mouth
he feels something pinch so
he pulls back his hand
and his finger's gone that damn sow's
bit him off he looked all round
and didn't find that finger nowhere
he guessed that sow swallered it

I don't much like to talk about how I lost
mine it still bothers me some
mebbe I'm just too drunk but I started thinking
about it. This all happened before
I went to work for the lectric company
I was younger and hired on for the oil
oh I made good money and it wasn't bad work
I don't think I'd do it again
anyways we's in Texas up on that panhandle
and had a rig drilling about 8 mile
outa town. We'd work 36 on and 12 off
at least I would cause I could make so much
I'd run chain awhile and then crow-nest
it never made no different
I was just after the paycheck on Fridays
I'd do bout anything they wanted as long
as the money kept coming in and they
seemed to like that
so anyways we was down over a mile
damn near 7 fousand foot
and we knew the oil was right there
we had to be coming thu any time
you just get the feeling it's gonna blow
so here comes the foman cause we sent for him
cause he has to sez when we can cap off
to get ready for the last push thu

so we don't blow all to hell and mebbe catch fire
that foman he's so goddam drunk
he caint tell shit from dog puke
he starts raising all kind of hell saying
you get this damn rig running right NOW
we won't hit no fucking oil
for 2 weeks nobody paid you to think
that's what I'm by god paid for
you just drill till I say stop and then
you just ast how long that's all
now git back to goddam work and stop
trying to set round fucking off
he left and we's so mad we couldn't see straight
for a man to talk to us that way
whether he's drunk or not didn't matter
so we set the bit back down in the night
and let her go wot the fuck
and about midnight the crewboss he sez to me
John you go up to the crow-nest we lifting
that pipe out I aint getting blowed up
for nobody and that was fine by me
we's all getting scairt to where we's just working
and not saying nothing just thinking
bout how long fore morning or till we got off
it's funny how you think the day'll take
the being scairt away but it never really does
anyways I climbt up the derrick to the top
and we's getting ready to pull that pipe out
when all of a sudden the whole thing starts shaking
to where I'm bout to get slung off
and I can hear the crewboss yelling
get down get DOWN this fucker's gonna blow
by god I burnt the palms off my hands
coming down I slid the wire guy rope
to the platform and then jumped off on the ground
the rest of the crews arredy running ahead
so's I try to catch up and then I hear
that big sonofabitch touch off K-BOOM
right behint me and caught on fire

it blew me down on the ground and started
me burning by god I was ascairt
I jumped up and started running and I'd of
burnt to death if this nigger hadn't grapt me
and thowed me down in this ditch and
put the fire out on my clothes
so's we look and that whole rig's burning
and we can see 2 guys from the crew laying
between us and the rig burning up
and we know they's dead and
the rest of us is burnt bad where we might die
the crewboss he takes off running
into the fire and we can see he's gonna
try to bring the pickup out
he goes to it and grabs the doorhandle
and it's so hot part of his hand
sticks to the door and just comes off
but he gets in and somehows
he gets that damn truck started and drives out
of that fire I won't never know how
all the wires was burnt up
it got so hot that that trucks paint was all
scorcht off to where you couldn't tell even
what kind of a truck it was
and he brings it to us and we get in
I'm so burnt they had to put me in the back
and I'm laying in this feller's lap
who put out the fire in my clothes
and we pull out of there driving like hell
to get to town and by then the fire
was so hot it burnt up the whole goddam rig
there wasn't nothing left and I
seen it bend over just like it was plastic
I wanted to pass out so bad I couldn't stand it
but I didn't I just laid there and felt it all
and saw it all so's we're going to town
as fast as we can go and we pass this law
and he turns on his red light and chases us
till he gets close to see and then

he pulls ahead and leads us thu town
about 90 mile a hour to the hospital
where he jumps out and runs over and opens
the door and he just puked like hell
3 up front was arredy dead 2 of them
stuck together they's burnt so bad
and the crewboss's hand was off and he
didn't have no face left
how he drove God knows I don't
and there was only one other still alive and
he died that night so then they come
to get us out of the back and they started to lift me
out I sez get him first he saved my life
the man sez its too late he's done dead
and I was laying in his lap

the onliest 2 that made it was me and
the crewboss. He was in the hospital for
96 days and I was in for 104
a week and a day more
I member cause he come to see me
when they let him out
he was burnt so bad I couldn't tell
who he was till he sed something
he ast if I's okay and I sed yas
we just looked at each other for a minute
and then he walked off
I sez be seeing you but he just waved
3 days later he drove his car
into a bridge and killed hisself
they buried him exactly one week after they
let him out and then let me out
the next day after his funeral was over

I don't have no bad scars left that show
my legs is burnt good
but I still feel it I get cold
and have to wear them long underwears
all year long on my legs

and my hands is so thin they bleed easy
my skin's bout as thick as a cigarette paper
and I don't have no feelings in my face
but I'm lucky I guess
all the rest is dead cept me

I went back to work for the oil
the next day because I didn't have nothing
else to do and they put me on chain
wrapping the pipes and that's when I done it
I hadn't been working a hour
when this feller on the other side
thew his chain and I felt it hurt
so's I finished and took off my glove
and the finger stayed in
I sez you sonofabitch you done
cut my finger off but I don't think
he heard he didn't say nothing
well I had it I went to
the man and sez that's it pay me off
oh he tried to get me to stay on
but I lost the taste
and didn't care no more

it was after that I went down South
and got my stomach cut out and
then I come here to die
it was a pretty place and I didn't have nothing better
ever day LaVerne'd pack me a lunch and
I'd draw her a map of where
I'd be if I didn't make it home
I was weak and couldn't hardly
stand so I'd drive up in the hills
where I'd take off my clothes
and let the sun shine on me
the muscles wouldn't heal up
on my stomach where I'd been burned
there was just ugly skin there you could see thu
I only weight 96 pounds and I'd lay

on a quilt and look back at the valley
and just wait to be dead and have it done

you know by god I guess I'd still
be laying up there waiting
cept after awhile LaVerne she went
and bought these 2 hogs for me
she knew I'd like that
I got to coming down early to feed them
and when I was up there
I'd get to thinking about the market
and making money
I got so cited I come down one day early
and went to looking for a boar
to get a herd started
and the next day I forgot to go up to die
then pretty soon I bout quit
thinking about it altogether
it just don't take much to keep
some people going

and that gets us about to here
which is nearly home
time for one last beer
they say God takes special care
of children and idiots
I guess he's been watching out for me
by god I'll always member them times
they was good times for the most
but I do hope to Christ they
don't never ever come back

35

Thomas James (1946–1973)

Mummy Of A Lady Named Jemutesonekh
XXI Dynasty

My body holds its shape. The genius is intact.
Will I return to Thebes? In that lost country
The eucalyptus trees have turned to stone.
Once, branches nudged me, dropping swollen blossoms,
And passionflowers lit my father's garden.
Is it still there, that place of mottled shadow,
The scarlet flowers breathing in the darkness?

I remember how I died. It was so simple!
One morning the garden faded. My face blacked out.
On my left side they made the first incision.
They washed my heart and liver in palm wine —
My lungs were two dark fruit they stuffed with spices.
They smeared my innards with a sticky unguent
And sealed them in a crock of alabaster.

My brain was next. A pointed instrument
Hooked it through my nostrils, strand by strand.
A voice swayed over me. I paid no notice.
For weeks my body swam in sweet perfume.
I came out scoured. I was skin and bone.
They lifted me into the sun again
And packed my empty skull with cinnamon.

They slit my toes; a razor gashed my fingertips.
Stitched shut at last, my limbs were chaste and valuable,
Stuffed with a paste of cloves and wild honey.
My eyes were empty, so they filled them up,
Inserting little nuggets of obsidian.
A basalt scarab wedged between my breasts

Replaced the tinny music of my heart.
Hands touched my sutures. I was so important!
They oiled my pores, rubbing a fragrance in.
An amber gum oozed down to soothe my temples.
I wanted to sit up. My skin was luminous,
Frail as the shadow of an emerald.
Before I learned to love myself too much,
My body wound itself in spools of linen.

Shut in my painted box, I am a precious object.
I wear a wooden mask. These are my eyelids,
Two flakes of bronze, and here is my new mouth,
Chiseled with care, guarding its ruby facets.
I will last forever. I am not impatient —
My skin will wait to greet its old complexions.
I'll lie here till the world swims back again.

When I come home the garden will be budding,
White petals breaking open, clusters of night flowers,
The far-off music of a tambourine.
A boy will pace among the passionflowers,
His eyes no longer two bruised surfaces.
I'll know the mouth of my young groom, I'll touch
His hands. Why do people lie to one another?

36

Marilyn Nelson (1946–)

Tuskegee Airfield

for the Tuskegee Airmen

These men,
these proud black men:
our first to touch
their fingers to the sky.

The Germans learned to call them
Die Schwarzen Vogelmenschen.
They called themselves
The Spookwaffe.

Laughing.
And marching to class under officers
whose thin-lipped ambition
was to *wash the niggers out.*

Sitting at attention
for lectures about ailerons, airspeed, altimeters
from boring lieutenants who believed
you monkeys ain't meant to fly.

Oh, there were parties,
cadet-dances, guest appearances
by the Count
and the lovely Lena.

There was the embarrassing
adulation of Negro civilians.
A woman approached my father in a bar
where he was drinking with his buddies.

Hello, Airman. She held out her palm.
Will you tell me my future?

There was that,
like a breath of pure oxygen.
But first,
they had to earn wings.

There was this one instructor
who was pretty nice.
I mean, we just sat around
and *talked* when a flight had gone well.

But he was from Minnesota,
and he made us sing
the Minnesota Fight Song
before we took off.

If you didn't sing it,
your days were numbered.
"Minnesota, hats off to thee . . ."
That bastard!

One time I had a check-flight
with an instructor from Louisiana.
As we were about to head for base,
he chopped the power.

Forced landing, nigger,
There were trees everywhere I looked.
Except on that little island . . .
I began my approach.

The instructor said, *Pull up,*
That was an excellent approach,
Real surprised.
But where would you have taken off, wise guy?

I said, *Sir,*

I was ordered
to land the plane.
Not take off.

The instructor grinned.
Boy, if your ass
is as hard as your head,
you'll go far in this world.

Freeman Field

for Edward Wilson Woodward, Captain USAF (ret.)
and the 101 of the 477th

It was a cool evening
in the middle of April.
The 477th, the only Negro
bombardier group in the Air Corps,
had just been transferred
to Freeman Field.

Some of the guys
said they were hungry
and left to find food.
The others went on
playing bridge,
mending socks,
writing letters home.

A few minutes later
the hungry guys came back,
still hungry.
We're under arrest.

The others thought they were kidding.

The next morning

the Base Commander
issued new regulations:
Negro officers were assigned
to the NCO Club;
white officers were assigned
to the Officers' Club.

The Base Commander,
who had deliberately busted
an entire Negro outfit
so he wouldn't have to be
their flight-leader in combat,
was a graduate of West Point.

He issued a statement:
If we do not allow
Negro and white officers to mix,
the accident rate
will go down two
and two-tenths
percent.

Sixty-one Negro officers
were ordered to report
one by one
to his office.
Lieutenant, have you read the regulations?
Sign here if you have read and understood.

Sixty-one Negro officers
refused to sign.
A man of your intelligence
must he able to recognize
the dangers of fraternization.

They refused to sign.
This is an order:
Sign the document,

They refused to sign.
This is a direct order!
You will sign the document!

Six cargo planes were called in;
pilots, navigators, and bombardiers
were shoved on board and flown
to Godman Field, Kentucky.

Across the river
was Fort Knox.
The sixty-one
had grown by now
to one hundred and one
American fliers trained
to fight Nazis.
They were confined
to the BOQ
under guard
of armed MPs.

By night, searchlights watched
every window. By daylight
the men leaned in the windows
to smoke, watching
the German POWs pump gas,
wash windshields
and laugh
at the motorpool
across the street.

37

AI (1947–)

The Ravine

I wake, sweating, reach for your rosary and drop it.
I roll over on the straw and sit up. It's light out.
I pull on my pants, slip into my rope sandals
and go outside, where you sit
against a sack of beans.
I touch the chicken feathers
stuck to the purple splotches of salve on your stomach.
Your eyes, two tiny bowls of tar
set deep in your skull, stare straight ahead
and your skin is almost the color of your eyes,
because Death pressed his black face against yours.
I put our daughter in your lap,
lift you both and walk to the ravine's edge.
I step over —

— the years fly up in my face like a fine gray dust.
I'm twenty. I buy you with matches, a mirror and a rifle.
You don't talk. While I ride the mule downhill,
you walk beside me in a blue cotton dress.
Your flat Indian face shines with boar grease.
Your wide feet sink deep in the spring mud.
You raise your hands to shade your eyes
from the sudden explosion of sunlight
through the umber clouds.
In that brightness, you separate into five stained-glass women.
Four of you are floating north, south, east and west.
I reach out, shatter you in each direction.
I start to fall, catch myself,
get off the mule and make you ride.
You cry silently, ashamed to let me walk.
At bottom, you look back.

I keep going. Up a few yards,
I strip two thin pieces of bark off a tamarisk tree,
and we chew on them, sweetening the only way home.

The Kid

My sister rubs the doll's face in mud,
then climbs through the truck window.
She ignores me as I walk around it,
hitting the flat tires with an iron rod.
The old man yells for me to help hitch the team,
but I keep walking around the truck, hitting harder,
until my mother calls.
I pick up a rock and throw it at the kitchen window,
but it falls short.
The old man's voice bounces off the air like a ball
I can't lift my leg over.

I stand beside him, waiting, but he doesn't look up
and I squeeze the rod, raise it, his skull splits open.
Mother runs toward us. I stand still,
get her across the spine as she bends over him.
I drop the rod and take the rifle from the house.
Roses are red, violets are blue,
one bullet for the black horse, two for the brown.
They're down quick. I spit, my tongue's bloody;
I've bitten it. I laugh, remember the one out back.
I catch her climbing from the truck, shoot.
The doll lands on the ground with her.
I pick it up, rock it in my arms.
Yeah. I'm Jack, Hogarth's son.
I'm nimble, I'm quick.

In the house. I put on the old man's best suit
and his patent leather shoes
I Pack my mother's satin nightgown
and my sister's doll in the suitcase.

Then I go outside and cross the fields to the highway.
I'm fourteen. I'm a wind from nowhere.
I can break your heart.

38

Robert Shaw (1947–)

Waiting in the Wings

Here we are for the hundred-and tenth performance;
the leading man, downstage, is mixing cocktails
and flickering glances at the ingenue
prettily posed beside a vase of flowers,
calculating how many drams will do
to keep the evening flowing in planned channels.
I see this from the sidelines, trading weight
from one to another haunch on a hard chair.
This is the sort of touring company
where everyone except the star does chores;
I am the understudy not yet needed,
meanwhile the prompter that he never needs.
I do admire him. I realize more each night
how much resides in gesture. See the swish
he gives the martini pitcher (full of water,
as everyone wills to forget, and ice cubes made
of durable plastic, as perhaps fewer realize).
Look at his three-quarter turn to her, his thumb
nesting under the sash of his smoking jacket.
Costumes went over budget at some point:
there's only one such covetable bit
of old-wine-bottle-green glad rags.

But we are of a size. Were he to have
a fainting fit or a heart attack, they'd strip it
gently from his limp frame and stuff me into it.
And then I would be ON.
                                    No more of that.
Sitting with script in hand I notice what
a way he has with words. He makes them up
often enough, sometimes ten lines together
come out of nowhere framed in full aplomb.
But even when they're lines I have before me
like some disputed contract on my lap,
his lithe delivery does them something more
than justice, the words paced, the accents placed
like cat feet padding nimbly down a fence rail.
Would you, would I, would anyone have said
those lines the way he did a moment back?
"Darling, let's not ever discuss money.
I think of it as ... the least of my attractions."
Masterly, the positioning of that pause;
I'd have rushed through it, putting one over on her.
But he, although he knows that *she's* the heiress,
mingles his irony and self-esteem
in subtly measured parts, with, as it were,
the pitcher's final swish as he glides toward her.
It's no surprise he gets her in the end,
nor that she thinks *he's* the acquisition.

Ho hum. One act to go. The only acting
I've done this trip was in the greasy spoon
across the street last night. The new young waitress
was certain I must be the leading man.
She brought my coffee, asked for an autograph.
I signed a place mat with his name, and even
dotted the i with a sort of little star.
It somehow seemed too easy. So I said,
"You know that it's a stage name," wrote my own
right name beneath his wrong one. Then I paid
with a five dollar bill, told her to keep the change,
calming her flustered thanks over my shoulder

with "Darling, let's not ever discuss money."
That was it, at last, best of both worlds.
And even then it somehow seemed too easy—
would have even without the screen door's clapping
shut with such a curt vocational comment.
I came back feeling not so much disposed
to drop a sandbag on him. When the tour
bows out for good in the last sad prairie town
I'll step across the footlights, take a column,
crowd the press rows with the other critics.
A critic is the artist's guilty conscience,
skewering what he knows to be too easy
with that uneasy instrument, his pen.
I think you'd say I have a talent for it.

39

R. S. Gwynn (1948–)

Body Bags

I

Let's hear it for Dwayne Coburn, who was small
And mean without a single saving grace
Except for stealing—home from second base
Or out of teammates' lockers, it was all
The same to Dwayne. The Pep Club candy sale,
However, proved his downfall. He was held
Briefly on various charges, then expelled
And given a choice: enlist or go to jail.

He finished basic and came home from Bragg
For Christmas on his reassignment leave
With one prize in his pack he thought unique,
Which went off prematurely New Year's Eve.
The student body got the folded flag
And flew it in his memory for a week.

II

Good pulling guards were scarce in high-school ball.
The ones who had the weight were usually slow
As lumber trucks. A scaled-down wild man, though,
Like Dennis "Wampus" Peterson, could hall
His ass around right end for me to slip
Behind his blocks. Played college ball a year—
Red-shirted when they yanked his scholarship
Because he majored, so he claimed, in Beer.

I saw him one last time. He'd added weight
Around the neck, using words like "grunt" and "slope,"
And said he'd swap his Harley and his dope
And both balls for a 4-F knee like mine.
This happened in the spring of '68.
He hanged himself in 1969.

III

Jay Swinney did a great Ray Orbison
Impersonation once at Lyn-Rock Park,
Lip-synching to "It's Over" in his dark
Glasses beside the jukebox. He was one
Who'd want no better for an epitaph
Than he was good with girls and charmed them by
Opening his billfold to a photograph:
Big brother. The Marine. Who didn't die.

He comes to mind, years from that summer night,
In class for no good reason while I talk
About Thoreau's remark that one injustice

Makes prisoners of us all. The piece of chalk
Splinters and flakes in fragments as I write,
To settle in the tray, where all the dust is.

40

Rachel Hadas (1948–)

Visiting the Gypsy

A cool May night, green leaves
exuberant against the lamplit rain.
In an unfamiliar part of town
we went to hear the stories of our lives.
How soft and warm the gypsy's hands. And do
we patients put one palm in them, or two?
You, I remember, gave yourself to her
equivocal pink and black
magic right away. I felt held back
(craning from the arm of the single chair)

by the first lesson that the gypsy taught:
to learn your fortune you must pay in coin
you yourself have scooped from deep within.
Without such cash no answers can be bought.
Her lap and hands were soft, but not her eyes.
They probed our faces, weighing truth and lies.
Lovers' confusion. Homesick. Pregnancy
desired, difficult. People envy you.
You smile but you are torn between these two
men. Someone's giving you the Evil Eye.

All this I write as if it were declared,
oracular; but rather it was fished,
questioningly. We answered as we wished,
you more, I less. Our mysteries were shared—
that, as I see it retroactively,
presented her with our one certainty.
Secret disappointment with your lot.
Anger. You're nice to people but they're not
nice to you back. Some person in your house
loves to give orders. I see nervousness.

Whoever claimed this dirty linen could
wear it (what's the proverb?). Separate
lifelines, loves, and histories were old hat.
But for one evening that we somehow should
merge into one; that we could, skittish, peer
through the gypsy's window; sit in her
overstuffed chair; could trust her with a hand—
that was the true adventure for us two,
that was the spell that both of us could brew.
Her Delphic lines took two to understand.

We deconstructed generalities
no feeble human creature could deny.
All of us suffer from the Evil Eye.
What seemed to one of us obscurities
the other would decipher. You don't see
that other people envy you? That he
is the man who takes but never gives?
We each found means to reassure the other:
She said a change was coming to your lives!
The gypsy watched us, silent as my mother

Her plateglass window boasted painted hands
at prayer. Behind it were arranged two packs
of cards, tarot and ordinary; wax
candles; several statuettes on stands;
old incense; knives; a spoon; a purple book;
cigarettes; herbs. A passer-by could look

in at our threesome's archetypal scene,
cartoon of fortune-telling ritual,
with the new wrinkle that here was a twin
client who proffered her four palms for tall

tales, for cliché and mystery and fable,
for human aspirations scaled to size.
For us to sift, as best we both were able,
her farrago of guesses, truths, and lies.
Out into the green evening, and on
our way—henceforth as sisters of the palm,
bound by the power of an unwritten tongue?
The first time that I saw a caravan,
in Corfu, I turned to my companion,
knowing no Greek. I gestured; said *tzigánes?*—

the ancient language ringing through me like a gong.

41

Beth Joselow (1948–)

The Head Cosmetician Tells a Story

I had a man once gave me everything
I could have dreamed. I had a dress for every
day in the month and a Thunderbird on order
when it all blew up.

I had some good times but I want to be
the one to tell you it was not the paradise
you think. He was a man who couldn't stand

to leave a thing without putting his mark on it,
and people paid their dues for knowing him.

Of course, I had my looks then and had done
some traveling on them. You could make a little
something for yourself before it was too late
if you played it right. I knew the boys
on Vice, and you would be surprised
how all the kingpins were their pals.
They'd make you some connections if you just
behaved a little nice.

My mother saw reward for those who walked
the straight and narrow, but she never got
her just reward. First thing I learned is that
there is no straightaway.
I made it all up as I went along,
all twists and turns and that seems smart to me,
even knowing the mistakes I've made.

It was Pinkie made the match of me and Roger,
Pinkie out of Second District Vice.
He worked plainclothes at all the downtown joints,
but he didn't like work much. So I would keep
an eye out while he'd lay up
in some dolly's bed, and naturally,
he'd do for me.

One night he introduced us all to Roger
and asked if I'd show him around, I was
hostessing at Danny's and I had on
a red silk dress—that was a classy place.
I never worked the joints myself,
but I knew the girls who sold champagne
and conversation at the Two O'Clock.
I guess Pinkie thought
I'd pass better than the rest.
Roger, he was out of Boston, Mass.
His father was a judge. He wore

three-hundred-dollar suits and smoked some fancy
cigarettes in a holder. Now you know
suits like that would never mean
nothing to me now, but at the time
I thought he was a fine thing come into
my life, and blessed sweet Pinkie for it.

I don't remember how you wear
your hair when you go out.
Do you keep it back like this?
Well then I'd stick with Twilight Sky—
it gives your eyes more definition than
a shade like Pearl, which anyway is aging.

Now Roger's hair was mostly grey but he
was hardly more than thirty at the time
when I was saying I was thirty-five. He had
a boxer's build and cool eyes, but I couldn't
tell you now if they were blue or grey.
He didn't like to talk or dance or drink.
What he liked was to watch
me take my clothes off slow,
and neither of us saying
a word. Then he'd hold me a little—
not sexy, not at all. He'd never
stay the night. He'd leave me there alone.
But after just a week he made it
plain he didn't want no other guys
around. He paid my rent and sent me flowers
every Friday. Still he didn't get it on
with me, except one time which left me bruised
all up my legs. And left his teeth marks
in me, too.

Even in those younger days the men were not
so much what mattered. I liked to have them
look, liked having them around, but sex was always
better if I'd had a few,
and if I was on the wagon I didn't miss it.

Ha! You said it, girl.
They always want the other.
It wasn't money, either. He bought clothes
and jewelry that I wore, but I hung on
to find out what it was he really wanted.
And if I let myself go off and think
about it when I was alone,
I saw a dark spot deep in Leakin Park
and him bent over me,
my neck all black and blue.
Still, I had to know the wind-up even though
I knew I should have told the man goodbye.

Pinkie had always been my friend and when
things weren't going right for him he'd take
to drinking and coming around my place all hours
of the night. His wife was such a pig—
she'd let the dishes pile up in the sink
'cause she said they were Pinkie's job and she
was not the maid. She never had a smile
or fixed herself for Pinkie like he liked.
And maybe six months after Roger came
around, Pink started in on one of his bad times
and he knocked on my door a couple nights
a week. He could have been the one told Roger.
I never did.

One day Pinkie gets a phone call at the station
when he's there on his paperwork. You know,
it had to have been planned, 'cause Pinkie's
on the street most times. It's Roger saying
I been hurt real bad, and says he'll come
and get him on his way to the hospital.

Pink says okay and walks the block
till Roger drives up in his Continental.
The two of them head straight for Hopkins.
They're almost halfway there when Roger pulls
a .38 and shoots Pink in the neck

and kicks the door and dumps him right on Broadway
in broad daylight!

Pinkie saved his own life. I was fine,
you know, I wasn't even in the hospital.
But Pinkie had to haul himself out of
the gutter, with his knees scraped all to hell
and blood shooting everywhere.
He clamped his hand on his neck and hailed
the first car that could bring itself to stop
at the sight of this lunatic cop waving one arm
and cursing like an Arab.
It took two weeks of tubes and dope
to put the scars on Roger's handiwork.
Pinkie's wife came down to sit beside him
and held his hand and later brought him ice cream.
The following year they had a little boy.

Of course, I've never done what mother told me.
But at fifty-three I'm older than mine was
when she died, and I have brought no harm
to nobody I know, except for Pinkie,
who'd be the first to say he was the one
brought Roger to us.
Well—and the wives. I didn't
know them for the most part. I was only
party to a bargain they had made
with no one asking me a thing about it.

I felt real bad for Pink, but here's the thing:
Of course he told them it was Roger, and
he was an easy find.
You might imagine, Pinkie being a cop,
they'd have gone hard on him, but
as we know, there's different sets of rules.
Roger's father bought the judge
just like some little birthday card.

So Roger made it back to Boston and
about that time I stopped my nightly check-ins
at the Two O'Clock. I never saw him
again, not even to give back the things
he'd given me, although I would have if
he'd asked.

You have a good time, now, you hear?
And come and let me hear about it soon.

We none of us party like we used to do.

42

David Lehman (1948–)

The Secret Life

She was strange. Even as a child she had been able
To picture her own death, as a prisoner pictures freedom.
The first time they met, he walked her to her third-floor walkup
On a city landmark block, tiny but with a lot of light.

The first time they went to bed, Mahler's Fourth Symphony
Was on the record player. They traded insults, had a fight
To juice themselves up for the main event, and in the morning,
Her guilt and his anger were gone. Neither of them could remember

The reason for the delay: hadn't their analysts explained
The loss of his wallet, her keys, that weekend at the shore?
The last time they went to bed, both of them knew it;

The neighbors knew it in the morning when her mother came
To collect her things, and her father mentioned his lawyer.
He felt like a burglar in his own living room when they left.

It started in the subway in Boston, where he thought he saw her
Before he knew who she was. The Red Sox were scheduled to play
Oakland that night at Fenway, but it rained all day
And he went to see a Hitchcock double feature instead.

He met her there, in the second half of *Vertigo*
And the first half of *Rear Window.* Afterwards they walked.
Neither of them was hungry, and both of them
Had something they wanted to keep quiet about.

He kept comparing Grace Kelly and Kim Novak in his mind,
Wondering about the woman he was with, and how little
He knew about her. Was it enough to get him to follow her

Into the Spanish church with the high tower
Where he was sure to have a dizzy spell
At dusk, after he rescued her from drowning?

Every time she left him she took off her wedding ring,
Slammed it on the dresser top, stormed out. Four hours later,
Sex was better than ever. They stayed up late to watch
The debonair husband bring his fragile wife a glass of milk.

Had he put poison in it? Or was it just his wife's bad nerves?
Clearly, *he* got on hers. She said he was too contentious.
They could never just enjoy a movie like ordinary people,
They had to analyze it to death. One day she locked herself

In the bathroom, sobbing, saying she had taken a lethal dose
Of Dalmane. It wasn't true, but he believed her, and made her drink
The vile stuff prescribed by the emergency-room guy on the phone.

She was scared of him, and basked in the fear, egging him on
To see him lose his temper while she kept cool and sarcastic,
Playing the role of the bitch, knowing how much he liked it.

As phone sex is to sex, so was their strained dialogue
To the quarrel they should have had. He brought up the baby.
All she could think of was the casserole in the oven.
She rehearsed the day's doings: X made a pass at her, Y frowned

When he said good morning, and Z is up a creek because
Her boyfriend has AIDS. He listened with one ear tuned
To the Mets game on the radio, down six to four in the eighth
But with the bases loaded and Hojo at the plate. Ball one.

He kept turning over sentences in his mind: "Her husband
Never suspected, not because he was dense but because
It hadn't occurred to him that other men might desire her

As he did not." And, "Maybe she needed to treat herself
To a breakdown, or maybe just a glass of water and a pill."
Every time he left her, he phoned her two weeks after.

Should she listen to his shrink sessions on tape, which
He had left behind—deliberately, she supposed?
Her shrink would have called it "an accident with intent,"
On the grounds that there were no accidents, no errors,

No false prophets or dreams, no mistakes that weren't messages
From the unconscious, texts for her to interpret and complete.
The tapes were meant for her ears only. Love abolished ethics:
That was her philosophy, and she would take it into the street

And see what happened. The prospect exhilarated her. Here at last
Was a project commensurate with her energy, her fanatical zeal
To do good works and get her hands dirty, be among the people,

Until she heard his voice on tape, going on and on about his moral
Dilemmas. His feelings had changed. He didn't want to hurt hers.
All this talk about feelings....She wanted to slug him.

He brought up the baby, which was strange because
They didn't have a baby She tried to reason with him, but
Humoring him was smarter. He was mixed up. One drink too many,

An extra toke of exceptional grass. No appetite, no sleep.

His lawyer explained how he could cheat her. He got indignant.
"I don't want to cheat her," he said. His lawyer sighed,
"It's your funeral." His favorite expression.
The object of the game was to make the ball disappear.

They checked in. He asked for a double room
With a king-sized bed. "You're very sure of yourself,"
She said, when the clerk went to get the key.

Raindrops in the sun, on the windshield, on the roses,
Blackening their crimson; on her cheek, a tear; in the air,
The trace of her giveaway smile in the getaway car.

She used to visit him before he knew who she was,
What she looked like, and why she came to him
At night, when the others were asleep. And now...
Was it possible? Was she the same woman

Framed in the window's tall landscape
Of pine trees receiving the evening's blue powder?
He had thrown away the frame, wanting her to enter the picture,
And he would go there with her, down country lanes

In France, where the pears were ripening
In poems of pleasure that had not yet been written,
For he could imagine an embrace as fierce as the one she fled from,

As cold as the taste of snow on burning lips,
And was prepared to love her in a shabby unlighted corner
Of the attic, on the shortest day of the year.

43

David Bottoms (1949–)

Under the Boathouse

Out of my clothes, I ran past the boathouse
to the edge of the dock
and stood before the naked silence of the lake,
on the drive behind me, my wife
rattling keys, calling for help with the grill,
the groceries wedged into the trunk.
Near the tail end of her voice, I sprang
from the homemade board, bent body
like a hinge, and speared the surface,
cut through water I would not open my eyes in,
to hear the junked depth pop in both ears
as my right hand dug silt and mud,
my left clawed around a pain.
In a fog of rust I opened my eyes to see
what had me, and couldn't but knew
the fire in my hand and the weight of the thing
holding me under, knew the shock of all
things caught by the unknown
as I kicked off the bottom like a frog,
my limbs doing fearfully strange strokes,
lungs collapsed in a confusion of bubbles,
all air rising back to its element.
I flailed after it, rose toward the bubbles
breaking on light, then felt down my arm
a tug running from a taut line.
Halfway between the bottom of the lake
and the bottom of the sky, I hung like a buoy
on a short rope, an effigy
flown in an underwater parade,
and imagined myself hanging there forever,
a curiosity among fishes, a bait hanging up

instead of down. In the lung-ache,
in the loud pulsing of the temples, what gave first
was something in my head, a burst
of colors like the blind see, and I saw
against the surface a shadow like an angel
quivering in a dead-man's float,
then a shower of plastic knives and forks
spilling past me in the lightened water, a can
of barbequed beans, a bottle of A.1, napkins
drifting down like white leaves,
heavenly litter from the world I struggled toward.
What gave then was something on the other end,
and my hand rose on its own and touched my face.
Into the splintered light under the boathouse,
the loved, suffocating air hovering over the lake,
the cry of my wife leaning dangerously
over the dock, empty grocery bags at her feet,
I bobbed with a hook through the palm of my hand.

44

Lynn Emanuel (1949–)

The Dig

Beyond the dark souks of the old city, beyond the Dome of the Rock
gray and humped and haunted, beyond the eyes of the men at the café
where they drink their thimblefuls of hot tea, beyond the valley
with its scar of naked pipe, the perfect geometrical arcs of irrigation,
and someone incising a dark furrow in a field, some plowman's black
gutter opening through the green, she is waist deep in this open grave,
staring at the delicate puzzle of my feet. Beyond her, in the shadow

of Tel Hesi, daubing and dampening the earth, another woman finds
the faint brickwork of floor spidering the dust, on the hearth's
wedge-shaped arc of shadow a scattering of charred millet.
Nothing else for miles. Nothing but this bluff of ruin,
one decapitated tower, one "window" staved into the brick,
the bougainvillea crawling across a wall dragging its little bloody rags.
She is standing here thinking she cannot bear the way this foot—
my foot—wants to step out of the earth. I don't care. I am using her
to leave the grave. And so we go on. We go on until we cannot go on
deepening my grave, and the trowel hits stone and I lie staring
while she makes the earth recede, reaches in and pulls me out,
my jaw wired shut by roots, my skull so full of dirt that suddenly
the intricate sutures come loose and, in her hands, the whole head
opens.
In the shallow setting where I lay is the small triangular sail
of a scapula, the ribs like the grill of a car. She bones me like a fish.
She lays the little pieces, the puzzling odds and ends, into the dishes
of shellac and formalin. One carpal still wears the faint blue
stain of a ring. Wearily, I lean my reassembled head,
sutures rich with glue, against the wall of the filled beaker.
A fine sweat of bubbles on my chin. All night, through the window
of my jar, I watch her mend with glue and wire the shallow
saucer of my pelvis. We are nothing. Earth staring at earth.

Liam Rector (1949–)

Old Coat

Dressed in an old coat I lumber
Down a street in the East Village, time itself
Whistling up my ass and looking to punish me
For all the undone business I have walked away from,

And I think I might have stayed
In that last tower by the ocean,

The one I built with my hands and furnished
Using funds which came to me at nightfall, in a windfall. . . .

Just ahead of me, under the telephone wires
On this long lane of troubles, I notice a gathering

Of viciously insane criminals I'll have to pass
Getting to the end of this long block in eternity.

There's nothing between us. Good
I look so dangerous in this coat.

Getting Over Cookie, a Made-for-TV-Movie

In the ninth grade I met a fantastic number of times
With Cookie Harris in the woods. . . . Under the pretense
Of going over our Algebra notes, given the pressure
Of the pop quizzes being served up then
With an alarming frequency, we'd have at
Each other, kissing and squishing against
Each other. . . . She'd stop, in a manner

Peculiar to those times, once I had my first full feel
Of her breasts (enormous and soft, as I remember,
A source of fascination and grief
To every frenzied boy I knew),
And then we'd go into the dry-humping
Segment of our routine until one of us
Rolled over and it would all be over. . . .
We would return, sitting on the invariably damp ground
And in utter depression, to the formulas
And to the grade-gettings of the day. . . .
She wanted me to be her boyfriend and led me
To believe I could go farther, much farther,
Should I but make the noises of consent
On that front, but I had eyes
For one of the DiFilippo twins
Who lived across the tracks and resented me
For the poverty of my parents and my acne
(Which Cookie had a touch of as well—
We were poor kids on the outs, with only
Bad skin to inherit), so with an eye cocked
Towards Cheryl DiFilippo I withheld what was then
The violent tumult of my callow affections. . . .
This kind of Marxist melodrama, rife
With all its underpinnings of dominance
And submission, haunted me well
Into my twenty-fifth year when I met and married,
In a veritable dither, one Alison Cromwither,
In a ceremony covered by the *New York Times*
Which took place at the estate of her approving parents.
Alison's father was a bull-boy broker and her mother
Was left-leaning and as cultural as they came
In those days. . . . Between them
They sponsored a fine literary press which issued
Its four slender volumes each year, and as it happened
My own debut in verse was soon among those in
The next batch to appear. . . . The book became known,
Befamed immediately for the surge and pith by which
It dismantled the hidden injuries of class in America,
And her father was soon convinced I was just the fellow

To restore the meanness and the juices he was certain
Bryn Mawr had taken out of his increasingly anorexic Alison.
Far from snubbing me owing to my humble origins,
Bull-Boy saw in me the stirrings of his own early anger
And hysteria, and trusted that fire-in-the-belly intensity
To lift Alison suddenly into the bounties of nature
And make for the bellowings which had in the past attended
His own breakthrough, business successes. . . .
He told me it seemed as though I had just come in
Out of the forest. . . . And I could see that the mother,
Whatever her misgivings, could hardly wait
To get her affluent mitts on me, to lie down with another
Of "her" authors. . . . Alison made an ideology
Out of everything in those days, a habit of mind
I took to be remarkably transcendent and high-minded
Until it became clear, altogether too clear,
That this was part of an irrefutable (and not political)
Sorrow and anger eating at her, all the while
Saddening and outraging her, blurring, in effect, whatever accuracy
Her thinking might otherwise have held. . . . As alluring as she was,
She was always perilously close to being committed,
Never far from the mental ward of it all.
And given how confused and co-opted I was, after my efforts
To administer to Alison and urge her, with not a whit of luck,
To place herself in the hands of an expensive professional,
I took to cavorting in the kick-ass bars of my beginnings,
Looking to recapture there some semblance of a wilder world
Still in the lurid process of getting-ahead
Or looking to forget that discreet stampede
Within the waters of yet another squat and guzzle. . . .
When I was soused I felt like a boy again,
And all I could think of was Cookie, Cookie.
Even when hungover and having to face myself in the morning,
Gratefully handsome after the crater-faced rigors of my adolescence,
All I could see through the clearing was Cookie's face. . . .
What began as the python thirst of pleasure soon turned
Into the worm of need and habit and I was spirited off
To a clinic myself, where Bull-Boy assured me
It was all part of the game and urged me forward again,

Back into the ring. His wife was off to a spa,
Longing for weight loss, and he desperately needed someone
In whom he could confide. . . . Things went on this way well
Into my thirties, by which time I was chairperson
Of many philanthropic organizations (so many pigs,
So few troughs; so many sluts, so few slots),
And I continued to write savage,
If irony-crippled, verses, until one day
Alison announced she would be gone
For the weekend, sequestering herself, as had become
Her debilitating gesture, in our cottage on Nantucket
By the incessant ocean, where she would undoubtedly
Sit by her "grieving window" and run her bony fingers
Up and down the chill of the pane, while moaning. . . .
Rather than accompany her, I decided to jump
Into our Alfa Romeo, given to us recently
By Alison's mother and used by Mummy and me for our sordid trysts
In the surrounding countryside, and I floored it
For the Middle Atlantic section of the country,
From whence I had so long ago come. . . . and there she *was,*
Perched in the same squalid neighborhood, getting by
In a mean but well-kept hovel, and with a dignity
Well beyond her years. . . . Cookie was there, ineluctably
There, as were tales of abortion, betrayal
Tales of lugging impossible tracts by Trotsky
Off to her job as a receptionist, to be read
When her boss wasn't looking or promising her a raise
If he could but once stare upon the naked flesh
Of her "jugs" revealed (and she all the while trying
To delineate through her reading what historical forces
Had brought her to this abyss of desolation). Her autodidact obsessions
Moved me beyond all belief, and I was on the phone to New York
Immediately: I would not be coming back. I would be
Staying here with Cookie. . . . Bull-Boy, older now and damaged
Beyond redemption himself, saw this for what it was—
My *last chance,* and one he might well have given himself
Had he but the foresight, the opportunity, or the still-burning-fire.
He vowed to notify Alison as soon as he could penetrate her
Solitary vigil on the Cape, and said were she not answering

He would leave a message for the idiot on her desperate tape. . . .
And he said to go ahead and keep the car!
I could not then, nor as things came to pass
Did I ever, abandon my romantic Tory sense of reality,
But coupled with Cookie's Commie zeal I was certain
We could make a go of things, and for many years
We did....We looked out for each other,
Laid down fully in the firm grip of each other,
And though we were too soon swallowed
In the deeper forests to come,
My sole measure of triumph and loss rises and falls
Around those final years with Cookie before she left me driving
An aging sports car without her
With too much, finally, to ever get over.

45

Dana Gioia (1950–)

Counting the Children

I.

"This must have been her bedroom, Mr. Choi.
It's hard to tell. The only other time
I came back here was when I found her body"

Neither of us belonged there. She lived next door.
I was the accountant sent out by the State
To take an inventory of the house.

When someone wealthy dies without a will,

The court sends me to audit the estate.
They know that strangers trust a man who listens.

The neighbor led me down an unlit hall.
We came up to a double door and stopped.
She whispered as if someone else were near.

"She used to wander around town at night
And rifle through the trash. We all knew that.
But what we didn't know about was *them*."
She stepped inside and fumbled for a switch.
It didn't work, but light leaked through the curtains.
"Come in," she said. "I want to show you hell."

I walked into a room of wooden shelves
Stretching from floor to ceiling, wall to wall,
With smaller shelves arranged along the center.

A crowd of faces looked up silently
Shoulder to shoulder, standing all in rows,
Hundreds of dolls were lining every wall.

Not a collection anyone would want—
Just ordinary dolls salvaged from the trash
With dozens of each kind all set together.

Some battered, others missing arms and legs,
Shelf after shelf of the same dusty stare
As if despair could be assuaged by order.

They looked like sisters huddling in the dark,
Forgotten brides abandoned at the altar,
Their veils turned yellow, dresses stiff and soiled.

Rows of discarded little girls and babies—
Some naked, others dressed for play—they wore
Whatever lives their owners left them in.

Where were the children who promised them love?

The small, caressing hands, the lips which whispered
Secrets in the dark? Once they were woken,

Each by name. Now they have become each other—
Anonymous except for injury,
The beautiful and headless side by side.

Was this where all lost childhoods go? These dim
Abandoned rooms, these crude arrangements staged
For settled dust and shadow, left to prove

That all affection is outgrown, or show
The uniformity of our desire?
How dismal someone else's joy can be.

I stood between the speechless shelves and knew
Dust has a million lives, the heart has one.
I turned away and started my report.

II.

That night I dreamt of working on a ledger,
A book so large it stretched across my desk,
Thousands of numbers running down each page.

I knew I had to settle the account,
Yet as I tried to calculate the total,
The numbers started slipping down the page,

Suddenly breaking up like Scrabble letters
Brushed into a box to end a game,
Each strained-for word uncoupled back to nil.

But as I tried to add them back together
And hold each number on the thin green line
Where it belonged, I realized that now

Nothing I did would ever fit together.
In my hands even 2 + 2 + 2

No longer equaled anything at all.
And then I saw my father there beside me.
He asked me why I couldn't find the sum.
He held my daughter crying in his arms.

My family stood behind him in a row,
Uncles and aunts, cousins I'd never seen,
My grandparents from China and their parents,

All of my family, living and dead,
A line that stretched as far as I could see.
Even the strangers called to me by name.

And now I saw I wasn't at my desk
But working on the coffin of my daughter,
And she would die unless I found the sum.

But I had lost too many of the numbers.
They tumbled to the floor and blazed on fire.
I saw the dolls then—screaming in the flames.

III.

When I awoke, I sat up straight in bed.
The sweaty sheet was twisted in my hands.
My heart was pounding. Had I really screamed?

But no, my wife was still asleep beside me.
I got up quietly and found my robe,
Knowing I couldn't fall asleep again.

Then groping down the unlit hall, I saw
A soft-edged light beneath my daughter's door.
It was the night-light plugged in by her bed.

And I remembered when she was a baby,
How often I would get up in the night
And creep into that room to watch her sleep.

I never told my wife how many times
I came to check each night—or that I was
Always afraid of what I might discover.

I felt so helpless standing by her crib,
Watching the quiet motions of her breath
In the half-darkness of the faint night-light.

How delicate this vessel in our care,
This gentle soul we summoned to the world,
A life we treasured but could not protect.

This was the terror I could not confess—
Not even to my wife—and it was the joy
My daughter had no words to understand.

So standing at my pointless watch each night
In the bare nursery we had improvised,
I learned the loneliness that we call love.

IV

But I gave up those vigils years ago.
My daughter's seven now, and I don't worry—
At least no more than any father does,

But waking up last night after the dream,
Trembling in the hall, looking at her door,
I let myself be drawn into her room.

She was asleep—the blankets softly rising
And falling with each breath, the faint light tracing
The sleek unfoldings of her long black hair.

Then suddenly I felt myself go numb.
And though you won't believe that an accountant
Can have a vision, I will tell you mine.

Each of us thinks our own child beautiful,
But watching her and marveling at the sheer
Smoothness of skin without a scar or blemish,

I saw beyond my daughter to all children,
And, though elated, still I felt confused
Because I wondered why I never sensed
That thrill of joy when looking at adults
No matter how refined or beautiful,
Why lust or envy always intervened.

There is no *tabula rasa* for the soul.
Each spirit, be it infant, bird or flower,
Comes to the world perfected and complete,

And only time proves its unraveling.
But I'm digressing from my point, my vision.
What I meant to ask is merely this:

What if completion comes only in beginnings?
The naked tree exploding into flower?
And all our prim assumptions about time

Prove wrong? What if we cannot read the future
Because our destiny moves back in time,
And only memory speaks prophetically?

We long for immortality, a soul
To rise up flaming from the body's dust.
I know that it exists. I felt it there,

Perfect and eternal in the way
That only numbers are, intangible but real,
Infinitely divisible yet whole.

But we do not possess it in ourselves.
We die, and it abides, and we are one
With all our ancestors, while it divides

Over and over, common to us all,
The ancient face returning in the child,
The distant arms embracing us, the salt

Of our blind origins filling our veins.
I stood confused beside my daughter's bed
Surprised to find the room around me dim.

Then glancing at the bookshelf in the corner,
I saw she'd lined her dolls up in a row.
Three little girls were sitting in the dark.

Their sharp glass eyes surveyed me with contempt
They recognized me only as a rival,
The one whose world would keep no place for them.

I felt like holding them tight in my arms,
Promising I would never let them go,
But they would trust no promises of mine.

I feared that if I touched one, it would scream.

46

Rodney Jones (1950–)

The Troubles That Women Start Are Men

On the porch, unbreeched shotgun dangling
Across one arm, just after the killing,
The murderer, Billy Winkles, made polite
Small talk with my father while we waited

For the sheriff to come. The reek of cordite
Still loomed above the sheeted corpse, his uncle
Ben, whose various dark and viscous organs
Jeweled the lawn. "Want some coffee, Von?"
I heard, and thought, A man is dead. And then:
Why had my father brought me there to stand
Alone, out of place, half-terrified, bored
With the slow yammer of weather and crops?

I stepped carefully across the rotted planks
Toward an oak where an engine block
Depended from a blackened limb and watched
A dull dazzle of horseflies, a few puddles
Hounds had dug like chocolate ruffles
Hemming the chicken yard. "I told the son
Of a bitch, come back, I'll shoot you dead,"
And he sure had, for sniffing round his wife.
He said, "It just ain't right." He rolled
A smoke and dragged a steady flame alive
While neighbors shyly stomped from pickups
And lifted the sheet to poke and peek.

"That's Ben," one said. "That's Ben to a T."
But was it? Was any of it real, the empty
House, the creek? My father saying, "Now
Your mother, she was a Partain, wasn't she?"
"Naw, she was a Winkles, too. My wife was
A Partain, she's over at Mai-Maw's now."
It went like that, and this. The wind drove
Up and set the shirts to popping on the line.
A red tricycle leaned above a one-eyed doll.

The mountain's blue escarpment unwound
Green bolts of fields, the white shelters
Where we lived, all of it somehow wrong,
And magical not to have changed while
Trucks backed up along the ditch and men
With their grown boys clambered uphill
To gawk at Uncle Ben who lay like shortcakes
Lined up on sawhorses on decoration days.

How strange, I thought, that no one prayed,
And strange that I was there, actually there,
With grown men, not sad or happy, but proud,
Knowing even then, the years would mostly
Amount to sleep, my father would come back
As history, and still there would be
To say the strobe of the ambulance light;
The sheriff, a tall, portly man, stooping
To help the handcuffed killer into the car;
And on the grass, bits of liver or spleen —
Whatever I'd dream, the world is not a lie.

47

Mary Swander (1950–)

The Doctor Explains

In all my forty years of practice,
I've only had two similar cases.
And let's get clear from the start:
1 deal with difficult patients
presenting a myriad of symptoms—I don't
have to tell you-ranging from minor
skin irritations to cardiac arrest.
Of course, those of you hospitalized
here are without doubt the most
severe, given little hope of recovery
until you made the discovery
on your own that my research has proven
effective and I am one of a handful
of doctors in the country who can help.

Toxic poisoning. I am the world's
foremost authority, the first man
called in on the scene in the early
hours of the Bhopal accident.
I went over with a team of physicians
specially picked by the president.
But back to the present and our event
last night. As I said, I've had only
two other similar experiences.
One was a man from Arizona who owned mines,
worked his way up, a true Horatio Alger,
dirt poor kid, picked copper and lead
from the canyons until his hands bled,
then put himself through school at night.
The man became photophobic among other things,
he lived so much in the dark, and later,
perhaps unrelated, his retina detached.
Blind, he ran his whole business by phone.
He'd come for appointments and wrap up
a million dollar deal in the waiting room
on the cellular he carried in his briefcase.
When he wheeled back to my office,
(after his eyes came crippling joint pain)
he always had an investment he wanted
to sell me and was rather funny in his
single-minded determination to make his
business his life. He wouldn't bend
for a soul and kept on urging me to jump
in when the market was hot. I found seven
different kinds of metal filings in his bloodstream
and a residue of dangerous gases in his lungs.
He had begun my detoxification program
and was making slow progress until
several of his veins began to dry up
and his sons fought each other silly
over which one was to become heir apparent
once the father went. The night he did,
he called me from South Africa in terrible pain,
and was throwing all the blame on himself

for his failures. This was new for a guy
who all along had suspected others—
his brother-in-law, his workers,
even his lawyers of plotting his ruin.
But there was nothing I could do from
so far away to adjust his medication.
The second patient, oddly enough, was the man's
daughter whom I first glimpsed when she pushed
his chair into my clinic. "My seeing eye dog,"
he joked and gestured toward her.
She was willowy, thin, but had the same
determined lines around the chin, the same
patch of baldness over the parietal bone,
unusual for a woman. But I sensed
a strong genetic link in all clinical
aspects that had perhaps been exaggerated
by the mother's early death. Or again,
the daughter's thyroid gland may have
become suppressed by radiation she picked up
in the desert where she lived alone with
her father and kept his books. Right next
to a nuclear testing site. At any rate,
she called me at home (I can still
remember, interrupting dinner. We were
just about to sit down to a plate of
pesto. I have a mind to never again
answer the phone.) and complained of
weight loss, that anything she put
in her mouth made her sick—many of you
have experienced a like condition—
and would I see her that very evening.
Of course, she'd also developed
a sensitivity to all chemicals in the air:
perfume, smoke, new carpet smell,
that sort of exposure most of you know,
a function of a damaged immune system.
I told her to come in first thing
in the morning and she agreed that
would be fine, but then at ten,

she called back, more upset, and we
made arrangements for her to be hospitalized
the next day early as possible. At noon,
I ran my finger down the list of new admits
and found her name instead on the print-out
from the morgue. I have no idea what happened
between our last conversation and the time
the maid found her in the motel
up the street. Which brings us down
to Kathleen and the incident in 551.
A code was called by the nurses
at four a.m. and this was the first
I heard anything was out of the ordinary.
Oh, we were all aware Kathleen was
down, but you couldn't be here
and not have faced a lot. Just yesterday
afternoon, the psychologist wrote a report
stating that things were not yet desperate,
so I didn't put the nurses on alert.
No, there are moments out of our control.
And I suppose this will always be
a mystery. I have informed her husband
in California and he will fly in tonight.
That's all I have to say.
Since there are no questions, you may
all go back to your rooms, record your
own temperatures on your charts and
the staff and I will continue our rounds.

48

Chase Twichell (1950–)

A Suckling Pig

What's the difference
between hard and dark?
It stays dark all night.

That's a woman's joke,
"prized for the friendly fire it draws,
especially in mixed company.

A joke like that has the ring
of a true story, as does the saying
"a man's brain is in his pants."

The painters and poets all drink
at the Twilight Café,
a farmers' bar on the edge of town,

and that was where Jerome,
the day he sold
tile painting of the trailer park,

passed out the invitations
requesting the honor of their presence
among gentlemen of like kind

for an evening of
drunkenness & debauchery,
excesses & excrescences. Black tie.

Jerome proposed to celebrate
three things: his fortieth year,
his rocketing fame, and his divorce.

The women laughed it off.
No one needed to remind us
how high hard drinking counts

among the principles
of thermodynamics.
Art thrives on tension,

yin and yang, their holy friction.
When you live in a small town
in New England,

each shovelful of snow
repeats the credo
or is meaningless exertion.

The month of March
distends with sap and knobby branches.
Tractors rut in the black acres,

the birds come back
to raid the feeders,
cattle emerge from steaming barns.

Jerome ransacked his attic.
The cardboard boxes
crumbled as he opened them:

his grandmother's linens,
limp with age, spilled from tissue,
and through the tarnish

and protective flannels,
silver flashed its costly light.
He had in mind

a feast of visuals:
black, hand-dipped, beeswax
candles from the specialty shop,

red dozens of anthurium,
each waxy, high-veined heart
split by a miniature penis,

curved, pale yellow, dusted with pollens.
Often they had spoken of
the clean dynamic,

how artifice can force
a loveliness from marriages
devoid of loveliness,

as the dented aluminum
and corrugated shadows
of the trailer park

well up in the twilight
Jerome found for them.
They lived entangled

in their brotherhood of work,
where paint and words can spur
anything to tenderness.

At eight o'clock the whole room
rose from a bath of candlelight,
breathing the laden atmosphere

of forced narcissus, so that the air
itself seemed bruisable, and colored
by Scarlatti's luscious harpsichord.

Tucked into each creaseless,
softly folded, immaculate napkin
monogrammed by hand

in another age,
was the crisp, black and gold
foil packet of a condom.

Jerome contrived that his guests
should pass through a doorway into a dream
composed by someone else,

a dream each man could fully enter,
abandoning the old self for a new,
the way a snake bequeaths

its paper ghost to a stone wall.
But at the point where form becomes
determinate, Jerome stopped painting.

The caterers slipped out the back,
leaving behind a suckling pig,
golden, shiny, roasted on its knees,

a wreath of greens around its neck.
Sharpened on a stone, the carving knife
glittered among the smoking candles.

With the sound turned off,
Jerome's expensive video
flickered like the waters of aquariums

at feeding time, nurses and cheerleaders
romping in their luminous elsewhere.
He knew the kind of man

aesthetics could seduce.
Also, they had a history:
the drinking to blackout,

the kidney stones and gout,
and all the vivid, half-believed
versions of their lives before.

So the night was a loaded pistol
right from the start,
a slow burn with a dirt sweetness.

We all make allowances
in the name of humanity,
the name we pray to, if we pray.

But which allowances?
As the first champagne
foamed in the long-stemmed glasses,

Jerome sent his young protégé
down to Springfield to fetch
the entertainment.

Just how detached
should art and artists be?
Did lie suspect they'd find

a correlation
in an evening of debauchery?
He must have seen himself

as Bacchus then, plunging with
his flock of satyrs deeper into youth.
Besides, how far is too far?

Once such a question
occurs to a man,
isn't he obliged to answer it?

A man walks into a bar and says,
"Barkeep! Ten shots of your worst scotch."
Pouring the tenth, the barkeep

asks what the occasion is. The man
shudders as the drink goes down
"Celebrating my first blow-job," he confides.

"No shit," says the barkeep,
reaching for the bottle.
"Here, have one on the house."

"No thanks," says the man.
"If ten shots of that camel piss
won't kill the taste, nothing will."

What's left of the pig
forms their centerpiece,
platter of bones, the head caved in.

For their uniform, they sport
the Mars-black rented tuxedo,
color of the soot that drowns

the candles as the stubs burn down.
Their flags of white linen
are soiled and cast aside.

Fired by brandy, they rise to toast
Saint Jude, patron of lost causes,
who speaks to their stiffening nerve.

The tremulous flames of a birthday cake
appear in the kitchen door,
flanked on either side

by the two muses from Springfield,
crowned by Jerome with plastic ivy.
Cigars flare up like hazard lights.

Large with fraternity,
the white shirts open at the neck,
undone by the slow hypnosis

of women dancing themselves
out of their clothing,
dancing for the faces that form

and reform in the amber smoke,
dancing for men.
A trembling moment comes,

overburdened like liquid in a spoon,
when the boundaries themselves
are the thing that spills.

What begins as a mere flirtation—
the mountain climber starting home
an hour too late,

so that he cannot help but lose
the trail to darkness—
swells to the plural story

of everyone present,
a story of war.
They slip across the lines

in the dark, on their bellies,
tranced by the dream-palette video
pulsing its intimate heat,

its clouds of honey.
The clenched fist and forearm
are a kind of cock.

That moment is followed by another
in which the weapon
no longer seems strange,

and the women's perfume
can be held in the hands
like a bruised peach.

The devil is dissociation.
No one wakes them.
He strings his scabrous wire

around them as they sleep,
stalking in their dreams
the multifarious flesh,

the dresses, damp and confining,
that chafe in the boulevards,
slaves to instinctual fire.

There is another dream
that ends another way.
From high above the curving map,

the explosions resemble floral sea-forms,
huge roses blown open by the storm.
The aircraft trembles in the sweet

air that rises,
green with torn leaves.
Rocking in its harness,

the pilot's camouflage
will slip unnoticed into heaven.
The moment of waking

is a moment of relief.
Gone, the untranslatable troops.
Gone, the trucks that marked

the road with red drippings,
the small, inflaming sun,
the soldier's luck.

The women danced to calm the men.
They danced a dance called
fear of getting caught,

and then the one called
fear of catching something,
They sat in each man's lap

to comfort him, and whispered
private things into his ears,
things with the tongue,

until each longed for the coiled
amnesia of the cobra,
rigid and transfixed

in its straw basket,
caressed by the cold
and hooded music of the flute.

No one expected Jerome's young painter,
newly married, to bolt out the door
with the redhead in tow,

and come downstairs
no more than ten minutes later
for the other one.

The catalog of weapons is endless,
inventions to pry loose
the simple griefs of the world,

and compound them.
Jerome's ex-wife
misunderstood the plan,

and dropped the ten-year-old
off around eleven. Shirttails out,
Jerome carried his son like a baby

into the musical darkness,
the boy's bare feet
latched around his father's waist,

and they danced off -balance
in the guttering candlelight,
the coarse salt of the father's check

shielding the child's unblemished face,
the green grass of his breath,
the women laughing and saying

he was handsome like his daddy.
A close call is straw for the fire,
for the smoldering sleep that swallows

even the artillery's close concussions.
All the countries of red clay,
the tricycles and groceries,

were washed away
by monsoons of forgetfulness.
Logy with medals, fictions, old scars,

they bowed their heads
before the holy suckling beast,
which looked like death

if anything ever did,
and drank to it
with glasses uplifted,

those pure pariahs,
to life, to language, and to paint,
and to each other,

because they recognized
the sniper in the soul, and feared
what he might father there that night.

A man calls his wife from the office.
"Honey," he says, "I have some bad news.
You know those stocks I gambled on?

It was a big mistake.
I had to sell the condo in Palm Beach,
the yacht, the string of thoroughbreds,

the ski chalet, and all the cars but two."
"Is that the worst of it?" she wants to know.
"We'll have to let the gardener go,

the butler, and the kitchen staff.
I fear, my love,
you'll have to learn to cook."

I have a better idea," says the wife.
"Let's fire the chauffeur,
and you can learn to fuck."

49

Nicholas Christopher (1951–)

Jupiter Place, 1955

The three sisters who lived in the house surrounded
by hedges elaborately set a redwood table in their backyard:
twelve miniature cups and saucers, plates, spoons, and forks,
on a white paper tablecloth the wind, at any moment,
threatened to lift skyward, where it would crumple,
then billow, indistinguishable from the clouds.
I had often wondered what went on behind those hedges
down the street: I knew the girls were twice my age—
I was four—and that I was the youngest
of the nine guests invited to their tea party;
the only other boy, around six, was someone
I had never seen before on our street.
He had hair pomaded so flat it shone like a mirror,
and on his starched collar he wore a clip-on bow tie.
"He's our cousin from Syracuse," the eldest sister informed me,
and, seated beside me, he didn't speak to anyone.
I had never heard of Syracuse, and even now I do not know
if he had journeyed from upstate New York or the coast of Sicily.

Expecting cake, I was served crab apples, acorns, and a pinecone,
and from the teapot an imaginary arc of "Darjeeling"—
the word rolled off the second sister's tongue—
filled my cup to the brim before she offered me
first a sugar bowl without sugar, then a pitcher and a yellow dish,
murmuring, "Cream or lemon," at which point, vastly
disappointed but getting the hang of things, I took an imaginary
wedge of lemon, squeezed it into my cup, and refrained
from biting into the one edible prop, my crab apple.
Then I noticed that the youngest sister had wandered
across the lawn and was dancing under an enormous
weeping willow, up high on her toes—
the first piece of ballet I ever witnessed—
trailing a chiffon shawl and tossing her dark hair
first over one shoulder, then the other.
The cousin from Syracuse looked away with set jaw,
and the other girls never left off their chattering,
but, empty cup raised to my lips, I couldn't take my eyes off her.
Every day after that, from my window or front walk,
I watched her amble past my house on the way to school,
loitering well behind the other children.
She must have always been late:
the bookbag in one hand and the lunch pail in the other
appeared to weigh her down terribly as she zigzagged
down the street from sidewalk to sidewalk,
pausing whenever a bird or flower caught her eye.
Never once did she speak to me, or I to her.
And I was not invited back for another tea party,
even though—unlike her cousin, who had nodded off unhappily—
I thought I had played my part well,
repeatedly emptying my empty cup with gusto.
Then, in the spring, I stopped seeing her altogether,
no matter when I planted myself at the window.
I worked up the nerve to ask her sisters about her,
but without replying they brushed past me.
Other inquiries I made came to nothing.
Until just before my family moved away that summer
when suddenly everyone on Jupiter Place was talking
about her in lowered voices, with veiled expressions,

for in those days there was still a stigma attached
to anyone who contracted polio—another word
I had never heard before but would forever associate
with the name of that girl who had danced slowly
into the twilight beneath the enormous darkening tree
even as her sisters cleared the table
and the rest of us were sent home.
A name I heard in a whisper twenty years later,
at the reenactment of an ancient festival on Rhodes,
when in the whirl of dancers moonlit in sheer robes
one collapsed by a precipice high over the sea;
a name I wanted to call out twenty years after that—
just today—as a woman on crutches passed me,
tossing her hair over her shoulder before disappearing
down the sidewalk, descending along the shadows
of the trees that ran like a ladder as far as I could see.
Kathryn.

50

Garrett Hongo (1951–)

The Legend

In memory of Jay Kashiwamura

In Chicago, it is snowing softly
and a man has just done his wash for the week.
He steps into the twilight of early evening,
carrying a wrinkled shopping bag
full of neatly folded clothes,
and, for a moment, enjoys

the feel of warm laundry and crinkled paper,
flannellike against his gloveless hands.
There's a Rembrandt glow on his face,
a triangle of orange in the hollow of his cheek
as a last flash of sunset
blazes the storefronts and lit windows of the street.

He is Asian, Thai or Vietnamese,
and very skinny, dressed as one of the poor
in rumpled suit pants and a plaid mackinaw,
dingy and too large.
He negotiates the slick of ice
on the sidewalk by his car,
opens the Fairlane's back door,
leans to place the laundry in,
and turns, for an instant,
toward the flurry of footsteps
and cries of pedestrians
as a boy—that's all he was—
backs from the corner package store
shooting a pistol, firing it,
once, at the dumbfounded man
who falls forward,
grabbing at his chest.

A few sounds escape from his mouth,
a babbling no one understands
as people surround him
bewildered at his speech.
The noises he makes are nothing to them.
The boy has gone, lost
in the light array of foot traffic
dappling the snow with fresh prints.

Tonight, I read about Descartes'
grand courage to doubt everything
except his own miraculous existence
and I feel so distinct
from the wounded man lying on the concrete

I am ashamed.

Let the night sky cover him as he dies.
Let the weaver girl cross the bridge of heaven
and take up his cold hands.

Pinoy at the Coming World

Waialua Plantation, 1919

I thought, when I left the fields
and hauling cane and hoeing out the furrows
for this job of counting and writing and palaver
in the rough, sing-song English of the store,
I had it made and could scheme a little,
put away something, so long as I made
the balance at the end of the day
and nobody squawked to the bosses
that I cheated or sassed them.
And I shamed no one, reading the paper
or some cowboy dime-novel like a *haole*
showing off my literacy as they shuffled into the store
dressed in their grimed khakis,
cuff and gloves sticky with juice,
and nettled head to toe with cane fiber.
I could speak Ilocano like a king or a muleteer,
a Visayan pidgin, a Portuguese,
a Chinese, and a Puerto Rican.
Simple words for service.
But for jokes, for talk story,
we used the English—chop suey at first—
then, year by year, even better,
smooth as love between old partners.
And the insults—*bayow, salabit, bagoong!*—
no matter if affectionate or joshing,
never entered my speech again
from the day I left the ditches,

tied on the apron, and stepped behind this counter.
No more '*manong*,' no more 'rat-eater' or 'fish-brain.'
No more garbage-talk to anybody.
How I see it, we all pull a load,
glory across the same river.
So, when I brought the wife in and the babies
start to coming—American citizens every one,
born, not smuggled here—I had every reason to figure,
'*Pinoy*, no worry, you going to the top.'

Even when the strike came and the black market
started to cut me out, I wasn't surprised.
The union had told me to stay on,
keep open even though they picketed.
When they needed cigarettes, sugar, or coffee,
when they needed box matches to light
torches at the labor rally,
they still came to me, calling from the back door,
and I sold in secret, out of pity,
and, for the plantation, at a profit.
Nobody lost. And I had the good will,
fish or vegetables or papayas whenever anyone had extra.
They came to the back, just as during the strike,
handing things through the door in old rice sacks
and smiling, bowing if they were Japanese,
and running off down the street past the Cook pines
without much to say, bowing each time they glanced back,
framed in the green monkey-tails of the trees.

But none of us was ready for the flu that hit,
first the Mainland and all the reports of dead
on newspapers wrapped around the canned meats I stocked—
drawings of mourners joining hands in long processions
following a single cow draped in white,
a black parade on an unholy day—
then here at Pearl by cargo and troop ship,
through the military and workers at the docks,
finally to all of us here on the plantations,
diggers and *lunas* and storekeepers all alike,

sick with it, some of us writhing on the beaches,
sleeping naked and in the running wash from the waves,
shivering, trying to cool our fevers down.

My boys were worse with it at first,
all of them groaning like diseased cattle,
helpless and open-eyed all through the night.
But they slipped the worst punch
and came back strong, eating soup
and fruits and putting the weight back on.

The oldest even went back to school
and took over for us behind the counter
times when my wife left to nurse the sick
and I boarded the stage for Honolulu,
hoping to fetch medicines from the wholesalers
and maybe a vaccine from the doctors at Pearl.

But it's my youngest now that has it bad,
so weak in years English is her only tongue,
fevers all the time and a mask of sweat
always on her face. It's worse because
she doesn't groan or call out or say anything much,
only cries and coughs and rasps in her breathing
like a dull saw cutting through rotten wood.
We pray, bathe her face and neck and arms
in a cheesecloth soaked in witch hazel,
light a few candles, and call on the saints
to cure her and to ease her pain.

But I know it's near her time
and that no faith doctor or traveling *hilot*,
our village healers expert in herbs and massage,
will bring her back from this final sickness.

Last night, when waiting was all there was to do,
I dressed myself in khakis again
and a pair of work boots so new
the laces were still full of wax

and soles like iron against the soft heels of my feet.
I closed up and walked past
the mill and the raw sugar bins,
by the union hall used for a morgue
and past the locomotive bedded down for the night.
I wanted to walk completely off plantation grounds
and get all the way out of town to where
sugar cane can't grow and no moon or stars
rose over pineapple fields. I wanted to get up
on a ridge someplace where kings
and their holy men might have sacrificed
or buried, in secret, some intruder's
unholy bones. I wanted rain to fall
and streams to churn and waterfalls, as they fell
from the Pali across mossy stone, to glow
with the homely, yellow light of mourning, our candles
lit for souls unwinding in their shrouds
and shrieking off the cliff-coasts of these islands.
I wanted the roar from the sea, from falling water,
and from the wind over mounds and stones
to be the echo of my own grief, keening within,
making pure my heart for the death I know is to come.

51

Andrew Hudgins (1951–)

One of Solomon's Concubines, Dying, Exults in Her Virginity

They tell me it's a fever. So
I'm right again. I bum and bum
and then go cold. And in between
they balance off and I can think
as clearly as I ever have.
A clearing in the brain is like
a clearing in the woods, a place
to stand and watch the circling trees
go up in flames, to study fire
while red and orange swirls dose in
on me.
       I came to Israel
at seventeen: an offer made
was ridiculed by his eunuch.
So I was added to a deal
for twenty others, rounding out
the bargain. He always has
a poverty of virgin girls,
for whom he has a private need.

During a childhood fever I
lost all my hair; it grew back white.
One eye turned brown and doesn't work
in concert with the violet one.
Since then I've had a tendency
to fits, a talent I've advanced
till I can see the future like
a master huntsman sees a tiger
crouched in a thicket, while the beaters see
a wall of leaves. Sharp leaves.

He touched my breast and called me sweet.
Then I fell victim to a spell
and called out loudly of a sudden,
Something is burning! He touched me
with practiced hands, firmer this time,
and called me sweet again and said
I was imagining, a common fault
of virgins. *When I tell you some-*
thing's burning, something is burning, I said.
Something is burning in Israel.
Is it a foreign ship in port,
a mendicant's poor desert fire,
or a stranger's soul I smelled in passing?
It's burning now and will be here
sometime tonight, burnt to a cinder.
He sent me back and had the eunuch
send up another, calmer virgin.
They brought me to him only once.
If I'd been beautiful or young,
he would have thrown me to the bed
and breached me anyway.

That very night inside the walls
an olive merchant's son burst into flames,
ran shrieking up the midnight streets,
and died not fifty feet from here.
I don't need confirmation for
myself. I've learned to trust my feelings
as they come to me. Yet the thing itself
is nice to flaunt at skeptics like
the king's most trusted eunuch,
whose noncommittal, boy-girl smile
I've seen before on poisonous lizards.

If he, the king, had raped me then,
I would have lost my gift of prophecy—
it's my one small comfort to know,
in some ways, what will happen next.
You've no idea what it does

for a woman's sense of grace to hear
the tune her life's unfolding to.
A temple dancer's poise informs
her body long into marriage
and through the bloody rip of labor.
And even walking, burdened, through
the marketplace, she senses where
to set her feet most gracefully
and how her aging torso sways.
Although it isn't quite the same,
my gift has given me that sense
of knowing things instinctively,
not being taken by surprise.

        For instance I
have seen the face of my old age
arrange itself as visage on
the mottled back of my brown hand
and known my flesh is wholly mine.
Though I will never live to know
the vision's truth, I've seen that face
smile off my hand at me, and I
have laughed at it and it at me.
Then I have kissed my old age on
the mouth, and it has kissed me back.

Saints and Strangers

You teach a Baptist etiquette, she turns
Episcopalian. I did. It's calm.
And Daddy, who shudders when I take the host,
stays home and worships with the TV set.
He's scared to leave the house. Incontinence.
When he's wet himself, he lets us know
by standing grimly at our bedroom door
and reading from his Bible. We think about
a nursing home. If I put on Ray Charles

he huffs around the house and says, *Marie,*
that nigger jungle-thumping hurts my head.
But these are little things. In many ways
the stroke has helped. He's gentle with the girls.
For hours he'll ride them horsy on his knees.
Still, there are those damn demons. Mine are blue,
Jim's red. He whispers demons to the girls
and gets them so they don't know what to think
of us. Beth's asthma starts. I tell the girls,
You play pretend, don't you? Well, you can stop.
But Paw-paw can't. He always plays pretend.
They seem to understand. In some ways, though,
I think he's even purer now—a saint
of all his biases, almost beyond
the brute correction of our daily lives.
Strangeness is part of it. And rage and will.
There's something noble in that suffering
and something stupid too. I'm not a saint,
of course, but as a child I had a rage
I've lost to age, to sex, to understanding,
which takes the edge off everything. Perhaps
it's my metabolism cooling down.
Who knows? One glory of a family is
you'd never choose your kin and can't unchoose
your daddy's hazel eyes—no more than you
could unchoose your hand. You get to be,
in turn, someone you'd never choose to be.
When feeling strong, I'll ask him to give thanks.
If he goes on too long, I say amen
and pass whatever bowl is near at hand.
Jim carves the meat, the girls reach for their tea,
and Daddy takes the bowl and helps his plate.

52

Paul Lake (1951–)

Two Hitchhikers

Once driving down a dark stretch of state highway
Through moonless countryside, not far from home,
Our headlights caught, as in a flashbulb's flare,
A pair of hitchhikers:
                      One held a crutch
More than he leaned against it, and the other ...
But the negative dissolved as we swept past.
I felt the car lurch right (my friend was driving)
As the brakes took hold, then they were getting in
To the back seat. Both reeked of beer and whiskey.

"Say, why don't you boys drive us down to Midway
To get some beer... They kicked us out the bar."

"We're going the other way," my friend protested.
"We'll drop you on our way, just tell us where."

That silenced them—that is, until we slowed
At a stop sign at the next dark intersection,
And when they spoke, it was with more than words.
I heard a sudden snickering of steel,
Then saw the knife blade nipping my friend's ribs
As he clutched the wheel, and sensed near my own chin
The warm unsteady hand poised at my throat
And just the slightest kiss of silvery blade.
"Turn here," the one without the crutch commanded,
So we made a U-turn there and headed south.
That made them cordial. Putting away their knives,
One lounged across the back seat, one leaned forward
To share a joke, all beery fellowship,
And to pass the time, kept up a steady patter
For several miles.

"Say, you boys must be hippies—
I seen them beards. Well, hell, we're just like you—
We want some beer so we can go and get dizzy...."
And so on, always ending in the refrain,
"We're like you boys, we only want to get dizzy.
Yeah, we smoke pot ... and marijuana, too!"

After twenty miles, they both seemed harmless
enough—
Relatively, I mean, with their knives tucked in their
coats—
And since we had to, in a funny way,
We warmed up to them till we had to stop.

Then things got complicated. They got confused—
Should they leave us there while they went in to shop?
Of course not—we'd drive off and leave them stranded.
One stay with us, one knife against us two,
While one went in?
                    They didn't like that either.

At last, they hit upon the expedient:
They'd walk in single file, one behind each,
Hands in their pockets, fingering their knives,
And, after dire threats, so we paraded
Around the store, then through the check-out line.

I've told this story a hundred times, I know,
And always left out how we bought that six-pack,
Ashamed of how I'd sheepishly been steered
Out to the car, to get back in again
With our abductors. Because it seemed cowardly
Not to have clutched a magnum of champagne
And clubbed one over the head, crying bloody mur-
        der—
Or at least to have leapt a shelf of cut-rate gin
And waited for fireworks. Liquor stores have guns.

Instead, I skip right to the funny ending:

How after we'd retraced the same dark road
To where we'd picked them up, they made us turn
Suddenly off onto a dead-end lane
Along which three lights shone from three dark shacks.
We passed the first, the second, approached the third,
And just as we faced the woods where I envisioned
Our last life-and-death struggle or breakneck flight,
A voice said, "Turn in here," and they got out—
It must have been their house—and turning toward us,
Reached in a pocket, pulled out two dollar bills
And muttering, "Here, this is for your gas,"
Turned back around and lurched into the house.
We locked the doors and burned that dirt road up
Getting out of there....

        That's how the tale might end.

But seeing them in the store's bright parking lot
Confused and half afraid of us, scraggly and scrawny,
One gimp-legged, both just wanting to get dizzy,"
But without a car to fetch their beer back home,
I guess we thought that it would be less trouble
To trust our lives to their humanity,
Or luck—and, anyway, all made it home.

As we spun out to the hard-topped county road,
My friend reached out and handed me one dollar.
"Here, you've earned half of this."
           We couldn't stop laughing.

That's how a tale should end—in dizzying laughter,
Though some won't be arranged to end that way.

53

Robert Wrigley (1951–)

Invisible Men

1

For the mile past American Steel
I breathed in my cargo of roses,
but even in that sweetness I could feel
the lung grit and chronic bloody noses
of my childhood. It was my last day
delivering flowers, and the dead man
these were meant to honor couldn't stay
dead in the town he lived in,
where the undertakers were all white.
Like me, doing my buck-an-hour duty,
driving deep into Venice, Illinois, and its blighted
air with a perfect spray of American Beauty
roses, Boston fern, and baby's breath for the casket.
What did I know? I was nineteen, a week
away from the army, and if you'd asked
I'd have just said, "Luck, bad luck,"
And looked away, believing for the moment in flowers.
I don't remember. Maybe I was told
it was all cosmetic, that even after hours
of trying, of dabbing at dead skin as cold
as any, no white man could make a black face
presentable. Maybe I believed that
the way I believed I'd go anyplace
the army sent me, the way I believed what
we'd all been told—dominoes and honor,
fine and fitting things, the old lies.
How could I have known any different? Conned or
gullible, probably both, I honed my eyes
on beer and smoke, my ears ringing
with wild guitars. In Venice that day,
late winter, young black men gathered singing

around trash-can fires, and no one looked my way.
A white boy with a job, a longhair,
I couldn't outshine the package store lights.
I was out of focus in the noxious air,
in March, when not even clouds were white.

2

What is that smell in funeral homes?
formaldehyde? ammonia? Chrysanthemums,
gladiolas, carnations, the roses I followed,
held out before me and nodding like beggars,
like mourners—*amen, amen,* my steps
murmuring down the carpeted hall. They were
gathered in the chapel, the family I slipped
past, though I felt them watch
while I nestled the casket-piece in place.
Flag-draped and sealed, steel-cold to the touch,
the coffin held a soldier, whose black face
grinned at me from an 8 x 10 portrait.
And what I don't understand today
is how I looked back at him without
so much as a blink, how I eased away,
cool and professional, slowly making sure
the roses were right, balanced and symmetrical,
how, until I turned toward where
the family waited, I could not tell
they were crying. Silent, emptied, they
didn't look at me at all as I left,
but at one another, or at the plush gray
floor, or at the roses and fern and baby's breath—
expensive, short-lived, and meager. In that air
so full with dying, I moved like a wrist,
like sleep, impossible, invisible, there
and not there, like the people I passed
on the smoke-killed streets of Venice,
like the dead man I looked at but didn't see,
like the country itself imagining a menace
from across the world, while back home we

trucked our darker dead away and paid
ourselves little more than nothing to buy it:
the lie, the dazzling flag, frayed
to the edge of its true colors, white on white on white.

54

Judith Ortiz Cofer (1952–)

Quinceañera

My dolls have been put away like dead
children in a chest I will carry
with me when I marry.
I reach under my skirt to feel
a satin slip bought for this day. It is soft
as the inside of my thighs. My hair
has been nailed back with my mother's
black hairpins to my skull. Her hands
stretched my eyes open as she twisted
braids into a tight circle at the nape
of my neck. I am to wash my own clothes
and sheets from this day on, as if
the fluids of my body were poison, as if
the little trickle of blood I believe
travels from my heart to the world were
shameful. Is not the blood of saints and
men in battle beautiful? Do Christ's hands
not bleed into your eyes from His cross?
At night I hear myself growing and wake
to find my hands drifting of their own will
to soothe skin stretched tight

over my bones.
I am wound like the guts of a clock,
waiting for each hour to release me.

55

Rita Dove (1952–)

Agosta the Winged Man and Rasha the Black Dove

Schad paced the length of his studio
and stopped at the wall,
                              staring
at a blank space. Behind him
the clang and hum of Hardenbergstrasse, its
automobiles and organ grinders.
                              Quarter to five.
His eyes traveled
to the plaster scrollwork
on the ceiling. Did *that*
                              hold back heaven?
He could not leave his skin—once
he'd painted himself in a new one,
silk green, worn
like a shirt.
            He thought
of Rasha, so far from Madagascar,
turning slowly in place as
the boa constrictor
coiled counterwise its
            heavy love. How
the spectators gawked, exhaling

beer and sour herring sighs.
When the tent lights dimmed,
Rasha went back to her trailer and plucked
a chicken for dinner.
                    The canvas,

not his eye, was merciless.
He remembered Katja the Russian
aristocrat, late
for every sitting,
            still fleeing
the October Revolution—
how she clutched her sides
and said not
            one word. Whereas Agosta
(the doorbell rang)
was always on time, lip curled
as he spoke in wonder of women
                        trailing
backstage to offer him
the consummate bloom of their lust.

Schad would place him
on a throne, a white sheet tucked
over his loins, the black suit jacket
thrown off like a cloak.
Agosta had told him
            of the medical students
at the Charité.
that chill arena
            where he perched on
a cot, his torso
exposed, its crests and fins
a colony of birds, trying
to get out...
            and the students,
lumps caught
in their throats, taking notes.

Ah, Rasha's
     foot on the stair.
She moved slowly, as if she carried
the snake around her body
always.
      Once
she brought fresh eggs into
the studio, flecked and
warm as breath.
      Agosta in
classical drapery, then,
and Rasha at his feet.
Without passion. Not
the canvas
     but their gaze,
     so calm,
was merciless.

Cholera

At the outset, hysteria.
Destruction, the conjurers intoned.
Some dragged themselves off at night
to die in the swamp, to lie down
with the voices of mud and silk.

     I know moonrise. I know starrise

Against orders
the well and almost-well were assembled
and marched into the wood. When
a dry open place was found, halted.
The very weak got a piece of board
and fires were built, though the evening was warm.
Said the doctor, You'll live.

     I walk in de moonlight, I walk in de

Who could say but that it wasn't anger
had to come out somehow? Pocketed filth.
The pouring-away of pints of pale fluid.

> *I'll walk in de graveyard, I'll walk*
> *through de graveyard*

Movement, dark and silken.
The dry-skinned conjurers circling the fire.
Here is pain, they whispered, and it is all ours.
Who would want to resist them?
By camplight their faces had taken on
the frail finality of ash.

> *I'll lie in de grave and stretch out my*
> *arms*

Well,
that was too much for the doctor.
Strip 'em! he ordered. And they
were slicked down with bacon fat and
superstition strapped from them
to the beat of the tam-tam. Those strong enough
rose up too, and wailed as they leapt.
it was a dance of unusual ferocity.

Parsley

1. *The Cane Fields*

There is a parrot imitating spring
in the palace, its feathers parsley green.
Out of the swamp the cane appears

to haunt us, and we cut it down. El General
searches for a word; he is all the world

there is. Like a parrot imitating spring,

we lie down screaming as rain punches through
and we come up green. We cannot speak an R—
out of the swamp, the cane appears

and then the mountain we call in whispers *Katalina*.
The children gnaw their teeth to arrowheads.
There is a parrot imitating spring.

El General has found his word: *perejil*.
Who says it, lives. He laughs, teeth shining
out of the swamp. The cane appears

in our dreams, lashed by wind and streaming.
And we lie down. For every drop of blood
there is a parrot imitating spring.
Out of the swamp the cane appears.

2.   *The Palace*

The word the general's chosen is parsley.
It is fall, when thoughts turn
to love and death, the general thinks
of his mother, how she died in the fall
and he planted her walking cane at the grave
and it flowered, each spring stolidly forming
four-star blossoms. The general

pulls on his boots, he stomps to
her room in the palace, the one without
curtains, the one with a parrot
in a brass ring. As he paces he wonders
Who can I kill today. And for a moment
the little knot of screams
is still. The parrot, who has traveled

all the way from Australia in an ivory
cage, is, coy as a widow, practising

spring. Ever since the morning
his mother collapsed in the kitchen
while baking skull-shaped candies
for the Day of the Dead, the general
has hated sweets. He orders pastries
brought up for the bird, they arrive

dusted with sugar on a bed of lace.
The knot in his throat starts to twitch,
he sees his boots the first day in battle
splashed with mud and urine
as a soldier falls at his feet amazed—
how stupid he looked'—at the sound
of artillery. *I never thought it would sing*
the soldier said, and died. Now

the general sees the fields of sugar
cane, lashed by ram and streaming.
He sees his mother's smile, the teeth
gnawed to arrowheads. He hears
the Haitians sing without R's
as they swing the great machetes:
Katalina, they sing, *Katalina,*

mi madle, mi amol en muelte. God knows
his mother was no stupid woman, she
could roll an R like a queen. Even
a parrot can roll an R! In the bare
room the bright feathers arch in a parody
of greenery, as the last pale crumbs
disappear under the blackened tongue. Someone

calls out his name m a voice
so like his mother's, a startled tear
splashes the tip of his right boot.
My mother, my love in death.
 The general remembers the tiny green sprigs
men of his village wore in their capes
to honor the birth of a son. He will

order many, this time, to be killed

for a single, beautiful word.

56

Mark Jarman (1952–)

Liechtenstein

For Audrey Rugg

Two white whales, the father and the bolster
He hugs to his sour guts. Something he ate.
High up in the hotel room the roof beams,
Carved with bluebirds and red crocuses,
Are thatched with shadows. Hammocks
Of cobweb luff in the rising heat. His wife
Is leafing through a guide. His children finger
New purchases, the girl her dirndl skirt,
The boy his Swiss watch with its 17 jewels,
Already a glinting scratch across the crystal.
August, a rainy month in this small country.
Window-framed, the castle's topped with mist.
Now he is snoring, whom the doctor sighed for
Listening to his chronicle that accused
Last night's Italian dinner: "Ah, but you're
A foreigner." At last now, he's asleep,
The bolster, a man-long pillow, in his arms.

Out in the little capital, the day
Above the mother and her boy and girl

Combs out a cloud of rain that hangs and drifts
And lapses over the castle's roofs and windows.
The children ask her questions about the prince
And reason that, because he's just a prince
And his castle small, he might accept a visit.
But Mother says the way looks wet and steep.
They find a *Konditorei* of covered tables,
Sober as snow in a deserted square,
Where statuelike two pairs of men are seated
At separate tables. All four eat ice cream.
Two of them whisper head to head. The others,
An old man and his younger version, smile.
The mother lets her children say the French
For ice cream, and at once the old man speaks.
His elephant ears are nests of silver hair,
His bald head faintly blue with broken vessels.
He compliments the girl's black braids, the boy's
White-blondness and their mother's youth and beauty,
Nimble with English and with flattery.
The pale ice cream tastes sweeter than its color,
Like the flesh of pears and apples, and comes heaped
In glasses shaped like tulips that, when empty,
Reveal a smoky tinge and weigh no more,
It seems, than ash or cobwebs. "A pretty place,
Our country," says the old man. And they nod,
Despite the weather. He admires the watch,
The dirndl skirt now spotted with ice cream,
And frowns to learn that Father, at the hotel,
Is sick and sleeping. "It is a pretty place,"
He says again, as rain begins, clear strands
That catch the window, then the falling rush.
"You would not think it an unhappy place.
Yet, like America, it has a past,
An older past, of course, and just as sad.
Our little country gave up one in ten,
Three hundred years ago, three hundred out of
Three thousand—one in ten. But you, too, know
Of hunting witches in America.
Yet a *Kleinstaat* is like a little town.

Its jealousies let loose the wild assumption
Salvation could be won for the accused
And for the living peace of mind—with fire."

The woman and her children stare, enclosed
Now by the rain and this familiar voice.
"I know a tale of witches for your children."
The boy and girl swallow their ice cream slowly
And feel it down their throats, a cold paste.
The old man's young companion moves to speak,
But the woman looks intrigued. She leans and arches
Her fine American neck to hear. He sees it—
Sap gold as barkless fruitwood—and relaxes.
"The *Minnesängers* have an old love song.
My voice has hit its tree line or I'd sing it.
It goes that, hunting once for capercaillie
(You know them? Game birds, gallinaceous),
A hunter pierced a woman in a clearing.
When he bent down to her, to break the arrow,
He held a mass of feathers that squirted away.
He followed blood, like scarlet stitchery,
To a black hollow, slimy with dead leaves
Under a willow's root. There, he thrust in
His hand and found a passage he could walk down
Lit by a door ajar at the far end.
Through the door's crack he watched the witch, as you
Might watch one of your children dress for bed
When they are very young. He watched, but she
Was not a child and not a hag. The wound
Was near the heart. She wound the bandage—so."
And for the children, watching witnesses,
White O's of ice cream printed on their mouths,
He makes the winding motion, as if tying
The band around his chest. "She knew he watched.
Knew when the wound was dressed, he would be bound.
She made the knot. The door opened. She had him!
She gave him feathers, a capercaillie cock's,
And sent him out to do her autumn forage.
His plumage blurred among the evergreens.

His will was mute, his protests. Then, an arrow
Caught him on his first flight, and he was free.
This hunter was the daughter of a count.
She found him lying as he'd found the witch.
But he stayed human in her hands, oh yes,
And spoke to her, healed only by her touch,
Which was like polished fruitwood, smooth and cool,
She was amazed that, in a blinding second,
A bird lay in her arms a man. He spoke...."

There is a flashbulb pop, without a light.
A second of dead breath. They turn to look
Beside them where the men were whispering,
The two men head to head with their ice cream.
And one of them looks back through his curled hands
And groans. The other holds the jagged stub
Of one of those glass tulips he has broken
In his friend's face. Now hubbub is translated
To tell the woman what the hurt man says.
"He says, 'What have you done?'" And the attacker,
Setting the broken glass down, shakes his head.
He says he does not know what he has done.
The children see the blood. Their mother sees,
And whisks them out the door. The rain has stopped.
At the hotel, the bolster against his thigh,
Like the pillar of salt Lot might have brought to bed,
Father's his old self, rolling out his greetings
Like timbers on a surge. He's ordered supper,
Been reading about Italy. What's wrong?
She tells him what she can, the men, the blood.
And the children tell him all about a story
Where birds are men and women hunt them, and
A bald man, witches burned here by the thousands.
Father feels weak again. The evening comes.

She meets the knock as if she knew and dreaded
That it would come, one hand against the door,
Pressing against it, the other on the knob,
A quiver from her running through the frame.

In bed, her husband, feeling better now,
Leans curiously. The children stand in bathrobes.
It is the storyteller's young companion,
The one who had translated the cries for her.
"I've come to make apologies, I hope.
That picture of our country was not true.
No truer than we get on television
Of your America. I came with gifts."
He gives each child a clear waxed envelope
That holds three postage stamps. "We make these things."
He draws his hand, the thumb and index pinched
Beside his temple, squinting. "We engrave them,
Uncle and I." The children peer at them,
Three rectangles of sun-struck reds and blues,
Embossed with charcoal tracery to make
Three windows of stained glass: a coat of arms,
A haloed woman holding a cathedral,
And one—they know her—Mary with her baby.
Small in the upper corners, there are landscapes
Made totally of sunlight. Bowing a little,
The children put the stamps back carefully,
Surprising Mother, and say, *"Merci. Danke."*
But when she turns to him as if to receive
A gift herself, he shows his empty hands.
"No, no." She smiles. "How did the story end?
The hunter was about to speak." "The story?
Ah, yes. First, let me say, it was not right
Even without an end. The enchanted bird
Makes many flights and comes back every time
With what he finds—grubs, grains—for the witch's winter.
He loves the witch, you see. His spell is love.
Shot by the countess, he is free. But still,
With the spell broken, he will have to die.
Another version has him just a bird
In love with a human being, doomed by his feelings.
They are big birds, these grouse. The horse of the woods."

Her husband nods and wakes, looking attentive,
A turtle poking out to catch the drift

He might have missed, doubting it was important.
She sees between them a fraternal sign—
Two men about to speak, turning away
From a woman and her children to that language
That, now she knows, can break glass in a face.
A splinter of this place, this little nowhere,
Glints as it works into her memory.
What has he suffered but an upset stomach?
What has he done but missed it all and made her
Witness to it alone, with children watching?
He nods inside his snowy mountain shell.
"You are ill, sir," the stamp engraver says.
"Yes. Something I ate last night. Cannelloni?"
"Possibly. But, of course, you are a stranger."

Unholy Sonnet 12

There was a pious man upright as Job,
In fact, more pious, more upright, who prayed
The way most people thoughtlessly enjoy
Their stream of consciousness. He concentrated
On glorifying God, as some men let
Their minds create and fondle curving shadows.
And as he gained in bumper crops and cattle,
He greeted each success with grave amens.

So he was shocked, returning from the bank,
To see a flood bearing his farm away—
His cows, his kids, his wife, and all his stuff.
Swept off his feet, he cried out, "Why?" and sank.
And God grumped from his rain cloud, "I can't say.
Just something about you pisses me off."

Questions for Ecclesiastes

What if on a foggy night in a beachtown, a night when
      the Pacific leans close like the face of a wet cliff, a
      preacher were called to the house of a suicide, a
      house of strangers, where a child had discharged a
      rifle through the roof of her mouth and the top of
      her skull?

What if he went to the house where the parents, stunned
      into plaster statues, sat behind their coffee table,
      and what if he assured them that the sun would rise
      and go down, the wind blow south, then turn north,
      whirling constantly, rivers—even the concrete flume
      of the great Los Angeles—run into the sea, and four-
      teen year old girls would manage to spirit themselves
      out of life, nothing was new under the sun?

What if he said the eye is not satisfied with seeing, nor the
      ear filled with hearing? Would he want to view the
      bedroom vandalized by self-murder or hear the
      quiet before the tremendous shout of the gun or the
      people inside the shout, shouting or screaming,
      crying and pounding to get into the room, kicking
      through the hollow-core door and making a new
      sound and becoming a new silence—the silence he
      entered with his comfort?

What if as comfort he said to the survivors I praise the
      dead which are dead already more than the living,
      and better is he than both dead and living who is
      not yet alive? What if he folded his hands together
      and ate his own flesh in prayer? For he did pray
      with them. He asked them, the mother and father, if
      they wished to pray to do so in any way they felt
      comfortable, and the father knelt at the coffee table
      and the mother turned to squeeze her eyes into a
      corner of the couch, and they prayed by first listen-

ing to his prayer, then clawing at his measured
cadences with tears (the man cried) and curses (the
woman swore). What if, then, the preacher said be
not rash with thy mouth and let not thine heart be
hasty to utter anything before God: for God is in
heaven?

What if the parents collected themselves, then, and asked
him to follow them to their daughter's room, and
stood at the shattered door, the darkness of the
room beyond, and the father reached in to put his
hand on the light switch and asked if the comforter,
the preacher they were meeting for the first time in
their lives, would like to see the aftermath, and
instead of recoiling and apologizing, he said that
the dead know not anything for the memory of
them is forgotten? And while standing in the hall-
way, he noticed the shag carpet underfoot, like the
fur of a cartoon animal, the sort that requires comb-
ing with a plastic rake, leading into the bedroom,
where it would have to be taken up, skinned off the
concrete slab of floor, and still he said for their
love and hatred and envy are now perished, neither
have the dead any more portion for ever in anything
that is done under the sun?

What if as an act of mercy so acute it pierced the preacher's
skull and traveled the length of his spine, the man
did not make him regard the memory of his daugh-
ter as it must have filled her room, but guided the
wise man, the comforter, to the front door, with his
wife with her arms crossed before her in that ges-
ture we use to show a stranger to the door, acting
out a rite of closure, compelled to be social, as we
try to extricate ourselves by breaking off the exten-
sions of our bodies, as raccoons gnaw their legs from
traps, turning aside our gaze, letting only the numb
tissue of valedictory speech ease us apart, and the
preacher said live joyfully all the days of the life of

thy vanity, for that is thy portion in this life?

They all seem worse than heartless, don't they, these stark
and irrelevant platitudes, albeit stoical and final,
oracular, stony, and comfortless? But they were at
the center of that night, even if they were unspoken.

And what if one with only a casual connection to the
tragedy remembers a man, younger than I am today,
going out after dinner and returning, then sitting in
the living room, drinking a cup of tea, slowly
finding the strength to say he had visited these
grieving strangers and spent some time with them?

Still that night exists for people I do not know in ways I do
not know, though I have tried to imagine them. I
remember my father going out and my father com-
ing back. The fog, like the underskin of a broken
wave, made a low ceiling that the street lights
pierced and illuminated. And God who shall bring
every work into judgement, with every secret thing,
whether it be good or whether it be evil, who could
have shared what he knew with people who needed
urgently to hear it, God kept a secret.

57

Dorianne Laux (1952–)

The Lovers

She is about to come. This time,
they are sitting up, joined below the belly,
feet cupped like sleek hands praying
at the base of each other's spines.
And when something lifts within her
toward a light she's sure, once again,
she can't bear, she opens her eyes
and sees his face is turned away,
one arm behind him, hand splayed
palm down on the mattress, to brace himself
so he can lever his hips, touch
with the bright tip the innermost spot.
And she finds she *can't* bear it—
not his beautiful neck, stretched and corded,
not his hair fallen to one side like beach grass,
not the curved wing of his ear, washed thin
with daylight, deep pink of the inner body.
What she can't bear is that she can't see his face,
not that she thinks this exactly—she is rocking
and breathing—it's more her body's thought,
opening, as it is, into its own sheer truth.
So that when her hand lifts of its own volition
and slaps him, twice on the chest,
on that pad of muscled flesh just above the nipple,
slaps him twice, fast, like a nursing child
trying to get a mother's attention,
she's startled by the sound,
though when he turns his face to hers—
which is what her body wants, his eyes
pulled open, as if she had bitten—

she does reach out and bite him, on the shoulder,
not hard, but with the power infants have
over those who have borne them, tied as they are
to the body, and so, tied to the pleasure,
the exquisite pain of this world.
And when she lifts her face she sees
where she's gone, knows she can't speak,
is traveling toward something essential,
toward the core of her need, so he simply
watches, steadily with an animal calm
as she arches and screams, watches the face that,
if she could see it, she would never let him see.

58

Kate Daniels (1953–)

In the Marvelous Dimension

Affliction is a marvel of divine technique. It is a simple and ingenious
device to introduce into the soul of a finite creature that immensity
of force, blind, brutal, and cold. The infinite distance which separates
God from the creature is concentrated into a point to transfix the centre
of a soul.... In this marvellous dimension, without leaving the
time and place to which the body is bound, the soul can traverse the
whole of space and time and come into the actual presence of God.
—*Simone Weil*

(John)

Until then, Id never liked

petunias, their heavy stems,
the peculiar spittooning sound
of their name. Now I loved
a petunia for all it was worth
—a purplish blue bloom
waving in a red clay pot outside
an office window, My right eye
could see it through the shattered
windshield. My left eye had gone
blank and the roof of the Camaro
pressed my head flat back on the seat.
I diminished to my right eye,
which could only see, past the wreckage,
that one little flower. I felt myself
growing smaller, like Alice,
a trick so I could travel
out of there, to that ledge
where a petunia waved in the dust rising
from a fallen-down freeway.

✝

(Mary)

I picked the kids up
at 4:45, as usual. As usual,
they were antsy
and fighting. Rose tore a hole
in her new knee socks
kicking Justin in the backseat.
Timmy sucked his thumb in the corner.
Then Justin wailed at another
abuse from Rose and I was just about
to yell, *Goddamnit, shut up for once,*
when the whole thing went. I mean
the whole thing, the whole world,
I thought. The car tilted, the road
buckled up and then something was falling
down on us with a horrible screaming.
I guess I stopped driving and turned

to my children with a face of horror.
I reached past the seatbelt for Timmy,
my baby, and that's when it hit us.
My hand, pressed by the roof, pinned
his leg to the seat and he screamed.
Blood flowed down. Rose, my sweet
little Rose, was already gone.
I couldn't find her beneath
the bulged-down roof. Justin and Timmy,
they looked to me. They didn't understand
I was not in charge. Id always been
their only God. They looked to me.
They wanted me to lift them up
and wipe them clean, to mend
with tenderness their shattered bodies.
But I was pinned in place. Blood
started seeping from Justin's
mouth. Timmy never spoke again.
And then I knew everything: how we
were going to die and how it didn't
really matter in the scheme of things.
My babies' suffering wouldn't matter.
It was a board game of gigantic
proportions. Our tokens
had been shaken out on the playing board
at 5:04 PM. on the 17th of October
in the year of our Lord, 1989.

(Jane)

I must have been unconscious.
Even now, I can't remember
anything about what happened
until that arm
reached in the broken window
of the passenger seat.
It was just an arm, a black
person's arm, very strong

looking with fine hairs
all over it. The fingers
moved on my face, felt
my mouth, and then I heard
a voice shouting, *Someone's
alive here, breathing.*
I knew then it was me.
I was alive but I must be
in trouble. My body
returned to me slowly.
I was laid out flat on my back.
The roof of the car seemed
to be on top of me.
I couldn't feel anything
but my face where the arm
had touched me. I couldn't help
thinking about sardines
in their little oily cans,
how, in college, I ate them
on saltines, to save money.

⊶

(John)

Years ago, on a lark,
I learned transcendental
meditation. Now I focused
on the blue petunia and slowed
my breathing as I began to understand,
I thought, what had happened.
The whole fucking thing fell down.
I can't begin to explain
that terror. I've put it
in a little box in my brain
and I'm afraid of the day
it will emerge again. That petunia
saved me. Now I have
a whole garden of them
and when I wake at night

with the shits and the sweats
I go out there and lie down
among them, blooming or not,
cold or hot, and I weep long
and deep into the earth.

+

(Mary)

My baby was the last
one to go. *And the last
shall be first. I* hope
it's true. My children
dead around me, I couldn't
think of anything to do
but sing the lullabies I sang
when they were infants in their cradles
and I was sending them away
to oblivion for the night.

(Jane)

When I meet people
now, I look at their hands.
I know I'm looking for *that*
hand, *that* arm, the one
that told the world
I lived, that proclaimed me
worth saving. My own hands
lie on the arms of the metal
chair, useless and heavy.
One finger on each has enough
strength left to press these buttons,
moving me forward, moving me
back. I don't think
it would matter, anyway, to still have
the use of my body. It's only hands
I care about, my mouth that still

loves. Even in sleep, I feel
his fingers reading my terrified face,
tracing my lips like a patient lover.
He found my breath. You bastards
can have my body.

—

I couldn't believe it
when I heard this little voice
singing We *Are Three Little Lambs.*
I thought it had already
gotten to me, like in 'Nam,
when I freaked out
on patrol before anything
had happened. But the voice
was real, coming from a dark blue
Toyota squashed almost flat.
When I shone the flash over it,
I could see the dark pool of blood
beneath. In the dark, I could
smell it. I yelled out, *Ma'am—*
I'm here to help you, and the song
stopped for a moment. Then a voice,
not little at all, harder than any
I've ever heard, said from deep in the wreck,
You might as well go away. Nobody
can ever help me again.

✝
(Mary)

People have actually asked me
what I thought about in there,
if I figured I would get out,
If I knew the children were dead.
The answer is: when I knew
the children were dead, I didn't want
to get out, couldn't get out
anyway. I was in there

forever with my three little lambs,
the smell of their blood,
and their dead faces, filled with questions,
looking at me.

⤝

(John)

When I do die, give me nothing
but petunias. Pots and pots
of them with their unpretentious
blossoms and their lack of smell.

⤝ ✝ ⤏

(John, Mary, Jane)

It suddenly struck me
that I believed
the unbelievable.

✝

(Mary)

The freeway had apparently
fallen down on top of us.
My children were dead
and dying. My head was locked
into position to watch that.
The only way to not see
was to close my eyes.
But my baby lived
a long time, I think.
I had to look at him
as long as he survived,
to say those things that mothers
say, *It's OK, Mama's here, it will be
all right.* All the while
I was not exactly remembering
my past, but feeling

the future. It had a shape now.
I knew what I was doing
and what I believed.
I was watching
all three of my children
die. More than ever
before I believed
in God. He was there
in that car. He caused
it, He saw it. And when
it was over, He'd gotten
what He wanted.
One more fearful
citizen bowed down
and kissed His feet.
And then, goddamnit,
I led my babies right up.
I put their little hands
in His, and delivered them over
for eternity to Him.

———

I was shaving at the sink
and drinking my second cup
of coffee when the story
about that woman and her three
dead children came on the news.
I'm a man, but I screamed
when I heard it, the saw
and all. How they had to
blindfold her, what they told her
they were doing. I'm a man
but I screamed about this world
men built.

✝

(Mary)

I never went to college

but I know now there's something
more than this world we see.
Trapped in that car, I felt it
when Timmy, Rose, and Justin
expired. They just left, and for awhile
I went with them. We eased
right out of that wreck
and floated in a void
—a marvelous dimension—
like big flecks of ash
freed from a fire.
That's why it didn't matter
when they took their bodies.
They had left them already,
and were part of me again, as they were
to begin with, making me bigger.

(John)

I'm lucky, I guess.
That petunia got me
through it. I came out
with fear and a limp.
Not like that poor woman
who lost her kids or the quadriplegic
in the car near mine.
The magazines all want to know
what it's like, but who could describe
your whole world reduced
to the size of a washer,
your body twisted
around the spindle, fear
churning through, and nothing
to help but your brain. I was in there
for three hours and forty-eight
minutes, thinking clearly every second,
reckoning nonstop. Oh, yeah,
I prayed, and I believed. I *saw*

my life. It had a shape
at last and I wasn't ashamed.
I knew if I made it, I would worship
the planet, the natural
world, eschew concrete,
deny the cities. I would plant
petunias, groom evergreen trees. In short,
I would worship the earth,
not men.

✝
(Mary)

Their father came over
from the city for the funeral.
He was drunk and terrified
to look at me. I wasn't drunk
and I wasn't scared. People looked
at me like I was a monster—dry
eyed and calm. But if they'd
touched me, they would have known:
hard as metal on the outside, empty
as a suit of armor within.

꙳
(Jane)

The most intense feeling
I've ever had was that man
touching my face. Even now,
when I can get
someone to do it,
I almost swoon with the shivering,
the delicious sensation
ascending my face.
I'm being born
again, being pulled
from my mother.

And a second chance is offering
itself in the form
of a hand,
    a simple
        proffered
           human hand.

          —

        I can't imagine
        going through that.
        Can you? Watching
        your own kids die.
        Or coming out paralyzed
        or soft in the head
        forever. Thank God
        it wasn't us. Life
        could never be the same,
        could it? How
        could you bear it? How
        could you live?

✝

(Mary)

I live somewhere else
now. With them. It's not
in space, not
in time. It's pure
feeling, spread out
like jelly on a warm piece
of bread, sinking down
out of sight, the sweetness
still there, sodden
and hidden.

(Jane)

I used to look at cripples
and wonder how

they stood it.
I never could, I thought.
Now I thank God every
day I'm alive and a crip.
I laugh with pleasure
and get the nurse
to run her fingers
on my lip.

—

Those motherfucker newscasters
stood in front of the freeway
and broadcast their pithy little
stories every evening while people
were dying inside. Now *that's*
my definition of indecent.

✝

(Mary)

A preacher came to see me afterwards.
He asked me not to be
so angry, to forgive God,
to try to see it as part
of a plan I could not understand.
I just looked at him and he saw something
in my eyes that scared him: those three
little babies, frightened as bunnies. I *can't imagine
your pain,* he finally said. I *wouldn't try to.*
*Can your affliction bring you closer
to Christ? Can you be with Him
in your suffering?* And then I did something
I'll never regret: I laughed
in his face, I brayed like a donkey,

—

She just kept
weeping for her babies
and he was raving

on and on about some
flower in a pot. The paralyzed
one had a beautiful smile
on her beautiful face. I don't think
she could feel
a thing.

(Jane)

When they pulled me out,
my body was dead
already but it didn't
matter. I felt the best
I've ever felt. That one hand
gave me hope. Other hands
pulled me back
into life. I wouldn't let
myself begin to believe
until I saw the sky
again. Widening and
widening, it revealed itself
in the shape of a lip
curved up.

Like everyone else, I watched it
on television for three straight days.
There was nothing a person like me
could do. The twentieth century
caved in finally. The earth
taught cement a permanent
lesson. Now, it's not
that I'm phobic. It's just
that I've seen postmodern light.
We're all insane
to live this way.

  ?
The earth settled.
The waters calmed.
The planet twirled
in the heavens
unconcernedly
again.

✝

(Mary)

When the priest raises
the pale white Host
something really does
happen if you want
to believe. If you don't,
it might still happen
anyway. Right?
Your past wiped out
by the force of the mystery.
The future emerging
from one huge moment ...

Once, at a student play
in seventh grade,
the whole backdrop collapsed
with the wheezy singing
of nails being forced
from cheap wood. Frayed ropes
dangling like live snakes
and sawdust rising in a smoky haze.
When the scene settled,
Reality was where
it had always been:
right *there,* lurking
behind the drapes:
a cinderblock wall
painted pale green and a red door
marked Emergency Exit chained shut.

For once, nothing
but an empty stage separated
me from It. I *was*
It, and It was this:
several million tons of concrete roadway
and steel beams smashed
down on top of
approximately 274 live human beings
when the San Andreas Fault flexed a tiny muscle.
39 died, including my children. I
survived, Hundreds
took part in the rescue effort.
The rest of you—Christ
have mercy—watched on TV.

⊷ ✝ ☞

(John, Mary, Jane)

The red door
was chained shut.
We went through it
anyway.

for Janet May

59

Robert McDowell (1953–)

Quiet Money

The bootlegger opens his eyes and stares
Down the gray runway, another Wednesday.
Bony, shivering in early bathroom weather,
He locates a glass of rye on the window ledge
And flicks on the light. Flight day.
The weather report on the wireless is good,
Though what he sees in his shaving mirror
Makes him think of mechanical foul-ups—
A slice of wing shooting past him,
Chips of propeller smacking his goggles.

Flicking his thumb across the straight razor
Joe tells himself it's good to feel the edge,
To remember it's only a membrane
That separates blood from the body intact.
He thinks of landing an office job and laughs.
He thinks of coffee in a field cup and he's warm.
Down in the alley two cats howl,
The soundtrack of a skirmish. A trash can topples.
"That's motivating music," he says,
And mutters the closing bars of "Over There"—

*

Betty sulks in a luncheonette on Fourth,
Daubing her nose with a hankie, stirring eggs,
She wants him. She wants him everywhere.
On the bus to work she thought of telling him,
"Give it up or stop coming around,"
But the words were too heavy to carry,
Like too much weight in her handbag
Throwing off her natural stride.

Now she laughs
At the thing she'd tried last night,
Pouring so many martinis, hoping he'd nosedive
Into sleep and miss this day.
But Joe can hold his liquor,
Especially when he's talking poets and war.
Later, filing claims at the office,
Betty can't fix on the hour she passed out,
Or the hour he pinned the note to her pillow:

> *See you Monday, Doll,*
> *With something pretty from Oslo!*

*

The airstrip flags point east at a quarter to five.
Joe rubs a compass in his flight-jacket pocket,
His fingers brushing the pages of Rupert Brooke,
And he's thinking of wings.
Not those of machines but of birds,
What he'd wanted as a child
Who had loved the bird's life of excess
And dramatic death down a chimney
Or in the talons of a larger bird.
Walking round the plane he whistles.

"Nobody knows," he says, "but some Norwegian 53,000 miles away.
'Nobody crosses The Pond alone,' the experts say.
Well, I won't be rubbing their noses in it,
Though there's plenty gearing up to do just that.
Circus flyboy stuff. There's money in it,
But fame comes, too—a suit you can't take off."

He lingers, checking the Wright Whirlwind engine.
The tailwind says *look out;*
His patience says *take off.*
Far to the north the lights of Jersey sparkle,
Calming down.

He scrambles up on the wing, his perch,
One step from home. The cockpit
Makes him think of the backyards of boyhood.
Clearing trees at the field's far edge
Joe banks to the left, circling a hill,
And levels out heading northeast.
He likes that initial turn, getting the feel of it,
Feeling the earthbound tug slip away.

He imagines gunning for stars,
But the stars are at peace, in collusion.
The sun balloons above the waterline;
The moon drops down to the sea.
Joe thinks of the money he's flying,
Of gin crates stacked in a hangar in Norway.
He thinks of a present for Betty,
Of the life he's making, up here, among prosperous currents.

*

She doesn't want to think of him all day,
But superstition bites. She takes off,
Daydreaming herself into flight beside him.
"Joe," she thinks, "the only thing I want is a home
With you on the sofa, drinking a soda."
After five, plodding home, her head
Keeps lifting toward a drone that isn't there.
"Monday isn't far," she tells herself.

*

Joe's gruff Norwegian contact waves
As he lifts off, climbing in the wind
That will take him back to the luncheonette.
He climbs with the current inside him,
The current Betty loves him for and fears.

Twelve hours out, twenty from home,
He fights it,

The drone of the motor stirring sleep.
He regrets staying up last night until two
Singing war songs, talking baseball,
Norwegian poets, and women—always women.
Joe nods behind his controls,
But something besides sleep isn't right.
Something in the sky is wrong.

He comes to long enough to focus
On a shadow image skimming the sea.
Bird, then *dolphin* occur to him. Then *plane.*
That can't be, so he tells himself *reflection*
And conjures the creature from an old story
That snatches plane and pilot
If they fly too close to water.
"That can't be anyone but me," he says.
The image below him fades, heading the other way.
That's wrong. So he cups his hand outside
To catch a breeze and deflect it into his face,
But sleep blows through him, too.

Now he's hunting for the brainstorm gadget he'd installed
Under his seat. He finds it, grazes the live wire
With his wrist, and sits up, back to himself.
And alone—as it should be.
Below him nothing angles but the sea.
Hitting fog he pulls back on the throttle
(Like flying inside a glass of milk)
Until he hits clear air at 4,500 feet.
He thinks of Betty asleep
And of Brown and Alcock
Teaming up to cross the Atlantic first in 1919.
He thinks of them losing their bearings in fog,
Flying upside down within 500 feet of the sea.
How many times did Brown crawl out on the wing,
Wiping snow and sleet from the fuel gauge? Joe smiles.
"Those clowns made good, alright, but what for? £10,000, knighthood,
And Alcock dead in a crack-up six months later."

Good night, Irene, good night . . . ©

Joe tips his wing to Alcock
And levels out over the coast of Newfoundland.

      *

Sweeping cups from the counter into a tray,
Madge winks as Joe saunters past the register.
Betty, raising a fork, freezes,
Riding out a tremor, and a wedge
Of lemon meringue free-falls to her lap.
"You can't have this and wear your food," he says.
One hand rests on her shoulder;
The other sets a hatbox on the table.
Tapping the left side of his jacket
He lowers his voice: "Tonight," he says,
"I'll show you what I've got in here."
Betty's face is like clearing weather
As she preens herself in the mirror,
Admires the way she looks in a smart Norwegian bonnet.
"Maybe in that hat you'll see things other ways,"
Joe says. Betty sits down.
Joe fidgets with a cup.
"You don't look well, she says. "What's up?"

"I pushed it to the limit on this run.
I let myself stay up all hours
And then I couldn't hold it off—
The Sandbag Eye—I saw things.
I saw the creature from that story you hate;
I saw myself as a child, grounded in a strange neighborhood.
I saw another plane. A reflection, I guess,
But that's what shook me most. Listen,
I got a bonus for the quick turnaround.
It's more than we've ever seen,
Why don't we get hitched?
Just don't make me give it all up."

"I know," she says,
And hammers one hard kiss across his chapped lips.

On the street Joe feels the slap of a newsboy's cry:

Lindbergh Lands in Paris!

He whistles like a punctured tire.
Betty hugs his arm and nods.
"I didn't want to bring it up," she says.
Joe leans against a lamppost, staring east.

"Lindbergh.
I never thought he'd beat them,
Byrd and the others with their cash.
I knew he was in the hunt, in a quiet way,
But I never figured this.
He'll get tickertape parades and medals now,
Money and keys to the mayor's w.c.
Think of it, honey. All that brotherly love."

On the landing, at the door to her walk-up,
Betty fumbles in her purse for keys.
"Lindbergh's never landed *here,* " Joe says.
Inside he pulls a bottle from his duffel bag.

"Sometimes a proud man
Doesn't wave himself around.
Headlines cut the pants off privacy.
They make you public, a pioneer.
I wonder if he knows what he's in for?"

Joe talks and talks.
The moon pins a spotlight on his face.
Betty wrings her hands and rocks,
The bottle open on the bureau-top,
But neither takes a drink.

Past three. Joe is flying blind, questioning.

Betty's breathing is a motor in good repair.
Joe hums under his partner's sleep.
"What?" she says, banking out of a dream.
"I'm thinking of getting a house in Jersey," he says,
But he's thinking of Lindbergh, too.
He's thinking of a plane below him,
Skimming the rooftops of Paris, beating him out.
"Anywhere," Betty says. "Anything you want."

What *does* he want?

Nearing five Joe looks down on his body in a restless sleep.
Sprawling so he looks a little like Italy on a globe.
Out of the body a body looks that way,
A smear of papier-mâché, a flare-up,
An ugly reminder on a fist of blue.
Joe, or Joe's double, wonders
If the quiet atmosphere he flew in was a cheat.
Betty, asleep, looks like a separate country.
How can she make him believe in home?
In peace? Can anyone? Undertakers, maybe—
White-jacketed illusionists keeping a low profile.
Why does Joe's double escape so many nights?
Why, when he returns, does he keep
What he's found to himself,
A country inside a country, unmapped?
The questions hound Joe out of sleep,
So wrapping himself in a blanket
He gropes his way into a chair
And flicks on a reading lamp.
Slowly the room settles, focuses,
And he picks up a copy of *Lear*
To whisper the Fool's lines, his favorites.
Their sound, the way it makes him feel,
Is enough. He rides it into the afternoon.

        *

On moving day they look like a couple

In a paperweight, their arms around each other.
Joe is Errol Flynn in a flight jacket;
Betty's lucky hair falls down like rain.

After the movers back over the curb
And putter north, the newlyweds
Climb the fire escape for a farewell drink.
"What are you thinking?" she asks.

"Nothing. just noticing the wind,
How it's turning nasty, how I wouldn't wait."
The winner in the paperweight dissolves;
A hard and lonely figure takes his place.

"Joe, how long before you face it,
Before you get it straight—what it means to you?"
"What are you talking about?"
"Not what," she says. "Who."

Joe faces her. "Don't push," he says,
And suddenly he sees himself as memory,
His image fraying like tapestry.
"I hope you can take it," he says. "Your man's obscurity."

                *

"Something Willy said just ticked Joe off,"
Betty tells her neighbor in the backyard.
The iron fence between them soaks up heat.
"I don't know what."

"I do," her neighbor says. "Willy was going on
About the Yankees and the Babe.
You know how men get hot when they talk sports.
Well, Joe claimed that there were players in bush leagues
Who were just as good as Ruth but never got the breaks.
Willy wasn't buying, and soon they were toe-to-toe.
Their faces got red.
The veins in Joe's neck popped out.

I noticed that just before he did it—
Threw his glass (I swear it nicked Willy's ear) in the pool."

"That's when I came out," Betty says.
"I saw Willy's eyes get big like balloons
And Joe just turning, walking away.
He passed right by me and didn't speak,
Though I could feel anger breathing out of him.
It goes back further than the Yanks or the Babe."
A drone out of the west breaks in
And both look up
As Betty's single-engine fly-boy tips his wing.
Anna gurgles in her playpen.
Chug, their terrier, snoozes on a plank of sunlight.
The plane levels out, descending
Toward the airstrip a couple of miles away.
Betty holds her breath. *Irrational*,
She tells herself, but she can't help it.
Only when he turns their Silver Ghost
Up the drive will the moment be enough,
His coming back in one piece
To lift Anna off his knee,
Catching her as she parachutes back.

*

"I had a case of the yips for years," Joe says.
His nephew sips lemonade and nods,
Not knowing what Joe means. He lets him talk.

"After we got hitched
The weather always indicated *stay*,
So I'd scrub a couple of flights a month,
Then two a week, and pretty soon
I was on the ground more hours
Than I was logging in my plane.
Imagine what that did to me!
You never feel the same
Once you've cut through weather

And known it topside.
You miss the motion, the nerve-and-bone collision.

"How many nights did I rock in my chair,
Spending in my head the cash I'd make
As soon as I got home safe? And *safe*—
That word would take me like a haunting
As I'd fall back knowing where I was.
I had it, yes. The Yank dream,
No rain, no sleet, no public pilot
Cutting his silver trail under me,
No flight I couldn't roundtrip in a day.
When I couldn't sleep I'd rock.
I don't know how I put her through
Those shifting moods, but Betty was great."
She'd touch me—stop me, really—
'Level out,' she'd murmur,
But if she strayed too long I'd veer off course.
My throttle hand squeezed nothing,
Making fingernail imprints on its palm.

"I had to face it,
The need for something to run up against,
A glass door, a garage wall,
An impassive, staring face on the front page.
Anna helped, and the dog, and this place,
But I needed more. I got it, too.
It's sad when I think of it.

"You're probably too young to recall
The scene I'm thinking of.
It was March of '32.
The Lindberghs had a house not far from here
Outside of Hopewell—ironic name!
The papers served up their grief like daily bread.
We memorized photos of ladders
And footprints in the mud,
A ransom note on the windowsill.
The baby, as near as we could tell,

Was stuffed, still sleeping, in a burlap bag.
'It looks like the work of pros,' the cops said,
Which was good for the kid's sake.

"And then the waiting. Ten weeks of dying,
Ten weeks of cranks and comforters,
Wheels (the cops called the crazies *wheels)* and volunteers.
I flew some for the cops, you know,
Shooting down false leads. It made me sick
Each time I landed with nothing to offer Lindbergh
But a negative shake of my head.
The look on his face will never leave me—
A mid-Atlantic look, your plane out of fuel.
The clocks ground on but didn't move.

"Mail buried their house like lava.
And all for nothing. Cruelty.
The body turned up in the woods
A few miles away—and this is the awful part—
He'd been dead since that first night.
The ladder-man had dropped the burlap sack
And the baby's head struck a window ledge.
Imagine how the 'nappers must have felt!

"And Lindbergh. How far out,
In after-years, did he push himself to feel secure?
And the rest of us...how many couldn't sleep
For fear of waking without sons or daughters?
We learned to love the sounds of words
That covered us—words like *lock* and *alarm,*
And we raised you on them.
Now you can't look strangers in the eye,
And there may be things you can't even tell your closest friend.

"Son, you have to lose to win.
That notion settled in with us
And we passed it on to you.
Thank God. You know what it meant to me?
My daughter safe, first of all,

And all of it, really.
I spent so many nights in her room
Just watching her sleep,
Convincing myself no gang would take her
From me—ex-fly-boy, average businessman—
And suddenly I was happy.
My life's course felt fair.
I thought of fame and money, and still do,
How what we do to get them can make us sorry."

Young Richard on the Road

For Richard Wilbur

Our neighbor fed the wanderer and called
To see if we had any work to give.
I met him at the drainage ditch that cut
Between her place and mine. A rabbit dove

Into the hedge where the bindlestick stood
Talking of trains, the barn needing repair.
All day without a word we labored there
Inside the ping of tools, the sussh of wood

Until I stopped. He stopped because I did,
And side by side we trekked along the fence
Down to the house, a wash, a meal, then bed.
For three days we smoothed corners, banged out dents

And when we finished the barn breathed easier.
Then Wilbur said that it was time to go
And turned in early. My sleep was like my water,
Which stung and came down sudden or too slow,

So I got out of bed. I warmed the damp
With tea, a slice of buttered bread, and stepped
Out to admire the moonlit barn. The lamp
Still glowed in the back room where Wilbur slept.

I saw him in his long-johns, wearing specs
And writing in a book. I thought to say
What gives? But checked my curiosity
Before I broke whatever spell it was

That kept him there after a brutal day.
I went back up to bed, and when I woke
He'd already gone, his room as orderly
As if he'd never come. A page from his book
Lay on the table under a bolt of yarn.
I found it first and handed it to you
Who drank your tea and studied it twice through;
A poem it was, his poem of the barn.

I keep it in a ledger of accounts
And have occasion, once or twice a year,
To take it out and read it to the horses,
To you, or someone dropping by. No matter

That the man who wrote it is far from here
Or near, living or dead. He understood
That all we are is work if it is good.
Just like his poem, like our barn out there.

60

Gjertrud Schnackenberg (1953–)

The Resurrection

Piero della Francesca

In the 1550s a lantern maker, Marco, testified
That as a child he had "led Piero by the hand"
Through the streets of Borgo San Sepolcro.
Piero, blind, and following a child guide along

The chessboard of his native city's streets
To the Civic Palace, within the tumbled walls
Of the Town of the Holy Sepulchre. Piero, blind—
Who once, with earth imported from the Black Sea,

Had dusted pinhole pricks on tracing sheets,
To trace the *Dream of Constantine* on the wall,
And the serf who leaned against his shovel
Awaiting Helen's command to dig for the cross,

And Pilate, impassive, hooded in the judgment Seat,
And the beautiful Jew who was tortured in a well—
Piero, white-gowned, a cataract prisoner, now
Shuffling, with outstretched hands, while far-off bales

Of straw, in fields ignited by the sunset,
Smolder behind him, setting a broken wall on fire.
The hem of a mantle of tree roots flames up
Like a patch of ancient sewing work littered

With those pearls for which Duke Federigo paid
A great price back in the old life, stitched
With silver leaf, in luminous embroiderings,
Lying tossed like a discarded shroud over

Kindling sticks in the hedge of thorns
The goldfinch once inhabited, her nest
A torch's head fallen from its stick
Beyond the curb of the marbly dream-town,

Where towers, knocked down across the countryside,
Half crumble like sugar-cube constructions
For a wedding, or dissolve like knocked-over
Buckets of sand for children's battlements—

For a city left behind in the wake of the earthquake
Of 1352, or the quake at Christ's death,
Since history is behind Piero now, and
The goldfinch is saved, circling ecstatically

Above Piero's head as he climbs a cement staircase
Step by step. *When you were young, you girded*
Yourself and walked wherever you would. But
When you are old, you will stretch forth

Your hands, and another will gird you,
And carry you where you would not go.
Halting in the streets of Holy Sepulchre,
Grown old in the town of his nativity,

Taken by the hand to the Civic Palace,
He stops at the site of *The Resurrection*,
And lifts his outstretched hand from Marco's shoulder,
As if he groped for the lip of a stone coffin

From antiquity set only inches away from where
The blind man appears to be staring in fright
Into God's face. Behind him the pink twinkle
Of twilight is a banner moist with one drop

Of Jewish blood; before him, the distant
Blue mountain of Purgatory. His fingertips touch
Only picture-shadowing earth from the Black Sea.

Once he could squint at *The Resurrection* through
An ever-smaller pinhole of light, like
A pinhole pecked for him by the finch's beak,
Through which he sifted powder for his drawings—
She whose nest had fallen when the mowers

Burned away the branches, she who had let
Piero approach, but only so far, and then
Warned him off with her gaze of terror,
When he would have bent on his knees in the grass

To stroke her anxious, silky head with
A fingertip, touching the scarlet cap
That stained it like a tiny, bloody drop,
But he'd backed away, not wanting to scare her—

But the pinhole he had peered through closed.
Now his shoes press against the plaster wall
Of blind old age, backed up by the empty place
Brick walls depict, where paint is a scent

That still could conjure the belfries of papier-mâché
He had painted for an important Duke,
A famous humanist he'd once depicted traveling
At twilight in a straw wagon with angels

Conversing in seraphic languages
Along the outskirts of a shining thunderstorm
Before the distant prospect of Rome-Jerusalem-Urbino.
Now he stands sightless with his empty hand

Outstretched at the rough edge of the sepulchre
Recently broken open, before which
Jesus has turned to Piero, holding out to him
Death's unraveled, pitiful bandages.

61

David Wojahn (1953–)

In Hiding

After Franco's victory, Manuel Cortes, socialist and soldier of *the Republic, spent thirty years in hiding in the attic* of *his home.*

From the attic's shutter crack I watch
Juliana recede down the road to Malaga,
  her egg baskets aglow in dawnlight,
and I turn from yesterday's papers, the radio

  humming low so the neighbors won't hear:
Franco guiding Eisenhower through
  the NATO base at Torrejon, a marching band,
the B-47s grumbling as they rise

  laden with napalm and atom bombs, the way,
in '37, the Nazi Heinkels rumbled over Guernica,
  our battalion, the 101st, peering up
from the trenches as the bombs surged down,

  and if not for the noise it looked
like a man shelling peanuts on a sidewalk,
  innocent litter that pigeons would eat
on a sun-drenched day in the spring, when you smell,

  as you can today, the lemon blossoms—but yellow smoke
laddered the sky, and the faces
  of the dying in Cathedral San Xavier
we could only imagine, like images

  remembered from a film seen years
before. So much one can only *imagine:*
  this attic room unchanged for decades,
and Conchita now with a child of her own,

and Juliana tells me all along
the road from Torremolinos to Malaga
   the villas of the rich, Americans
and Madrillino doctors, gaze out

   on the sea, Hollywood men, their women
precious stones, sunning themselves
   each afternoon on the balconies.

But isn't this also a life of leisure?
   I weave, some mornings, mats of esparto grass
      Juliana will sell in the city,
and some nights try to read again

the difficult chapters of *Kapital.*
   Even those mornings when De Valente's
      Guardia Civil, all of them drunk,
would ransack Juliana's wardrobe, tear

her slips and nightgowns from the dresser
   to find some evidence of me,
      my waiting here, only this wall
between me and the firing squad—was leisure.

I counted time, like a blind accordionist
   tapping his boot to the music,
      his ears by now so acute
he still can hear his heartbeat

among the loud notes of his reel.
   Time, it comes down to, and timing.
      As mayor, as soldier, I believed in
The People, in bread for them, and land

To believe in them now, I believe
   in this waiting, asking to keep
      the waiting holy, uncompromised by memory,
though some nights I'm still faltering

knee-deep through snow in Catalonia,
   my boots turned rags, the wound
      in my neck, where the bullet passed,
stanched with a scarf, my comrade

a Jewish corporal from Mérida,
   moaning for his sweetheart on my back,
   the dark hole in his chest
all night dampening my shoulder.

   Last year Conchita, my only child,
married the village postal clerk,
a man who does not know I exist. With my
   smuggled champagne I stared through the shutters

   at the wedding dance in the courtyard below,
and wept, not for her, but for my own absence,
the way a ghost must weep, continually,
   for things it lived with and touched.

   But later, I found myself humming
to the band as it yelped its tunes,
yet softly, so no one would hear.
   Then the guests were home, yellow lights

   still strung in the olives. The musicians,
ties and jackets draped on wicker chairs
wiped sweat from their brows and gently placed
   in their cases the heavy accordions.

   Always people say you walk
ahead into the future, though in truth
you walk backwards toward it, and only
   the past spreads its vista before you,

   though always, my friends, it is fading.
And you try to remember what it is that you
believed in. You try very hard.
   You wait. You watch until it's gone.

62

Kim Addonizio (1954–)

Physics

In the darkness of the booth, you have to find
the slot blindly and fumble the quarter in. The black
shade goes up. Now there's a naked woman

dancing before you and you're looking
at her knees, then raising your eyes
to the patch of wiry hair which she obligingly parts

with two fingers while her other hand
palms her body from breast to hip
and it's you doing it, for a second

you're touching her like that and when
you lift your face to hers she's not
gazing into space as you expected but

looking back, right at you, with an expression
that says *I love you, I belong to you compl—*
but then the barrier descends. You shove

another quarter in but the thing has to close down
before slowly widening again like a pupil adjusting
to the absence of light and by the time it does

you've lost her. She's moved on to the next
low window holding someone's blurred face,
and another woman is coming nearer

under the stage lights and in the mirrors,
looking so happy to see you trapped there
like some poor fish in a plastic baggie

that will finally be released into a small bowl
with a ceramic castle and a few colored rocks,
and you open your mouth just like a fish waiting

for the flakes of food, understanding nothing
of what causes them to rain down
upon you. You can feel your hunger sharpening

as she thrusts herself over and over into
the air between you. And now, unbelievably,
there comes into your mind

not the image of fucking her
but an explanation you heard once
of what vast distances exist

between any two electrons. Suppose,
the scientist said, the atom were the size
of an orange; then imagine that orange as big

as the earth. The electrons inside it
would be only the size of cherries. *Cherries,*
you think, and inserting your quarter you see one

sitting on an ice floe in the Antarctic, a pinprick
of blood, and another in a village in north Africa
being rolled on the tongue of a dusty child

while the dancer shakes her breasts at you,
displaying nipples you'll never
bite into in this lifetime; all you can do

is hold tight to the last useless coins
and repeat to yourself that they're solid,
they're definitely solid, you can definitely feel them.

HA

A man walks into a bar. You think that's some kind of joke?
Actually he runs in, to get out of the freezing weather.
Who cares, you say. Nobody you know.
You've got your own troubles, could use a drink yourself
You get your coat, a long scarf. You trudge
to the corner over the scraped sidewalk, slip and fall down
on the ice. Actually a banana peel, but who's looking?
Only a priest, a rabbi, and a lawyer you vaguely recognize—
didn't she help with the divorce? Never mind, the marriage
is over, good riddance. You're thinking now
you'd better have a double. You get up, holding your hip,
and limp towards the neon martini glass.
Anyway a man goes into a bar, just like you do.
He's tired of life, tired of being alone. No one
takes him seriously; at work he's the butt of jokes,
the foreman calls him *Moron* all day long. It's true
he's not too bright. He wants to kill himself,
but doesn't know how to. He orders drink after drink,
cursing the angel who passed out brains.
You take the stool next to him. In half an hour
you're pals—two losers getting shitfaced.
You start to tell each other riddles. What's big and red
and eats rocks; what do you get when you cross a penis
with a potato? Why is there something rather than nothing?
If God is good, how is it that the weed of evil
takes root everywhere, and what is there to keep us
from murdering each other in despair? Why is pleasure always
a prelude to pain? The bartender takes your glasses, tells you
it's time to get out. You stumble through the door,
and there you are in the cold and the wind and a little snow
that's started to fall. Two losers stand on a corner.
One turns to the other and says, Why did our love end?
The other can't answer. Why do they torment me? he says.
The snowstorm begins in earnest but still they stand there,
determined to stay put until they finally get it.

David Baker (1954–)

Murder: Crows

I can't help it. The brute dawn brings the day.
The window where my coffee's steamed with me
blackly since four, my sleep gnawed open
by a scream, becomes a field, like prophecy.

We'll let her go, he breathed, *we'll see;*
so my blood-gloved neighbor released to the herd
the runted lamb already ruined in the womb.
He is a gentle man, who hopes. His sheep stand

now luminous, fatal as patchfog, huddled
around that shy heart where the fence should be.
I guess they've been that way all night
though only since the dawn has so slowly

beat away the dark have I been able to see
their deadly self-indulgence. He didn't lie.
The clean-cut stumps glow like cellar bulbs.
The field grows long and starved. Silently

a kitchen light labors to cross its backyard, high
with weeds. The dawn bleeds out inevitably.
And so, like negatives of stars reflected,
or like me, the crows begin to stir where they

have landed, attacking the fencerow and baled hay.
They throb among the clover. They hop, wait,
screaming with the certain glee of screaming there.
I see his sheep brood and suffer, shifting about.

I see my nightmare blacken in the broad daylight.

David Mason (1954–)

The Collector's Tale

When it was over I sat down last night,
shaken, and quite afraid I'd lost my mind.
The objects I have loved surrounded me
like friends in such composed society
they almost rid the atmosphere of fright.
I collected them, perhaps, as one inclined
to suffer other people stoically.

That's why, when I found Foley at my door—
not my shop, but here at my private home,
the smell of bourbon for his calling card—
I sighed and let him in without a word.
I'd only met the man two months before
and found his taste as tacky as they come,
his Indian ethic perfectly absurd.

The auction house in St. Paul where we met
was full that day of cherry furniture.
I still can't tell you why he'd chosen me
to lecture all about his Cherokee
obsessions, but I listened—that I regret.
My patience with a stranger's geniture
compelled him to describe his family tree.

He told me of his youth in Oklahoma,
his white father who steered clear of the Rez,
a grandma native healer who knew herbs
for every illness. Nothing like the 'burbs,
I guess. He learned to tell a real toma-
hawk from a handsaw, or lift his half-mad gaze
and "entertain" you with some acid barbs.

So he collected Indian artifacts,
the sort that sell for thousands in New York.
Beadwork, war shirts, arrowheads, shards of clay
beloved by dealers down in Santa Fe.
He lived to corner strangers, read them tracts
of his invention on the careful work
he would preserve and pridefully display.

Foley roamed the Great Plains in his van,
his thin hair tied back in a ponytail,
and people learned that he was smart enough
to deal. He made a living off this stuff,
became a more authenticated man.
But when he drank he would begin to rail
against the white world's trivializing fluff.

Last night when he came in, reeking of smoke
and liquor, gesticulating madly
as if we'd both returned from the same bar,
I heard him out a while, the drunken bore,
endured his leaning up against my oak
credenza there, until at last I gladly
offered him a drink and a kitchen chair.

I still see him, round as a medicine ball
with a three-day beard, wearing his ripped jeans
and ratty, unlaced Nikes without socks.
I see him searching through two empty packs
and casting them aside despite my scowl,
opening a third, lighting up—he careens
into my kitchen, leaving boozy tracks.

I offered brandy. He didn't mind the brand
or that I served it in a water glass.
He drank with simple greed, making no show
of thanks, and I could see he wouldn't go.
He told me nothing happened as he planned,
how he left Rasher's tiny shop a mess.
I killed him, Foley said. You got to know.

You know the place. Grand Avenue. The Great
White Way they built over my people's bones
after the western forts made stealing safe.
Safe for that fucking moneyed generation
F. Scott Fitzgerald tried to write about—
and here was Rasher, selling off such crap
no self-respecting dealer'd waste his time.

I heard he had good beadwork, Chippewa,
but when I went in all I saw was junk.
I'm thinking, Christ, the neighbors here must love him,
the one dusty-shuttered place on the block
and inside, counters filled with silver plate
so tarnished Mother wouldn't touch it, irons
with fraying cords and heaps of magazines.

He had the jawbone of a buffalo
from South Dakota, an old Enfield rifle,
a horn chair (or a cut-rate replica),
German Bible, a blue-eyed Jesus framed
in bottlecaps—I mean he had everything
but paint-by-number sunsets, so much junk
I bet he hadn't made a sale in years.

You got to know this guy—skinny bald head
and both his hands twisted from arthritis.
I wouldn't give his place a second look
except I heard so much about this beadwork.
He leads me to a case in the back room.
I take a look. The stuff is fucking new,
pure Disneyland, not even off the Rez.

Foley's glass was empty; I poured him more
to buy time while I thought of some excuse
to get him out of here. If homicide
indeed were his odd tale's conclusion, I'd
rather let him pass out on my floor,
then dash upstairs and telephone the police.
I wouldn't mind if "fucking" Foley fried.

It's crap, he said. I tell this slimy coot
he doesn't know an Indian from a dog.
I can't believe I drove five hundred miles
to handle sentimental tourist crap.
He rolled himself upright in my kitchen chair
and looked at me with such complete disdain
that I imagined Mr. Rasher's stare.

I knew the man. We dealers somehow sense
who we trust and who the characters are.
I looked at my inebriated guest
and saw the fool-as-warrior on a quest
for the authentic, final recompense
that would rub out, in endless, private war,
all but his own image of the best.

Pretty quick I see I hurt his feelings.
He gets all proud on me and walks around
pointing at this and that,
a World's Fair pin, a Maris autograph,
and then he takes me to a dark wood cupboard
and spins the combination on the lock
and shows me what's inside. The old man

shows me his motherfucking pride and joy.
I look inside his cupboard and it's there
all right—a black man's head with eyes sewn shut—
I mean this fucker's real, all dried and stuffed,
a metal ashtray planted in the skull.
I look and it's like the old man's nodding,
Yeah, yeah, you prick, now tell me this is nothing.

He's looking at me looking at this head,
telling me he found it in a house
just up the street. Some dead white guy's estate
here in the liberal north allowed this coot
whatever his twisted little hands could take,
and then he hoards it away for special guests.
I didn't say a thing. I just walked out.

Now Foley filled his glass, drinking it down.
His irises caught fire as he lit up.
I sat across from him and wiped my palms
but inside I was setting off alarms
as if I should alert this sleeping town
that murder lived inside it. I could stop
the story now, I thought, but nothing calms

a killer when he knows he must confess,
and Foley'd chosen me to hear the worst.
Weird, he said, looking straight at me beyond
his burning cigarette. I got so mad.
Like all I thought of was a hundred shelves
collecting dust in Rasher's shop, and how
a dead man's head lay at the center of it.

I had to get a drink. Some yuppie bar
that charged a fortune for its cheapest bourbon.
I'm in there while the sun sets on the street
and people drop in after leaving work.
I look at all these happy people there-
laughing, anyway; maybe they aren't happy—
the well-dressed women tossing back their hair,

the men who loosen their designer ties
and sip their single malts—living on bones
of other people, right?
And two blocks down the street, in Rasher's shop,
a head where someone flicked his ashes once,
because of course a darky can't be human,
and someone's family kept that darky's head.

These genteel people with their decent souls
must have been embarrassed finding it,
and Rasher got it for a fucking song
and even he could never sell the thing.
No, he showed it to me just to get me,
just to prove I hadn't seen it all.
Well, he was right, I hadn't seen it all.

I didn't know the worst that people do
could be collected like a beaded bag,
bad medicine or good, we keep the stuff
and let it molder in our precious cases.
Some fucker cared just how he dried that head
and stitched the skin and cut the hole in the top—
big medicine for a man who liked cigars.

It's just another piece of history,
human, like a slave yoke or a scalping knife,
and maybe I was drunk on yuppie booze,
but I knew some things had to be destroyed.
Hell, I could hardly walk, but I walked back,
knocked on Rasher's door until he opened,
pushed him aside like a bag of raked-up leaves.

Maybe I was shouting, I don't know.
I heard him shouting at my back, and then
he came around between me and the case,
a little twisted guy with yellow teeth
telling me he'd call the fucking cops.
I found the jawbone of that buffalo.
I mean I must have picked it up somewhere,

maybe to break the lock, but I swung hard
and hit that old fucker upside the head
and he went down so easy I was shocked.
He lay there moaning in a spreading pool
I stepped around. I broke that old jawbone
prizing the lock, but it snapped free, and I
snatched out the gruesome head.

I got it to my van all right, and then
went back to check on Rasher. He was dead.
For a while I tried to set his shop in fire
to see the heaps of garbage in it burn,
but you'd need gasoline to get it going
and besides, I couldn't burn away the thought
of that weird thing I took from there tonight.

It's out there, Foley said. I'm parked outside
a few blocks down—I couldn't find your house.
I knew you'd listen to me if I came.
I knew you'd never try to turn me in.
You want to see it? No? I didn't either,
and now I'll never lose that goddamned head,
even if I bury it and drive away.

By now the bluster'd left his shrinking frame
and I thought he would vomit in my glass,
but Foley had saved strength enough to stand,
while I let go of everything I'd planned—
the telephone, police and bitter fame
that might wash over my quiet life and pass
away at some inaudible command.

I thought of all the dead things in my shop.
No object I put up was poorly made.
Nothing of mine was inhumane, although
I felt death in a kind of undertow
pulling my life away. Make it stop,
I thought, as if poor Foley had betrayed
our best ideals. Of course I let him go.

The truth is, now he's left I feel relieved.
I locked the door behind him, but his smell
has lingered in my hallway all these hours.
I've mopped the floor, washed up, moved pots of flowers
to places that he touched. If I believed,
I would say Foley had emerged from hell.
I ask for help, but the silent house demurs.

65

Mary Jo Salter (1954–)

Argument

Lunch finished and pushed aside, lost
in a book, I hadn't registered
for some time what was going on
not ten feet from my table. But then
flew out one pointed, poisoned word—
"You"—and before turning my head,
I knew what I'd been hearing: the urgent,
stifled tones of an argument.

He (hunched in a black coat against
the backdrop of a window, one
fist jammed deep in a pocket) hissed
so near her face I couldn't view
either of them clearly. But
surely they were married, and to
each other. Had they been lovers, met
for an hour she would have left that skirt

home in the closet. She had some suffering
under her belt, in the telltale bulge
of her belly. Yes—she'd borne him children.
Oh, she'd borne so much from him,
and what gave him the right to berate
her now, especially here? He had
a secret to lie about, or divulge,
and no wonder she was crying...But wait;

women tend to side with women.
She could be a devil, and he a saint
she'd driven to the breaking point—
No again. The truth, whatever it was,

was (as always) a mess. They were too close
to see it, I was too far away,
and when he sprang up, scraping his chair
behind him (really leaving her

for good? Or was this the daily spat?
Little comfort to think of that),
I saw them both reduced, or heightened,
to something other than themselves,
cartoonish, tragic, archetypal:
Man rises, Woman dissolves.
Man rises and, having risen, has
to go through with it, through the door;

Woman stays, in her place
to be hurt, faced by her just dessert.
Striped like a flag, a three-layered piece
of cake she never should have ordered,
and no solace now; it promised only
the taste of tears and calories.
My lunch, too, sat less well. A spell
of solitude was what I'd had;

but the terror of being truly alone!
The pain we'll put up with, not to learn
how it feels...I heard her fork
clink on the plate, and couldn't look.
And, turning to the window, I thought
I saw the flapping tails of that black
coat tug at the man, as if to say,
You must go back to her, go back.

Ginger Andrews (1956–)

The Hurricane Sisters Work Regardless

Scrubbing the upstairs tub at our first housecleaning job of the day,
I hate to whine about some trivial fever, chills and sore throat. Instead,
I decide to sing Old MacDonald Had a Farm, starting with the *E I E I O*,
to my oven-cleaning downstairs sister who has a large uterine tumor
and knows it won't get removed unless it becomes absolutely necessary.
She doesn't have insurance, and free clinic patients have to make do
with whatever surgeon volunteers, whenever there's time.

My diabetic sister, who hasn't had a slice of pie, a doughnut
or a cigarette in years, who watched me hog down half a bag
of miniature Snickers on the way to work, and might not believe
I could eat like that with a fever, who is dusting mini blinds
on the middle-floor windows, while ignoring the nasty body aches
resulting from Wednesday's flu shot, joins in on the *moo-moo's here,
moo-moo's there.*

Also scrubbing a tub, my basement sister, who's on her second round
of antibiotics for her third sinus infection of the year, hollers
up the stairway, *here a moo, there a moo.*

My lungs full of Lysol Basin Tub & Tile cleaner, I'm hacking
on the *quack-quacks* when my oven-cleaning sister,
now singing along, says, Hey, are you all right up there?

Jim Daniels (1956–)

Where I'm At: Factory Education

My first week, I'm working the cover welder
when the automatic welding gun stops
being automatic halfway through a cover.

I rush down the aisle to find Santino,
biting my lip, sweat in my eyes.
The other guys stop working to watch.
Santino gets Old Green, the jobsetter,
to fix my machine.

Later, Spooner grabs me by the neck
pushes my head against the machine.
Old Green shouts into my face:
You ain't supposed to go get Santino,
he's got to find you, dig?
what's the big hurry, boy? Listen,
You get paid the same no matter.
Kissing ass good way
to get your lips burned.
He walks away. Spooner lets go,
stands there a minute, shakes his head:
Where you at, brother, where you at?

Santino shows me a new job:
After the machine cuts the tubes
hang them on these hooks.

I pick them up, hang them,
pick, hang, till the edges slice
moons into my hands. I stop.
The line backs up.

Santino slaps my bloody hands.
grabs my shirt: *Where's*
your goddamn gloves?

The plant nurse tapes my hands.
When I get back, Santino throws me
leather gloves: *Next time*
you're fired.

I shove anger deep
into rough leather. I forget
and work fast.

Where you at, brother?

Bush idles over from his broken machine
big pot sticking out tight
under a white t-shirt
grey hair slicked back, perfect.
He bends toward me and stares
at my greasy coveralls. I sweat
behind the washer, tossing
axle parts into baskets.

Hey, look at me.
Am I dirty? Am I sweating?
Look, you got to learn how to survive
around here, kid. If you don't know
how to break your machine
then you shouldn't be runnin' it.
He wanders off, shaking his head.

I push my safety glasses up my nose.
The parts start backing up
so I toss them sloppy in the baskets,
pause to straighten the rows,
get farther behind.

A part glides crooked down the conveyor

and I rush to straighten it
but catch myself. It catches
on the washer's inside edge.

Parts pile up behind the jammed piece.
The conveyor chain clicks, then snaps.
I press the *Stop* button.

Bush walks by and smiles,
patting his belly.
Sit your ass down, kid.
When Santino comes
look stupid. Like this.

Santino rushes over. His shirt says
"Your Safety is *Our* Business."
You bet I work safely—I just point
to the machine, and thumbs down.
He can't touch it—it's not his job.
See if you can fix it, he says.
Not my job, I say.
He calls Old Green
who looks at it and says
Not my job—
need an electrician.
The electrician shows up
but he just wants to jive
with Nita, the fox
who works at the next press.
Santino gets on his case
which *is* his job
and the electrician
fixes the machine
which is *his* job
and I go back to my idiot buttons,
Which *is my* job.
I work safely.

Where you at?

68

Amy Uyematsu (1956–)

Dreaming of Fire on the Night It Rained

I am trapped in a house owned by strangers with white skin. I do not
like it here but know I can't leave. Fires are burning throughout
the city. Though new fires break out randomly, the timing
between each new outburst is almost rhythmic. Everyone waits
in expectation for the next one. The flames get closer to this
old frame house. I am only nine or ten but try to convince the
white man who owns the house that it needs to be hosed down
with water. He ignores me. So I search outside and find a short
hose. The water pressure is low but I manage to get a small
stream, which I aim toward the roof and to the building's sides.
Some parts of the wooden structure are so weak they break under
the slightest pressure of the water. The white strangers in the house
frighten me but I know my fate is tied to them. I must keep
watering the dry, dry wood. For now it all I can do.

69

Chris Semansky (1960–)

The Girl Who Couldn't Stop It

Petrified, the little girl stood hugging the creamy white walls of the emergency room. Ugly words spewed randomly from her mouth: "shit, piss, cocksucker, cunt . . ."

It started that morning after a simple breakfast of fried eggs and bacon. A quick peck on the cheek by her father before school seemed to trigger it.

"Have a nice day sweetheart," he offered innocently, patting her on the head.

"Like hell I will you motherfucker!" the little girl snapped back. But she really didn't mean it. Actually, the little girl loved her father very much. She couldn't explain what was now happening. "Sonofabitch, prick, asshole . . ." She couldn't stop it, she just couldn't.

Frozen there like a mute popsicle on the edge of warmth, the little girl clung desperately to her father's jacket, absorbing stares and ridicule from the surrounding patients and nurses.

"Why doesn't he do something about her foul language?" one elderly woman whispered to her friend, who was picking at a gaping sore on the back of her hand.

"Yeah, like wash her mouth out with a laxative, and not one of them chocolate flavored ones neither!" the friend growled.

"White trash!" yelled an old black woman from the corner of the waiting room.

"Can't you shut up for one goddamn minute?!" the girl's father pleaded. He was trying to obtain a sedative or a tranquilizer to calm her, thinking her distress a simple nervous breakdown so many other young girls her age suffer.

But the little girl couldn't shut up, not even for a second. She couldn't stop it. She wanted to tell her father that. She wanted to tell him there was nothing she could do, that she was totally helpless, just a little girl hanging on the coat sleeves of her father. She wanted to tell him that she was all alone, that she was just a sad clown trapped inside her crumbling body of toys. But all she could do was stand there, tears streaming down the sides of her face, words seeping out: "pussy, dick, fuck, fuck, oh fuck . . ."

Appendix

Kim Addonizio: *Jimmy and Rita*

If Vikram Seth's *The Golden Gate* is a story about Bay Area yuppies, then Kim Addonizio's *Jimmy and Rita* is a story about Bay Area destitutes. The narrative is presented in a series of free verse vignettes, a gradual accumulation of events that creates something of an impressionistic collage. With stark imagery, Addonizio reveals a world of late night parties, drinking until blind, and fistfights. It is San Francisco's dark underbelly of drugs and prostitution, the homeless and the unemployed.

Rita is the oldest of seven kids who moved from Nevada to California. At seventeen, she attempts to buy Quaaludes and is rudely introduced to street life in a bathroom of an office building. Later, at a party, she meets Jimmy, a failed boxer who has a tattoo of a cartoon devil riding a panther on his right bicep and who moves cadavers for the medical school. Rita is enamoured with him. Together they slip into the sordid world of heroin where the only pressing concern is how they are going to get their next fix. Eventually, the turbulent couple get married but are soon evicted from their apartment. Jimmy goes to jail for helping a friend rob a guy on the street; their marriage falls apart, and Rita makes money the only way she knows how. Rita warns us, "No one/can live like this for long."

And the reader waits for what appears to be the obvious and expected tragedy. However, we are led to the edge of the tragic and are abruptly brought back to a world of uncertain futures. It is refreshingly different from the typically insipid postmodernist fiction in which authors revel in their cynicism with predictably dull, sneering conclusions. The point of view switches between observing Rita in the third person to experiencing life as Rita in the first. The same occurs with Jimmy's character. The reader must adjust the camera eye from one as witness to one of participation.

Addonizio makes these moves with inconspicuous ease as we are introduced to one scene then the next. Her language is both blatant and poetic, street-tough, yet tender. In the end, the reader is left with the cooked-down, raw essence of Jimmy and Rita. One thing the poem does lack, though, is humor. What humor does exist is through spare character self-mockery. Our sympathy for these characters' despondent lives could have been more pronounced with some lighter moments.

Nicholas Christopher: *Desperate Characters*

With the frantic pace of a Quentin Tarantino film, *Desperate Characters* is a tour-de-force poem that reads with cinematic speed. Nicholas Christopher presents a surreal world that employs pop-culture references and corkscrew twists in chronology. However, Christopher uses these techniques long before the term "Tarantinoism" became fashionable and Vincent Vega the rage.

Told in the second person, this free verse narrative uses the technique of introducing the reader as a character. This angle of vision has interesting advantages over the autobiographical "I" of first person narrative and the more distant third person perspective. Through the use of the second person, the narrator still captures a sense of immediacy while avoiding the first person's tendency to lapse into confession. In addition, the reader is intimately involved in the action of the story as opposed to being a witness.

You are being chased by the mob for gambling indiscretions in Las Vegas. You wear snakeskin boots and were a sixteen-hour millionaire. You escape to Hollywood and live with Stella, a nude, sombrero-wearing fortune-teller and encounter a cast of strange, circus-world characters: female impersonators who speak in tongues, Romanian opera singers posing as mutes in search of Thomas Jefferson's ghost and who rob savings and loans, the Human Cannonball, Rocco, and Zimmer, an undercover cop and theosophist. There are nightclubs where women in leopard-skins snatch coins from the air with lariats, caves where midgets in loincloth wrestle in a mock-lagoon, and a search for the stolen 24-karat Belinsky pineapples. All the while you are being sought by a mysterious woman who wears a necklace of snakebone, carries steel suitcases stamped BEDLAM in red and who, by the way, wants to kill you. This is a story that keeps you in eerie suspense and a world where it is difficult to distinguish between dream and reality.

Chekhov once said, if there's a gun in the first act, it had better go off in the third. We begin with a .38, but it's a .45 that's left smoking. You, the reader, are consistently caught off guard and, with each frantic turning of the page, you are left wondering if you will get out of this alive. With short, crisp lines, *Desperate Characters* leaves you exhausted, and we are left with a story that is definably Christopher-esque.

James Cummins: *The Whole Truth*

This verse narrative consisting of twenty-four sestinas employs all of the entertaining, low seriousness of detective fiction metaphors. This disturbing parody explores the psyche of the famous Perry Mason TV series' cast of characters in a witty, mocking fashion. One cannot help but grin at the absurdities while at the same time feel their despair. Cummins invents a fly that exposes the affair between Della Street and foot-fetishist Hamilton Burger, follows Paul Drake in his efforts to acquire evidence, and sits on a wall to uncover Perry Mason's own attempts to recover from a mental breakdown.

There is only a thin thread of narrative that connects the individual poems, but the use of the sestina form provides an economy of repeated and redistributed words that links the segments. Perry Mason is clever; so is the form. The sestinas shift their focus back and forth between the characters revealing a seedy, erotic underworld and strange, surreal probes of the self. This poetic recuperation of the detective genre is a good example of how contemporary narrative poetry can successfully gain back some of the lost ground ceded to prose forms. As the fly says, "Iff'n someone tells yo' a good story, man, yo' feel it deep in yo' bones."

Jim Daniels: *Digger's Territory*

This is a sequence of ten poems told in the second person about a character named Digger that reads more like a short story than a collection of poems. Yet, the action is compressed in lines that are almost aphoristic. It opens with "Digger Enjoys a Party" as Digger watches his son in a fistfight and enjoys it. Later, he is dismayed by his brother purchasing a slow, unmuscular Escort, even though they save his job at a Detroit auto factory. Digger is aging and balding, "40 years old. 20 at the plant," where the "Only things you do fast now are eat and drink." We follow Digger to church, then to the bar. He trains his dog to defecate on his neighbor's lawn. Digger's life is one of routine. It is one of boredom and lost youth and lost opportunities: "Some would say/there's not much to/a life lived on your street." In spite of it all, Digger finds life not to be so bad. He has the love of his family and can drink beer and talk with his friends on his porch. Jim Daniels tells Digger's blue-collar story in a deceptively simple free verse that is full of humor and tenderness. One gets the feeling he deeply cares for this character. Though *Digger's Territory* is only seventeen pages long, we intimately get to know Digger and his wrestle with what we call life.

Rita Dove: *Thomas and Beulah*

Winner of the Pulitzer Prize, Rita Dove's third book of poems is an affectionate, yet unsentimental, portrait of her maternal grandparents. Thomas was born in 1900 in Tennessee and "landed/in Akron, Ohio/1921,/on the dingy beach/of a man-made lake." Beulah was born in 1904 in Georgia whose family moved to Akron in 1906 and whose "Papa called her Pearl when he came home/drunk." The story tells of these two lives that interweave because of marriage, yet reveals their different perspectives of life, emphasized by the arrangement of the book into two halves.

The first half of the story is devoted to Thomas under the rubric "Mandolin." Beulah's story is told under the heading "Canary in Bloom."

In each section, time moves swiftly as we are transported from place to place in quick physical and temporal shifts. We first meet Thomas as he leaves Tennessee with his friend, Lem, for life on a riverboat. Three short poems later Thomas has arrived in Akron, and courts and marries Beulah. Soon after, Thomas and Beulah have their first child, but Thomas "doesn't feel a thing." We move just as quickly through Beulah's childhood to her perspective of her courtship with Thomas and the birth of her first child. Whereas Thomas has the urge to run away from his new family, Beulah spends a bit more time meditating on the wonders of her pregnancy until "she drops it and it explodes/like a watermelon."

Though there is no definitive plot, the thread of narrative is maintained by the beautifully detailed lives of these characters as we follow their struggles and successes: their movement northward, their marriage, the birth of their four daughters, and their death in the same month of April. The chronology at the end of the book provides a larger historical backdrop for these compelling biographies: the turbulent organization of unions and strikes, the Depression, World War II, the civil rights movement, and the March on Washington.

Dove's language is deceptively simple and shimmers like Thomas's "silver falsetto," and time is of the essence. Dove moves swiftly from scene to scene, which gives the reader the sensation of time passing by at eye-blinking speed. In the poem "Variation on Guilt," her presentation of Thomas in the waiting room, counting his life away by the waiting room clock, the lengthening of hangnails or by his buttons, realistically renders a complex character who senses an impending doom, as if his own life is slipping away. In contrast, we sense the slowing down of time as Beulah, in "Weathering Out," reflects on her pregnancy, which is evinced by longer lines peppered with dashes, commas, colons, and periods. Though the shifts are sudden, Dove has a fine sense of pacing that gives the narrative smooth transitions and poignancy.

Frederick Feirstein: *Manhattan Carnival*

A dramatic monologue told in heroic couplets, we open the book to a preface by X. J. Kennedy, who gives us a brief summary of the story in verse as well as endorsing its form in the manner of a literary underwriter. In the end he tells us "So read, enjoy. Even learn something," presenting his Horatian philosophy as a type of pedagogy, which reveals the neglected state of contemporary narrative poetry. What novel requires such an introduction to support and espouse its importance and virtues? Unfortunately, most contemporary readers, as well as non-readers, of poetry require this information.

We first encounter Mark Stern as he awakes to a nurse he picked up in a bar. However, he is still hung up on his estranged wife of ten years. Despondent and "fizzled out," Stern wanders the streets of New York. He says to himself in the mirror, "'You've lived on this stone island thirty years/And loved it for its faults; you are depressed./Get out, discover it again, get dressed.'" His roamings bring us into contact with the multifarious and colorful people and places of Manhattan. We meet Happy, a restaurateur who loves theater gossip, a dancing cowgirl, and come upon a sexual liaison between two adolescents in Central Park. We witness Stern as he heroically pulls a cabby from a blazing taxi and as he jogs, harassed by passerbys who shout, "'Watch it, you'll still get old!'" and sexual propositions. We lament with Stern as he watches with dismay as "wreckers mug and rape/The Greek Revival houses" and declares, "The New World's paved with dog-shit, not with gold/And tasteless in its art." For Stern, his inner life as well as New York is in a state of decay. Eventually, this odyssey of odd encounters leads Mark Stern back home and to a surprising conclusion about himself and the city in which he lives.

It is a story told with both tenderness and blatant honesty and is thoroughly entertaining. However, some of the lines are forced with transitions that are sometimes awkward. Despite Kennedy's assertion otherwise, the reader never really forgets *Manhattan Carnival* is told in five hundred and thirty-three rhyming couplets (in fact, much of the story's humor requires the turning of phrase that the rhyming couplet provides), but why should he? Feirstein's idiom fits the form well, which contains a music that counterpoints Stern's despair. As Kennedy notes, the poem can be seen as a larger metaphor where Stern's fractured life mirrors the condition of the city itself. Though life is often seen as painful and sad, there is much humor, and "Somehow love remains when love decays."

John Gery: *Davenport's Version*

Uncertainty, incongruity, and discontinuity are prevalent themes in John Gery's poetry. His book, *Davenport's Version*, is no different. In fact, the very provenance of the poem is elusive. Gery imitates the publicity campaign for Washington Irving's *A History of New York*, in which the fictitious landlord of a "small elderly gentleman" found a book that was later ascribed to a Diedrich Knickerbocker. However, this editor will leave the intriguing mystery of *Davenport's* origins to the reader.

Though variously influenced by Chaucer's *Troilus and Criseyde*, Boccaccio's *Il Filostrato*, and the Arthurian legend of *Tristram and Iseult*, *Davenport's Version* is more closely patterned after Shakespeare's *Troilus and Cressida*, particularly that play's nihilism. *Davenport* is told in five books, mirroring Shakespeare's five acts, and each section of each book closes with a couplet, again mirroring Shakepseare and his technique of ending soliloquies, scenes and acts with couplets. Set in New Orleans during the Civil War, as the Confederates blockade the mouth of the Mississippi, Davenport tells his version of the story of a young Creole widow, Bressie, who becomes romantically involved with Colonel Trosler, a Cavalry officer in the Confederate army. After the Union eventually occupies the city, many of New Orleans's citizens flee, as does Bressie. However, Davenport, a Union captain, is assigned to escort Bressie back to New Orleans from her exile along the Bayou Teche, and their encounter initiates a doomed relationship between them. Davenport writes the story in straight lines, "hoping they will help me remember /only what's important." The straight lines (trochaic pentameter) are unobtrusive and run smoothly, almost to the point of being prosaic, but Gery adroitly handles the line, sustaining the poetry, and the book reads swiftly like a good novel.

The comparisons with the Troilus and Cressida story are obvious. Trosler is Troilus; Davenport is Diomedes; Bressie is Cressida; Bressie's father, Charles, is Calchas; Cassie Mae is Cassandra, and so on. Though Bressie's namesake is Briseis, the female prize that caused so much strife between Achilles and Agamemnon during the Trojan War, her name is actually derived from Benoît de St. Maure's *Roman de Troye*, in which the seed of the story for Chaucer's Criseyde lies. Maure called her Briseida.

Trosler possesses the same lovesick emotions of Troilus and is just as ridiculous. Trosler faints at the feet of Bressie and relentlessly pines for her to the point that I found myself uttering the words of Ulysses when he reproved Troilus; "O, contain yourself." So go romantic heroes. Davenport, on the other hand, does not have the qualities of Diomedes, who Thersites called "a false-hearted rogue, a most unjust knave." Davenport is more intellectual and meditative and quite likeable. Uncle Bandeaux, who is really Briseis's second cousin once removed, plays the role of Pandarus. Bandeaux has the qualities of the effeminate and moody Albin of *La Cage aux Folles* and is a comic foil. His interests are his art shop and salon, Studio des Artistes, vicious gossip, and soirees, as well as playing Cupid for Bressie and Trosler. Bandeaux also has a touch of the deformed and scurrilous Thersites; he is hunch-backed, pigeon-toed, and is described as "different." Yet, Bandeaux does not possess the invective language of Thersites, nor is he as satirically sharp.

There are harrowing moments in the poem. Gery's phrasing rushes the reader headlong in anticipation when the Union troops invade New Orleans, and the reader enters a Hell more frightening than Dante's. He also provides erotic and intimate details and provocatively delays the undressing of Bressie. Ironically, instead of following poets such as Pound, Williams, or Ashbery, and write an elusive collage in which symbols and associative meanings dominate, Gery follows traditional storytelling techniques to produce a compelling and memorable story. A unique and welcome addition to the book are numerous paintings. The painting *Farragut's Fleet Passing the Forts Below New Orleans*, by Mauritz Frederik

Hendrik De Haas, is especially dramatic.

Despite the characters' nihilism, disorder, and vision of a world in pieces, the structure and order of the story contradicts the reductivist view of man. Gery's book is connected to the great tradition of Greek, Renaissance, and American literature, and through this connection, he creates value, coherence, and meaning.

Brooks Haxton: *Dead Reckoning*

Based on the King Conn and Queen Eda Irish tale found in Yeats's collected folklore, this is a fast-paced story about a decorated Vietnam vet named Conwell Eddy who quotes Catullus and describes himself as a "shell-shocked redneck gangster." The story opens with Eddy's father being hospitalized after drinking Green-Gro liquid plant food. Eddy then steals his father's body from the hospital to bury him in an ancient Indian burial mound. In the process, Amy, a beautiful strung-out junky, greets him with a .38, mistaking him for a doctor and needing drugs. Meanwhile, Amy's violent boyfriend, Vic, is in jail after punching a cop and beating her up. Together, they search the snake-infested swamps of Mississippi backwater to find Vic's dope and forge an unlikely relationship. Little do they know Vic has escaped and is after them, which leads to a midnight showdown in a canal tunnel. Along the way we encounter a strange cast of characters in this pulp fiction thriller: a black bank robber who dances naked on his pink Cadillac and sings praises to the rising sun, an MIA widow pregnant from her affair with a teenage orderly, a wealthy professor of Native American Culture, an ex-catfish farmer turned guided missile merchant.

A story about the uncertain navigation of our lives and the people who change them, *Dead Reckoning* is a suspenseful novel made even better by Haxton's use of a direct style in blank verse, which intensifies the drama. It is entertaining fiction as compelling as any pulp prose. It even contains a wheel-gripping car crash that thrusts us on a metaphysical journey. Haxton gives us a wild ride in his hometown of Greenville, Mississippi.

Daniel Hoffman: *Brotherly Love*

"There are ways of telling that poems can deliver better than prose," remarked Daniel Hoffman in an interview nine years after writing *Brotherly*

Love. What other form than poetry would be a better homage to William Penn and Philadelphia, the City of Brotherly Love? Hoffman has done what the best poets have done for centuries, combined history and poetry to create what could be called truth. Hoffman is concerned with history, a history that speaks us and the present into being and "is absorbed into our breath, our blood,/our selves." It is a history where past "deeds linger as a fragrance," as "an unseen hand laid on our consciences/in this place."

Told in three sections of sixty-one "chapters," the story opens in present-day Philadelphia where "Penn's statue spreads indulgent arms" over City Hall. The first section develops and probes the culture of the Indians, evoking the spirit of those who first occupied the land of Pennsylvania and Delaware. We are given a reconstruction of the Walam Olum—or How the World was Made—of the Lenni Lape based upon their pictographs on maple shingle and the words these served to recall. Hoffman attempts to give the verses metrical form. The section ends with the meeting of the white man. In the second section, we are transported to the seventeenth century and are given a history of the hero William Penn and his conversion and struggles with other Quakers. It is here we meet his father, Admiral William Penn, whose victory over the Dutch at sea is retold in heroic couplets, in a way reminiscent of Sir John Denham's satire on the same subject. The tone of this section is apocalyptic. The past is mysterious, as is the future; it "lies upon the present like a giant's dead body" or "a cast-iron railway coach of obsolete design" in which "we have come careening on that road" where "we rush precipitately toward a future we can neither see nor conceive." In the third and final section, the Indians and Penn meet to sign a treaty that grants tracts of land to Penn in exchange for goods. The final poem returns to contemporary Philadelphia, back to the "indulgent arms" of Penn over City Hall, where "yet there's a spirit.../that sifts through hands that clasp/what only time can grasp/—Here possibilities of grace/like fragrance from rich compost cling/to leaves where our each deed/and misdeed fall. The Seed/stirs, even now is quickening."

It is impossible to relate the many beautiful poetic moments, the richness of imagery, language, and history of this marvelous poem in such a short space. Paintings by Benjamin West and Edward Hicks included in the book are an integral part of Hoffman's attempt to present a representation of past events in image as in word. In addition, The Philadelphia Singers presented in March 2000 "A World Premier Oratorio Examining William Penn's Legacy" with *Brotherly Love* as the text and the music by Ezra Laderman.

Daniel Hoffman: *Middens of the Tribe*

Here, as in *Brotherly Love*, Hoffman is concerned with reconstructing the past. At first, the reader may feel that these forty-three untitled sections are indeed separate, unconnected poems. But as one reads further, it becomes clear that Hoffman is slowly unearthing lives that are accumulating into an integrated whole. Each poem is an artifact; the shards, flutes and axeheads of these people's lives come together, gradually collected into a perceptive whole like an archeologist gathering evidence to reconstruct, not just a primitive people's past, but the entire human race's past.

The story opens with a prologue of sorts in twenty quatrains where most of the characters are met or alluded to. We meet a doctor as he makes his rounds, encountering, among others, a boy dying of meningitis, a woman whose head was smashed in a trolley accident, a dying Wall Street tycoon, and the mother of a stillborn child. It is only later that we discover that each one is related to the others in a strange twist of chronology. I will refrain from revealing these encounters, for so much of the story depends on these surprising turns of fate. Even so, it is interesting to note that the archeologist of the poem, Bud, is a character whose dig of a primitive tribe compares and contrasts with the daily lives of these people. Bud's conclusions serve as an examination and as a reminder of our *Homo sapiens* lineage. All of the lives are illuminated through monologues and dream sequences, some of which are depicted through frightening hallucinations, as in poem number eleven. We grow distressed as we watch the Wall Street tycoon's harried attempt to get his sick daughter to the hospital. His car has no gas, the hospital has moved, and when finally he arrives the medical staff will not admit him because he has no insurance card. To our relief, a doctor agrees to come see the sick child still in the tycoon's car, but when he opens the door, there is no one there. The story ends with poem number forty-three and the archeologist's findings. He concludes, "my study of a culture at a distance/must, so little known of its inner life, be/fiction."

Hoffman reveals that little is known of our inner selves and that we are shaped by forces beyond our control. Even the most seemingly insignificant incidents and encounters can alter our life's pathway. In addition, whereas Tolstoy finds suffering to be what makes families different, Hoffman questions whether, indeed, all of our sufferings are the same: "Can the middens/of the tribe I study tell if family/strife always reveals a culture's dynamics,/if, amid bones, flints, sufferings are the same?"

Andrew Hudgins: *After the Lost War*

This long dramatic monologue is based on the life of the Georgia-born poet and musician Sidney Lanier, 1842-1881. Hudgins provides prose passages to set off each of the four sections of the book, dividing it into chronological sequences. Part one, "The Macon Volunteers," covers Sidney Lanier and his brother Clifford's experience as Confederate soldiers, Lanier's capture, his release at war's end and his long journey home. Part two, "After the Lost War," details Lanier and his family's life in Alabama, his move to Texas for his failing health and the pursuit of his love for music and poetry. In "Flauto Primo," the third section, Lanier accepts a position as first flautist in the Baltimore Symphony Orchestra. He returns home, has memories of Lookout Prison and describes the onset of tuberculosis. The final section, "Under Canvas," tells of Lanier's attempt to prolong his life by moving his family to the mountains of North Carolina.

The drama of this story is built slowly, gradually. It accumulates like memory itself. Hudgins subtly moves between iambic pentameter and iambic tetrameter lines, a technique that creates a natural, easy flow and fits concisely with the story's subject matter. Each poem is filled with lyrical intensity, but this intensity is cooled by a quiet aestivation, like the slow passing of a warm summer's day. However, this underlying halcyon spirit does not result in dull, dormant reading. The understated mixture of humor and tragedy only adds force to this compelling narrative. For example, in a poem titled "Serenades in Virginia," Lanier gives an account of a soldier who has his heel sliced off by a minié ball at Gettysburg. He "sings as deeply as he ever did/but does it leaning slightly to the left." In the very next poem, "Around the Campfire," the soldiers sing hymns, and there is one Texas boy who strums a homemade banjo. As they play music and drink liquid corn to the sounds of cannonfire, Lanier remembers "A shell exploded to our right./A piece of shrapnel nicked my ear,/and when the smoke cleared, I saw/him sitting, looking for his cup/and for the hand he'd held it in." Tender moments are interrupted by the grotesque, the cruel inhumanity of war. These wartime memories recur with mindnumbing weight: "But I see clear in memory/what I ignored back then: the dull/inhuman thud of lead on flesh,/the buckling of a shot man's knees,/the outward fling of arms, and the/short arc a head inscribes before it hits the ground."

But the story also moves from "suffering to grace." Through music and poetry, Sidney is able to experience the beauty of nature, humanity, and life itself. As we travel with Sidney Lanier, we watch, and hear, him become more meditative and poetic. The next to last poem, "Dying," swells with the inevitable, Sidney's diminishing mortality. Yet there is a gentle thoughtfulness that pervades this ending. His last days with his wife Mary reveals an enduring love that carries him into the hereafter. Like the marshes that are so prevalent in this story, *After the Lost War* reeks of humanity. It is a work of singular beauty.

Mark Jarman: *Iris*

Part one of *Iris* first appeared in *The Hudson Review* and is representative of the bold moves this publication has been making with long narratives. An homage to Robinson Jeffers, who wrote such narratives as *Roan Stallion*, the story reveals our need for poetry to give our lives significance. Told in three sections, Jarman tells the story of Iris, who is leaving her abusive husband to return to western Kentucky. While on the bus with her daughter Ruth, she reads the poetry of Robinson Jeffers, a poet she encountered in college and to whom she constantly returns: "He was her poet." She arrives to a hillbilly idyll, the mobile home where her boozing mother and drug-running brothers, Hoy and Rice, reside. Hoy is fat "like a friar" and Rice is "thin as a hoe handle."

After her brothers are murdered in a drug deal gone bad, Iris takes Ruth and her mother and leaves for California. Iris marries a salesman and spends section two as a housewife who is searching for "'the honey of peace.'" She is sustained by reading Jeffers. Years later, when her daughter marries, Iris makes the pilgrimage she has dreamed of and sets off for Carmel and Tor House, the landmark sea-cliff home of Robinson Jeffers, which marks the beginning of section three. Iris sees herself as "A ghost,/Haunting a life she imagined from a book of poems by a/poet who was dead."

Tom Disch states that *Iris* possesses "the virtues one associates with a good novel. There is a continuous action, developed characters, and a narrative momentum with none of those speed bumps that poets introduce into their longer works on purpose to slow the reader down to the statelier gait of Dame Poetry." Employing the capacious style of Jeffers, Jarman's long, ambling lines flow effortlessly and are a perfect vehicle for storytelling. Jarman also creates a deeply poetic story. There are long meditative passages that reveal the secret inner life of Iris and her connection to Jeffers, but

Jarman seamlessly incorporates these lyrical passages so as not to lose the narrative's energy. Jarman has numerous gifts, and his descriptions of landscapes and characters alone are worth the price of admission.

George Keithley: *The Donner Party*

Many have heard of the difficult, agonizing journey made in 1846 by the Donner family: how George Donner, his third wife, Tamsen, and their children joined the wagon train for the rich farm soil and eternal spring of California. Yet, George Keithley builds on historical fact to create an archetypal American adventure. George Donner tells the narrative in the first person, and the reader gets a direct account of this infamous journey West by wagon.

Though the story is written in the form of journalistic-type entries, the reader receives insights into the lives of the other pioneers that cut deeper than the surface reporting by newspapers and history books. Keithley illuminates everyday events, and there is a humanness to the violence and the death. The ironic foreshadowing, such as the heavy odor of the overturned loam of the Misssissippi Valley and the understatement of the horrible conditions, such as the cannibalism, the starvation and the disease, develop the drama and give the story its tension. But all is not bad. Along the way the group enjoys living in a veritable idyll: swimming, eating and drinking with the Indians, hunting game, picking wildflowers. An especially lyrical moment is when George makes love to Tamsen in Ash Hollow. These moments of timelessness provide a necessary relief from the time-haunted journey.

Throughout the story, the reader is in the mind of George Donner. When the family is taken into strange and unknown country, the reader is as lost as George, an effect that creates in the reader a sense of wonder and impending doom. Always present are the tragedy of responsibility and the consequences of bad decisions. When George Donner is made leader of the expedition at Little Sandy in Wyoming, he leads the group south toward the Utah desert on an unknown trail despite the protestations of his wife and the advice of expert mountain men. It is in "the slow intelligence of the snow" that George and Tamsen foresee their imminent deaths. George speaks of the family's great loss in a calm and eloquent manner: "After this we will listen/lying in the loose grains of dirt/with our eyes sealed shut against the roots/that reach for them. We will hear/our breath begin again. The engine of the brain/begin humming in the mulch, and we will climb...."

The Donner Party is narrated in the plain speech of the Midwest and in the vein of realist fiction. It is easy reading without all of the trappings of Modernist symbolism and obscure allusions, and the short, free verse lines and swift, chronological movement belie the book's length. There is no discernible rhythm except for the poem's intricate pattern. It is arranged into three-line stanzas, with quatrains to begin and end the chapters, contained in three books, each of nine chapters and is exactly five thousand lines long. This gives the poem its structure and unity. The stanza breaks and patterning provide an interesting effect on the journey, something of a spiritual trip across the continental divide, into an American purgatory, that is somehow equivalent to that other stygian excursion by Dante.

Brad Leithauser: *Darlington's Fall*

This engaging story begins in the summer of 1895 in Storey, Indiana. Russell Darlington is a seven-year-old boy chasing a frog, "the jewel of the world," and the "Little Mister Naturalist" is drawn to the natural world. His life is changed when his father takes him to Old University to get an expert to identify one of the butterfly specimens he has caught where he encounters his future mentor, the deformed Professor Schrock. Russ is fascinated with butterflies, "nothing born of earth can rival the glory/Of the butterflies," and he decides to go to college to become a lepidopterist. While in school, he falls in love with and marries the beautiful Pauline Beaudette. Wanting to make his mark, he sets out for Malaya in 1912, with Wordsworth's *The Prelude* to keep him company, to find the rarest and the fairest of the world's butterflies. Yet, on the Pacific island of Ponape, while hiking in precarious terrain, he views what he thinks to be a pure discovery. He reaches for the blue butterfly, loses his foothold, falls and is crippled. He returns home and separates from his wife.

In 1915, John Darlington, Russ's father, dreams of building something bigger than he's ever done before, yet death is at his doorstep. John leaves a large sum of money for a museum to be constructed, part library, laboratories, and repository. The story continues in 1922; the museum is built with the John Darlington Hall a site-in-progress. An artist has been commissioned to paint prehistoric murals to decorate the museum, a "four-part mural-cum-cyclorama," and Russ is intrigued by the artist and the art. He finds purpose again when he is commissioned to write a textbook, an intro to biology, that he titles *Life's Kingdoms*. Over the years, Russ suffers losses and loneliness, but, eventually, he finds love in the most unlikely of places. Leithauser himself makes several appearances, who is on "a pilgrimage of my own," to explain his tale's genesis, which I will leave to the reader to discover, and he recounts some of his own efforts to follow in Russ's footsteps. The story ends with "Darlington's Dream," an appropriate coda to this fine novel in verse.

The story is told in twelve chapters and in ten-line stanzas with rhymes that, according to the author's note, "fall catch-as-catch-can." He uses exact rhyme as well as rime riche and pararhymes. The rhythm of the lines is loose and easy-going, and the reader glides smoothly through the story. Russ is a fully realized character, and Leithauser's descriptions are rich and romantic, the details vivid and lush. Whimsical line drawings by Mark Leithauser complement the text.

Michael Lind: *The Alamo*

In an essay originally published in *Parnassus* and, subsequently, included in a collection under the title *The Castle of Indolence* released in 1995, Thomas M. Disch proclaimed "The epic poem on the '*Arma virumque canto*' model is now pretty much a lost cause...." Many poets and critics would tend to agree. However, two years later, Michael Lind produced his epic poem *The Alamo*, which has challenged the *ultima ratio* concerning the martial epic.

A native sixth-generation Texan, Lind has taken as his subject the Texas Revolution, one of the great mythic moments in U. S. history. The gradual takeover of northern Mexico by Anglo-Americans led to the Mexican War and drew the borders of two major nation-states of North America. For Lind, "This is not a story of merely regional interest. The history of Texas is of crucial importance to the history of the United States; the history of the United States, to that of modern global civilization." In this critical event, the ancient rivalry between Hector and Achilles is recreated in the hero William Barrett Travis and his nemesis General Antonio Lopez de Santa Anna. Lind has synthesized the major elements of classical epic, *The Odyssey*, *The Iliad* and *The Aeneid*, and medieval and Renaissance epic, *The Faerie Queene* and *Troilus and Criseyde*. The stanza, rhyme royal, was used by Shakespeare for *The Rape of Lucrece* and by Chaucer for *Troilus and Criseyde*, as well as in Provençal and Italian verse. The story is told in twelve books, à la Virgil. In Lind's world, there is no pantheon of gods taking sides to wreak havoc upon the mortals. For his supernatural "machinery," Lind incorporates the allegorical figure of La Llorna, the Weeper, from contemporary Mexican folklore, suggested by Chaucer's use of Tisiphone in *Troilus and Criseyde* who, in turn, got the idea from Statius. Lind also tells us that the design of the book goes beyond Virgil's twelve-book construction. *The Aeneid* combines an "Odyssey" in the first half with the second half being an "Iliad." The first third of *The Alamo* follows the episodic adventures of its hero, William Barrett Travis; the remaining two-thirds is devoted to the siege and battle of the Alamo. Lind blends these epic elements with more modern components, which he lists as "the realism of the historical novel, the pace of cinema, and the vividness of imagery characteristic of the best Romantic and Modernist lyric poetry."

The story begins *in medias res* with Santa Anna imposing his rule on liberal Zacatecas. Lieutenant Colonel William Barret Travis, at an all-time low, is forced to go into hiding for his attempt to launch a revolution. The reader is immediately swept into the conflict: "Confusion. All around is churning smoke,/a supernova's planet-flensing shroud, an embryonic solar system's yolk." Many readers will know the outcome of this war memorial, of how 187 men under the flag of the Republic of Texas held off 4,000 soldiers for eleven long days in an old mission. Yet each stanza will be read with eager anticipation to see where Lind will take the Texas rebels next. The suspension is enough that one may still hope the leader of the "War Dogs," Sam Houston, will arrive in San Antonio, "to come to our aid with all dispatch." In *The Alamo*, there is the destruction of a city, the conduct of a colony, and the foundation of an empire; three topics "of great consequence" that Samuel Johnson believed were the proper subjects of epic poetry.

An appendix is included that contains a glossary of people, places, animals, and items that appear in *The Alamo*, a chronology of events from the beginnings of Texas's rebellion in 1811 to the treaty of Guadalupe Hidalgo in 1848, and a substantial, intriguing essay on the nature of epic poetry and the method behind the writing of *The Alamo*. However, as some critics have noted, problems regarding the historical facts of this event arise. Did the Texans remain at the Alamo fully expecting reinforcements or did they make a suicide pact? Did Crockett die heroically, as he has often been depicted, or did he surrender, and later executed, as is told in the diary of De la Peña? Much of the truth about the Texas Revolution is still bitterly debated. Both sides of the conflict have dubious versions. Yet, such is the stuff of myth.

David Mason: *The Country I Remember*

Published by Story Line Press, this narrative poem also appeared, in its entirety, in the Summer 1995 issue of *The Hudson Review*, one of the few literary journals that has devoted its pages to long narrative poetry. *The Country I Remember*, whose title is taken from Trumbull Stickney's "Mnemosyne," is written in a loose iambic pentameter grouped into seven line stanzas with an occasional single line that serves as closure to a dramatic sequence. There are twelve titled sections that alternate between the parallel lives of John Mitchell, a lieutenant in the Union Army and prisoner in Libby Prison, and his daughter Maggie Gresham.

The story opens with the widowed Maggie Gresham in Los Angeles, two years before her death in 1956, as she recounts her family's railway journey West from Illinois to Oregon. The reader enters the rough-and-ready pioneer world and is given a real sense of Maggie's wanderlust: "We came this far, and maybe I could go/farther on my own." The story then shifts to Lt. Mitchell shortly before his death at Pomeroy, Washington, in 1918. This section depicts Mitchell and his troops during the Civil War. Instead of a battle scene, we find them searching for food by raiding orchards and bargaining with indignant Southerners. It is an episode which portrays a human dimension to the war: "'We have twenty-five thousand starving men,'/I told him. 'If you have any food to give/I will receipt you for it. Swear loyalty/and you'll get paid.' 'Damn your receipt,' he said." Later, Maggie, nearing thirty, leaves Pomeroy for an independent life, turning down several marriage proposals. In the mean time, Mitchell is captured at Chickamauga and sent to Libby Prison. The story ends with both of these sojourners finally finding roots as Maggie marries in California, enjoying her nieces and nephews, and Mitchell settles in with his family after the war, recalling his youth fighting in the Indian wars.

The similarities of temperament between Mitchell and Maggie provide, in addition to the genealogical link, a continuity of narrative that helps the reader to negotiate the temporal terrain of a story that spans one hundred years. The theme of rootlessness and the search for the self is prevalent throughout the poem. In fact, the two protagonists follow similar lives of unrest and settlement, which could be considered a metaphor for American history at large. Despite the historical impact of the Civil War, Mason demonstrates that the movement West, manifest destiny, the subsequent feeling of dislocation and disconnectedness and the agonizing search for roots are the prevailing subjects that define the American identity.

Robert McDowell: *The Diviners*

In the book's introduction, Dana Gioia states, "*The Diviners*...matter-of-factly presents middle class characters caught in the crisis of domestic existence." McDowell effectively captures the essence of mundane, colorless suburban life through a minimalist style. The characters are realized with few details, and he moves rapidly from scene to scene. "By eliminating the prosaic material of transitions," McDowell moves sharply in five chapters through five decades, from the 1950's to the 1990's.

The story opens in 1958 and is about the dysfunctional middle class family of Al, nicknamed "Boss," his wife Eleanor, and their son Tom. Al is often away on work, and his wife begins an affair with Bill, Tom's schoolteacher. In the spirit of film noir, Al hires a private detective and has Bill's legs broken. Eleanor leaves and "crisscrosses the bleak Southwest," working odd jobs. After six months, broke and bitter, she reluctantly returns. Al and Eleanor maintain a threadbare relationship in which "sadness surfaces and spreads." Tom becomes a "silent, grief-grown boy."

The Seventies begins with Tom sweating out the Vietnam lottery, but because of connections, he is able to avoid the draft. Later, while picketing against the draft, he meets up with a college buddy in Oakland who has returned from the war. Tom returns home to Santa Monica at Eleanor's behest and begins working for Al, even though he fights against his father's bullying philosophy. Tom falls in love with a black girl named Elaine, further distancing him from Al.

In the Eighties, Tom and Elaine, ironically, move to Ireland, a place from which Tom's ancestors once fled. They buy a small cottage and take up farming, living the simple life. However, their idyll is quickly interrupted as they receive news that Eleanor has cancer. During her funeral, Al and Tom are forced to confront one another.

In the Nineties, Tom and Elaine struggle to assess their life and future. Al becomes an increasingly pathetic and lonely figure, and the reader enters his disturbed psyche for a final time before he, too, dies. Tom and Elaine tie up loose ends and migrate back to Ireland.

The story is told in iambic pentameter. The narrative rhythm is carried throughout, yet the five beats per line are not conspicuous. McDowell uses a natural, plain speech appropriate to his characters, and the lines are never forced or awkward. He deftly moves from the mind of one character to another, an effect from Expressionist drama, which provides the groundwork for the emotional and physical distance that pervades so much of their lives. Since the story can be read in a single sitting, this tale of loss and loneliness is immediately felt.

R. F. McEwen: *Heartwood*

Written in a supple blank verse branching from ten-line stanzas to ten chapters, McEwen presents a strangely fascinating world never before realized in narrative verse. *Heartwood* is told in the language of treemen, both plain and eloquent, where we enter the forest world of tree trimmers. The comparison of life with a tree may sound hackneyed and a cliché, but this story is written in such an original and beautiful manner that the metaphor feels just right.

We become acquainted with John Price, a tree trimmer with rope-cut hands who has had broken ribs and a dislocated shoulder, what he describes as "markers on a calendar of pain." John is married to a woman called Danean; "Her pride was...in the climbing man who swung through death/In those great vaulted tops with more control/Than one who would take to walk the razor's edge." The story is full of the wonderment and the mesmerizing life of working in various types of trees: the cutting of Siberian and Green Ash over a cemetery in Hemingford, the climbing and swinging amidst Black, Burr and Southern Red, Chestnut, Oak, the Shingle and the White, Laurels, Cottonwoods, Green and Mountain Junipers, Elms, Shagbark Hickory and Silver Maples. But this family receives its fair share of troubles. After an accident, John works an unsuccessful five years at his father-in-law's bike shop. Danean and her father are distressed by John's need to work the trees and the cross-country treks his work takes him on. With much argument and many tears, John takes Patrick, their ten-year-old son, to Wounded Knee. Patrick is lost in a blizzard and found four days later in a haystack with frostbitten feet. Later, Danean is hospitalized after a mental breakdown, and John is severely hurt and spends two months in the hospital. Like the locust tree holding strong against a February wind, the Price family snaps its frozen tips but manages to hold through the harsh winters. It is a family that's "been through hell enough/To break, I'll bet, in these last hundred years." Yet, they mend themselves "back as good as green." In the distance remains the elusive dream of settling down and working in the luscious groves of Carbondale.

McEwen's *ars poetica* is made clear: "Once in their trees,/True climbers cleave to purpose, not to show." And *Heartwood*'s purpose is made perfectly clear by McEwen's haunting storytelling. It contains the perfect mixture of ideas and emotions. Reading this poem is like swaying in the treetops with the wind and the elements. After you come down, you look up in wonderment and realize what a great place to have been.

Frederick Pollack: *The Adventure*

This is a book-length fantasy tale that immediately engages the imagination and is immensely entertaining, much more so than its cinematic counterpart, *What Dreams May Come*. Though told in a lithe free verse that gallops down the page, Pollack's dream kingdom is not written in plain style poetry. The reader must be deliberate to absorb its lyrical intensity, the philosophical wit, and richly descriptive language.

The poem is divided into three sections and told in tercets, reminding the reader of that other otherworldly journey by Dante. Here on the other side is a sunless domain that is neither heaven nor hell, where one has the opportunity to rectify missed chances. Here one gets what one wants simply by wishing for it. The narrator endows himself with muscles and rides Juggernaut, "not a cow/or a bear though big and solid, a child's/drawing of an animal," across the strange new landscape on his adventure. Along the way he encounters a beautiful palace peopled with a Countess, a General, and a Painter, and has timeless days of sex with Yvette, a French maid. This idyll is abruptly ended as he enters the City, a seedy precinct rife with taverns and highways and a morose parody of death-in-life. He sets up house with his old flame, Susan, who committed suicide, as did he, in the former life. He also sees his parents who are rather indifferent to his arrival.

Of course, as one hopes, famous people are visitable as well. Here Picasso is back at work on paintings as well as on women. The narrator speaks with Kierkegaard on the nature of the afterlife and views a holographic drinking session involving Freud, Wittgenstein, and Marx. He hangs out with Gottfried Benn at a waterfront dive, Wolf's Tavern, where Benn explains the absence of such great men as Shakespeare, Mozart, and Kafka. Unfortunately, Elvis doesn't make an appearance as he is undoubtedly one of those celebrities inaccessible even after death. The hero-narrator eventually leaves the City and rides north, still in search of the "heavenly mansion."

Frederick Pollack: *Happiness*

This is a sci-fi novel in verse told in free verse quatrains in three sections and thirty-two "chapters." The story begins after X-Day, the day the universe has been turned inside out, and a great, garishly lit Wall has emerged. The Wall has been created because of an anomaly in a physics experiment masterminded by Stephen Hawking. On one side of the Wall is the old world, and on this side of the Wall, known as Aidenn, are those who would rid the world of capitalism, fundamentalists, anti-abortionists and the like. If you travel too close to the Wall, your ears bleed and you vomit.

> The Wall was
> ugly. Colors
> entered the mix—neon
> greens, electric
>
> pinks—lacking even the
> doubtful beauty
> of fractals,
> but would not settle
>
> into white
> or mud.

The story is told from the first person point of view of the Captain, the leader of a paramilitary force known as the Special Action Squad of the Provisional Revolutionary Government, which has been assembled to rid the new society of any undesirables. These "Avengers of Wrong" punish offenders such as cultists, crude racists and anti-Semites. Some "criminals" go through psychological reprogramming while others are zapped to the other side of the Wall. The squad also heals various physical and mental afflictions by the use of a Wand and a Glove.

Section two takes place at Ric's place, a joking nod to *Casablanca* no doubt, a restaurant that is within sight of the Wall. The laser pistol-toting commandos drink and talk metaphysics as the Captain waits on two appointments (the second one mysteriously never shows). This provides Pollack the opportunity to digress on philosophical matters, which lead to metaphysical contemplations that become the basis of the narrative.

Meanwhile, the squad watches the War Crimes Trials on television. Business executives are convicted and given punishments like shoveling toxic waste. Others are convicted of gender crimes and men are transposed to women's bodies and raped by androids. Renata, one of the commandos, says that after the Trials have ended, television will "be like/the old,/pre-cable PBS," though "Somewhat more leftish." However, in section three, Hawking warns that the anomaly and Aidenn will soon disappear because the field won't attract enough O-muon particles. The squad is disbanded, and the Captain goes AWOL, "away from/the Wall", and drives to Denver where he cultivates his garden and is "reborn."

The story reads rapidly; the short, enjambed lines and jagged syntax propel the reader down the page. The effect of such lines creates disorientation and can be frenetic, mirroring much of the story. Yet, this reader had difficulty in assessing whether this story was a Leftist paradise, a best of all possible worlds, or a satire. The tone is not sharp enough to be satire. Yet, the metaphor of the Wall, the obvious problems that arise from raising walls, as was done in Berlin and is going on in Israel, creates a society that we know cannot work. Is Pollack providing us with a political experiment, a brave new world that fails or with a metaphysical alternative? Though intellectually complex, the story seems a bit dry. The characters' motives are realized, but it is hard to be empathetic and emotionally engaged. Does the Captain eventually gain salvation through some kind of knowledge or recognition of spiritual truth? Even so, the fall of the Wall is not tragic. The story, however, is original and can, and should, be reread because it is fun and is necessary to grasp the various ideas presented.

Vikram Seth: *The Golden Gate*

Touting itself as a "novel-in-verse," *The Golden Gate* is a long narrative poem that employs as its model Sir Charles Johnston's "luminous translation" of Pushkin's *Eugene Onegin* (1977). However, the loose and diffuse lines and passages generally allowed to novelists are corralled by Seth's diligent application of fourteen line stanzas of rhyming iambic tetrameter. Pushkin's verse romance influences Seth's plot as well as his meter, and there is a nice balance between narrative momentum and poetic play. The four-beat line swiftly accelerates the reader through this story of entangled yuppie liaisons in "circa 1980" San Francisco.

At the story's outset, we meet the despondent and hapless John Brown, the upper-middle-class equivalent to Everyman. Janet Hayakawa, an ex-girl-friend, struggling sculptor, and drummer for Liquid Sheep, attempts to shake John from his despair by running a personal ad for him. After several disastrous encounters, John meets and becomes enamoured with Liz Dorati, a "golden-haired" attorney. Later, at a housewarming party, Phil, a former classmate and friend of John's, meets Ed, Liz's younger brother. Ed is a Catholic who falls in love with Phil and develops a deeply ingrained sense of sexual guilt, which stalls the affair. Eventually, the relationship ends as does John's with Liz, and in a strange twist of events, Phil proposes to Liz. John collapses back into embittered depression and seeks the solace of Janet. Soon after, their romance is rekindled only to be just as quickly extinguished by Janet's death in a traffic accident. Time passes and John bemoans his outcast state until friends reconcile, and all is good in the best of all possible worlds.

The poem does have its problems. One of them might be overextension: Pushkin limited himself to 400 stanzas whereas Seth gorges us with a corpulent 590. It is difficult to sustain a strict form over such a long stretch. Many of the lines scan only if forced like a square peg into a round hole, and there are rhymes that make one wince. Long soliloquies also seem to suffer. For instance, the grandiloquent political oration of Father O'Hare is nineteen stanzas long and tests the meter's breath as well as the reader's patience. One gets the feeling that the story would have been more with less. Despite these problems, however, *The Golden Gate* is an enjoyable story and the narrator's apologetic interjections are as rejuvenating as getting up to get a cup of coffee.

Mary Swander: *Driving the Body Back*

Mary Swander, in her second book, clearly establishes the narrative and dramatic force from the beginning. She uses the second person to draw the reader in as a character and as a vital member of the family. The narrator and you, her companion, tell stories of family members who have died. The poem has a strong dramatic element as the characters, through flashback, come alive again and relate their own accounts. However, the reader is not drawn into the world of the dead by some sort of chronicle of the afterlife. The dead return as a reminder that they are always with us. A major reason we tell stories is so that we do not forget those who came before us.

On our drive to return "my mother's body/back to the town/where we were born," we meet Jim, who strikes a bargain with a headless ghost and owns a butcher shop; George, who has one glass eye, smokes short cigars and blew up the still; Julia, who died at the age of ten; Phil, who was a pig farmer, ran rum for Al Capone, and who was found dead in a wooden crate labeled PURE LARD; Nell, a tough-minded aunt who lived to be eighty; Maud, an eccentric woman who died with a pack of dogs on top of her; Doc, Nell's husband, who spoke in tongues; Ed, a legislator who filibustered on the House floor by performing birdcalls; and Grandma, who had cancer.

We develop compassion for each of these characters as their stories are recounted. But there is no sentimentality or gush of emotion for the lost in this elegy. Instead, each family member is remembered for his or her eccentricities and gestures, which makes each of them wholly unique. Sometimes disturbing, oftentimes funny, Swander has created a loquacious family, which helps one to cope with the great silencer, death.

Frederick Turner: *The New World*

Frederick Turner is the former editor of *The Kenyon Review* and one of the founders of the New Formalism and the New Narrative or the Expansive Movement. His epic poem, *The New World* was published in 1985, between such novels in verse as Alfred Corn's *Notes from a Child of Paradise* (1984) and Vikram Seth's *The Golden Gate* (1986). What is so important about this particular poem is that, instead of being set in a mythopoeic past, it is situated in the more modern science-fictional future. He even names his own futuristic Muse, Sperimenh. By imagining an alternative universe, Turner is given freedom to critique the present.

The story is written in an unrhymed five-beat line with a natural tendency toward blank verse. Here is a brief synopsis. In 2376, the post-apocalyptic United States, or Uess as it is called, is divided into three parts, the utopian Free Counties of the Midwest, the fanatical theocratists of the Mad Counties in the Southeast, and the joyjuice-drinking Riots of the inner cities whose stupefying drug is supplied through the slave labor of the old middle-class Burbs. It is up to James Quincy with his inherited sword, Adamant, to become schooled in the martial arts and pass a Periclean test in order to marry Ruth McCloud, the poem's heroine. Eventually, war comes as Simon, the false Messiah of the Mad Counties, raids his old hometown and kills Ruth's father. So as not to ruin any of Turner's *coup de théâtre*, suffice it to say Simon's killer and the effect of the traitorous servant Judd's suicide will surprise the reader.

Any contemporary epic will inevitably have to contend with the epic poem's past. It is impossible to erase from memory the tradition given to us by way of *Gilgamesh*, The Bible, *The Iliad, The Odyssey, The Mahabharata, The Aeneid, The Shah-Namah, The Kalevala*, the Mandika versions of *The Sunjata* and the medieval and postclassical European epics such as *The Divine Comedy, Troilus and Criseide, Orlando Furioso*, and *Paradise Lost*, to name a few. In producing an epic, Turner must meet the demands of creating characters of heroic dimensions. That is, to borrow from Thomas Disch's EAS or Epic Achievement Scale, imagining a plot with moral meaning where the actions of the characters have a significance beyond mere romance and where the story as a whole has an emblematic reference to the larger patterns of history. Though Turner's characters tend toward epic proportions, they also tend to fall short. The darker figures of Simon and of both the Mad Counties and the Riots are not equal in nobility to the hero James Quincy and the Free Counties, which automatically devalues any heroic efforts by the protagonist. What would happen if Achilles had no Hector, Aeneas no Turnus?

New World, at times, is awkward. It does not have the smoothness of line or intense imagery of *Genesis*, Turner's second science fiction epic poem, possibly because of the numerous philosophical digressions. Though there are flat passages, Turner can still spin a simile as good as Homer, such as this one describing a battle scene: "They burst on the enemy line as surf on the breakwater/shatters in blossoms of phosphorescence and sweeps/in green tons over the wall...." Yet, the pseudo-medieval mixture of sword and circuitry seems like King Arthur with a light saber, and the black dialect of the Kingfish is silly. Which is to say, Turner learns from his mistakes and improves, dramatically, in his next attempt.

Frederick Turner: *Genesis*

Imagine a story that covers the major historical events of the period approximately from 2015 to 2070. Then imagine that a group of scientists and technologists, led by Chancellor ("Chance") Van Riebeck, is charged by the United Nations with the scientific survey of the planet Mars. Using theories from the Gaia hypothesis, they clandestinely introduce hardy genetically tailored bacteria into the Martian environment with the intention of transforming the planet so that it would be habitable by human beings. The Earth has fallen under the theocratic rule of the Ecotheist

Movement, which divides human beings from the rest of nature and regards all human interference with nature as evil. Chance and his followers are captured and put on trial, and war breaks out between the Martian colonists and the home planet.

Many critics have scoffed at Turner's science fiction poems as being adolescent fantasies; however, what else are *The Odyssey, Paradise Lost,* and *The Divine Comedy* but fantasy tales, or what touchy postmodernist critics might preferably call, magical realism? *Genesis* is truly an epic poem, part of the great lineage of Homer, Virgil, Dante, and Milton. It contains an absorbing plot and intriguing characters along with captivating philosophical discussions on beauty and the future of humanity. It is wholly original. It is a poem of social, cultural, and moral import, elements that Sir Philip Sidney requires of a poem. One of the world's most significant debates is that between those who would abandon technology for the sake of the planet's survival and those who would use technology for humanity's progress. According to Turner, it is technology that will eventually save the planet. In fact, he provides a note on the science of *Genesis*, a science that has become entirely plausible.

The art of *Genesis* is as complex as its science, much of it based on the current ideas of chaos theory. As Turner notes, "The scientific and technological material of the poem constitute not only a large part of the content but also a gigantic metaphor of its very structure and form." Told in the persona of a poet who will not be born until over a hundred years have passed, the poem is written in blank verse, the ancient epic meter of the English language used by Shakespeare and Milton, and in the fashion of Homer and Virgil. It is exactly 10,000 lines, in five Acts, each with five scenes, each of 400 lines. It represents the great branching, forking tree of evolution, story, and of the universe itself, a world of fractal geometries and collapsing wave functions.

Frederick Turner has created a distinctive body of poetry; it is individual in imagery, individual in language, individual in style. He "goeth," returning to Sidney, "hand in hand with nature, not enclosed within the narrow warrant of her gifts, but freely ranging only within the zodiac of his own wit."

Frederick Turner: *The Ballad of the Good Cowboy*

When one hears the name Frederick Turner, one immediately associates him with science and science fiction, most notably the sci-fi epics *The New*

World and *Genesis*. Yet, in this long narrative poem, we get another side, the cowboy poet. A mixture of Medieval Romance and Texas tall tale, three cowboy-knights are on a quest to rescue an imprisoned Christ. Sir Galahad, meet Clint Eastwood. *The Ballad of the Good Cowboy* originally appeared in the seventeenth issue of *The Reaper* and was later printed in an edition of 150 numbered hand-signed copies for The Maverick Press as part of the Southwest Poets Series.

The tale opens in a bar in Abilene when Jack McCall, the killer of Wild Bill Hickok stumbles through the doors. Jack is feeling suicidal, so Gabby Salvador, known for spinning yarns, tells him the story of the Good Cowboy. Tex Galahad, Red Boyce, and Jesse Passaval are employed as cow-punchers, a group that is counterpart to Jesus's disciples, Arthur's Round Table, and Robin Hood's Merry Men. While out on the range, they encounter a Mexican boy who unrolls a cope, which contains the image of an imprisoned Christ with a woman's face painted in his eyes, the veiled Sister of the Good Cowboy. After a miracle, they are inspired to look for the "shanghied Christ." Tex, Red, and Jesse, set off on their respective journeys. Tex rides to Telluride and plays cards with three seedy strangers clothed in black who are accompanied by a pretty whore in a red dress. As Tex attempts to protect the girl's honor, four hands slap leather, and we learn that Tex is not the greatest gunfighter. Big Red heads north to "Alasky" where he, too, gets in a gunfight at the crossroads. Later, thanks to his big Appaloosa, Red ends up in the mountains prospecting for gold. Killing four claimjumpers whose stake was actually fair, Red flees to the lands of the Tlingit, marries an Indian girl, and is transformed into a bear. Jesse heads south, Texas-way, to Galveston. He ends up fighting in the Alamo and, amazingly, escapes, but soon he is captured by a Mexican patrol.

So goes the beginning of their quest to find the Good Cowboy and, ultimately, the search for their own salvation. Turner mixes Mexican folklore, Native American legend, and chivalric romance and creates a strange cosmology where there is nothing east of Chicago, where San Francisco sits on the Gulf of Mexico, and where "Horizons didn't bend as they do now." The structure of the poem is also one of numerology based on the powers of 2: 2 to the power of 10 lines altogether, 2 to the power of 3 sections each containing 2 to the power of 5 stanzas of 2 to the power of 2 lines each. The story evokes the strange, surreal world of the Spaghetti Westerns, and I found myself sidling up to the bar because of Turner's perfect cowboy speech and the narrator's intimate connection to that small, Main Street bar in Texas.

Acknowledgments

Kim Addonizio, "Physics" and "Ha," *Tell Me*, BOA Editions, Ltd., 2000.

AI, "The Ravine" and "The Kid," *Killing Floor*, Houghton Mifflin, 1979.

Dick Allen, "Cliff Painting," *Flight and Pursuit*, Louisiana State University Press, 1987.

Ginger Andrews, "The Hurricane Sisters Work Regardless," *Hurricane Sisters*, Story Line Press, 2004.

David Baker, "Murder: Crows," *Sweet Home, Saturday Night*, University of Arkansas Press, 1991.

Frank Bidart, "Herbert White," *Golden State*, G. Braziller, 1973.

Elizabeth Bishop, "The Moose," *The Complete Poems 1927-1979*, 1979, 1983 by Alice Helen Methfessel. Reprinted with the permission of Farrar, Straus and Giroux, Inc.

David Bottoms, "Under the Boathouse," *Armored Hearts: Selected and New Poems*, Copper Canyon Press, 1995.

Gwendolyn Brooks, "In the Mecca," *In the Mecca*, Harper and Row, 1968.

Jared Carter, "The Measuring," *Work, for the Night is Coming*, Macmillan, 1981, and "The Gleaning," *After the Rain*, Cleveland State University Poetry Center, 1993.

Nicholas Christopher, "Jupiter Place, 1955," *The Creation of the Night Sky: Poems*, Harvest Books, 1999.

Judith Ortiz Cofer, "Quinceañera," *Terms of Survival*, Arte Público Press, University of Houston, 1987.

Jim Daniels, "Where I'm At: Factory Education," *Punching Out*, Wayne Sate University Press, 1990.

Kate Daniels, "In the Marvelous Dimension," *Four Testimonies*, Louisiana State University Press, 1998.

James Dickey, "The Lifeguard," *Drowning with Others*, Wesleyan University Press, 1961.

Tom Disch, "La Venganza de Los Muertos Vivientes," *Dark Verses and Light*, Johns Hopkins University Press, 1991.

Stephen Dobyns, "Black Dog, Red Dog," *Black Dog, Red Dog*. Carnegie-Mellon University Press, 1997.

Rita Dove, "Agosta the Winged Man and Rasha the Black Dove" and "Parsley, " *Museum*, Carnegie-Mellon University Press, 1983, "Cholera," *The Yellow House on the Corner*, Carnegie-Mellon University Press, 1980.

Russell Edson, "The Terrible Angel" and "Ape," *The Tunnel: Selected Poems of Russell Edson*, Oberlin College Press, 1994.

Lynn Emanuel, "The Dig," *The Dig: Poems*, University of Illinois Press, 1992.

B. H. Fairchild, "The Welder, Visited by the Angel of Mercy," *The Art of the Lathe*, Alice James Books, 1998.

Frederick Feirstein, "The Witch," *New and Selected Poems*, Story Line Press, 1998.

Edward Field, "The Bride of Frankenstein" and "The Curse of the Cat Woman," *Variety Photoplays*, Grove Press, 1967.

Dana Gioia, "Counting the Children," *The Gods of Winter*, Graywolf Press, 1991.

R. S. Gwynn, "Body Bags," *No Word of Farewell: Selected Poems 1970-2000*, Story Line Press, 2001.

Rachel Hadas, "Visiting the Gypsy," *Mirrors of Astonishment*, Rutgers University Press, 1994.

Donald Hall, "Wolf Knife," *Kicking the Leaves*, Harper and Row, 1978.

Anthony Hecht, "Behold the Lilies of the Field," *The Hard Hours*, Atheneum, 1967.

Garrett Hongo, "Pinoy at the Coming World" and "The Legend," *The River of Heaven*, Knopf, 1988.

Andrew Hudgins, "One of Solomon's Concubines, Dying, Exults in Her Virginity" and "Saints and Strangers," *Saints and Strangers*, Houghton Mifflin, 1985.

Linda Hussa, "Fate's Child," *Ride the Silence*, The Black Rock Press, 1995.

Lawson Inada, "Legends from the Camp," *Legends from the Camp*, Coffee House Press, 1992.

Thomas James, "Mummy of a Lady Named Jemutesonekh XXI Dynasty," *Letters to a Stranger*, Houghton Mifflin, 1973.

Mark Jarman, "Liechtenstein," *Black Riviera*, Wesleyan University Press, 1990, "Unholy Sonnet 12" and "Questions for Ecclesiastes," *Questions for Ecclesiastes*, Story Line Press, 1997.

Rodney Jones, "The Troubles That Women Start Are Men," *Things That Happen Once: New Poems*, Houghton Mifflin, 1996.

Beth Joselow, "The Head Cosmetician Tells a Story," *Broad Daylight*, Story Line Press, 1989.

Donald Justice, "Ralph: A Love Story," First appeared in *The New Criterion*.

George Keithley, "Silver," *Earth's Eye*, Story Line Press, 1994.

X. J. Kennedy, "What She Told the Sheriff," *Cross Ties: Selected Poems*, University of Georgia Press, 1985.

Etheridge Knight, "Hard Rock Returns to Prison from the Hospital of the Criminal Insane" and "A Poem for Black Relocation Centers," *The Essential Etheridge Knight*, University of Pittsburgh Press, 1986.

Maxine Kumin, "The Selling of the Slaves," *Our Grand Time Here Will Be Brief*, Viking Press, 1982.

Paul Lake, "Two Hitchhikers," *Walking Backward*, Story Line Press, 1999.

Dorianne Laux, "The Lovers," *What We Carry*, BOA Editions, Ltd., 1994.

Sydney Lea, "The Feud," *To the Bone: New and Selected Poems*, University of Illinois Press, 1996.

David Lee, "Back to the Valley," *A Legacy of Shadows*, Copper Canyon Press, 1999.

David Lehman, "The Secret Life," *Valentine Place*, Simon and Schuster, 1995.

David Mason, "The Collector's Tale," by permission of the author. First appeared in *Pivot*.

Linda McCarriston, "Le Coursier De Jeanne D'Arc," *Eva-Mary*, Northwestern University Press, 1991.

Robert McDowell, "Quiet Money," *Quiet Money*, Holt, 1987, "Young Richard on the Road," reprinted from the forthcoming collection, *Sweet Wolf*, by permission of the author.

James Merrill, "Days of 1935," *Collected Poems*, Knopf, 2001.

Frederick Morgan, "Captain Blaze," *Northbook*, University of Illinois Press, 1982.

Marilyn Nelson, "Tuskegee Airfield" and "Freeman Field," *The Homeplace*, Louisiana State University Press, 1990.

Robert Pinsky, "The Saving," *History of My Heart*, The Ecco Press, 1984.

Liam Rector, "Old Coat" and "Getting Over Cookie, a Made-for-TV-Movie," *American Prodigal*, Story Line Press, 1994.

Mary Jo Salter, "Argument," *Sunday Skaters*, Knopf, 1996.

Gjertrud Schnackenberg, "The Resurrection," *Gilded Lapse of Time*, Farrar, Straus and Giroux, 1992.

Chris Semansky, "The Girl Who Couldn't Stop It," *Death, But at a Good Price*, Story Line Press, 1991.

Anne Sexton, "The Moss of His Skin," *The Complete Poems*, Houghton Mifflin, 1981.

Robert Shaw, "Waiting in the Wings," *The // Wonder // of // Seeing // Double*, University of Massachusettes Press, 1988.

Louis Simpson, "The Previous Tenant" and "Sway," *Collected Poems*, Paragon House, 1988.

Dave Smith, "The Colors of Our Age: Pink and Black," *The Wick of Memory: New and Selected Poems 1970-2000*, Louisiana State University Press, 2000.

Mary Swander, "The Doctor Explains," *Heaven-and-Earth House*, Knopf, 1994.

Fred Turner, "Libbard's Last Case," *Between Two Lives*, Wesleyan University Press, 1972.

Chase Twichell, "A Suckling Pig," *The Odds*, University of Pittsburgh Press, 1986.

Amy Uyematsu, "Dreaming of Fire on the Night It Rained," *Nights of Fire, Nights of Rain*, Story Line Press, 1998.

Robert Penn Warren, "Audubon, a vision," *Audubon, a vision*, Random House, 1969.

Richard Wilbur, "The Mind Reader," *The Mind Reader: New Poems*, Harcourt Brace, 1976.

Nancy Willard, "Pish, Posh, said Hieronymous Bosch," *Pish, Posh, said Hieronymous Bosch*, Harcourt, 1991.

David Wojahn, "In Hiding," *Mystery Train*, University of Pittsburgh Press, 1990.

Robert Wrigley, "Invisible Men," *What My Father Believed*, University of Illinois Press, 1991.

Index of Authors and Titles